POLITICAL ECONOMY OF HUMAN RIGHTS

POLITICAL ECONOMY OF HUMAN RIGHTS

SN Bhaskar

MD PUBLICATIONS PVT LTD
NEW DELHI
www.mdppl.com

Published by:

MD Publications Pvt Ltd
"MD House", 11, Darya Ganj,
New Delhi - 110 002
Phone : +91-11-45355555
E-mail : contact@mdppl.com
website : www.mdppl.com

ISBN: 978-81-7533-298-0

Published and Printed by Mr. Pranav Gupta on behalf of **MD Publications Pvt Ltd** at JJ offset Printers, Delhi.

Preface

Since the 1980's, we have experienced the acceleration of globalisation, a process driven primarily by the rapid integration of the world's economy. Globalisation has led to new challenges and opportunities for the protection and promotion of human rights. Although the current trade and human rights regimes are both post-war phenomena, they have developed on parallel, separate and sometimes inconsistent tracks. Globalisation has required a change in our way of considering and teaching human rights, gender and justice. Gender equality had hardly begun at the national level when transnational developments called attention to the need to think about the condition of women on a global scale. The relationship between human rights and women's equality has indeed assumed a place of prominence in the debates on globalisation and international law, including universal human norms to guide the conduct of public life as well as private realms.

As the post-war GATT regime evolved into the World Trade Organisation in late 1994, so its rules and those of its accompanying agreements evolved into a detailed legal code, which is interpreted and defined through a dispute settlement process. This process, however, has not been transparent and has not viewed dispute resolution through the lens of human rights impacts. Provisions of WTO Agreements on domestic food safety and other technical standards, as well as on intellectual property directly affect the ability of governments to fulfill their human rights obligations to their citizens. This is especially true in the case of social and economic rights, which should be understood in connection with, not in isolation from, civil and political rights.

The trade and human rights regimes need not be in conflict, so long as the trade regime is interpreted and applied in a manner consistent with the human rights obligations of states. This interpretation respects the hierarchy of norms in international law, where human rights, to the extent that they have the status of custom in international law, and certainly where they have the status of preemptory norms, will normally prevail over specific, conflicting provisions of any treaties including trade agreements. The preamble of the WTO Agreement, which establishes the framework for the entire WTO system, does not make free trade an end in itself. Rather, it establishes the objectives of the system as related to the fulfillment of basic human values, including the improvement of living standards for all people and sustainable development. As is widely recognized now, both in development literature as well as in numerous documents of international policy, these objectives cannot be reached without respect for human rights.

I am very grateful to Mr. Pranav Gupta, Director of MD Publications Pvt Ltd, New Delhi, for his kind cooperation and support for this book.

SN Bhaskar

Contents

1

Introduction

Political Economy

Political economy originally was the term for studying production, buying and selling, and their relations with law, custom, and government. Political economy originated in moral philosophy. It developed in the 18th century as the study of the economies of states — polities, hence political economy. In late nineteenth century, the term "political economy" was generally replaced by the term economics, used by those seeking to place the study of economy upon mathematical and axiomatic bases, rather than the structural relationships of production and consumption.

Originally, political economy meant the study of the conditions under which production or consumption within limited parameters was organized in the nation-states. The phrase économie politique (translated in English as political economy) first appeared in France in 1615 with the well known book by Antoine de Montchrétien: Traité de l'economie politique. French physiocrats, Adam Smith, David Ricardo and Karl Marx were some of the exponents of political economy. In 1805, Thomas Malthus became England's first professor of political economy, at the East India Company College, Haileybury, and Hertfordshire. The world's first professorship in political economy was established in 1763 at the University of Vienna, Austria; Joseph von Sonnenfels was the first tenured professor.

In the United States, political economy first was taught at the College of William and Mary; in 1784 Adam Smith's Wealth of Nations was a required textbook. Glasgow University, where Smith was Professor of Logic and Moral Philosophy, changed the name of its Department of Political Economy to the Department of Economics (ostensibly to avoid confusing prospective undergraduates) in academic year 1797–1798, leaving the graduating class of 1798 as the last to be graduated with a Scottish Master of Arts degree in Political Economy.

Current Approaches to Political Economy

Contemporarily, political economy refers to different, but related, approaches to studying economic and political behaviours, ranging from the combining of economics with other fields, to the using of different, fundamental assumptions that challenge orthodox economic assumptions:

- Political economy most commonly refers to interdisciplinary studies drawing upon economics, law, and political science in explaining how political institutions, the political environment, and the economic system — capitalist, socialist, mixed — influence each other. When narrowly construed, it refers to applied topics in economics implicating public policy, such as monopoly, market protection, government fiscal policy, and rent seeking.
- Historians have employed political economy to explore the ways in the past that persons and groups with common economic interests have used politics to effect changes beneficial to their interests.
- "International political economy" (IPE) is an interdisciplinary field comprising approaches to international trade and finance, and state policies affecting international trade, i.e. monetary and fiscal policies. In the U.S., these

approaches are associated with the journal International Organization, which, in the 1970s, became the leading journal of international political economy under the editorship of Robert Keohane, Peter J. Katzenstein, and Stephen Krasner. They are also associated with the journal The Review of International Political Economy. There also is a more critical school of IPE, inspired by Karl Polanyi's work; two major figures are Susan Strange and Robert W. Cox.

- Economists and political scientists often associate the term with approaches using rational choice assumptions, especially game theory, in explaining phenomena beyond economics' standard remit, in which context the term "positive political economy" is common.
- Anthropologists, sociologists, and geographers, use political economy in referring to the neo-Marxian approaches to development and underdevelopment postulated by André Gunder Frank and Immanuel Wallerstein.
- Contemporary political economy students treat economic ideologies as the phenomenon to explain, per the traditions of Marxian political economy. Thus, Charles S. Maier suggests that a political economy approach: interrogates economic doctrines to disclose their sociological and political premises....in sum, [it] regards economic ideas and behaviour not as frameworks for analysis, but as beliefs and actions that must themselves be explained. This approach informs Andrew Gamble's The Free Economy and the Strong State, and Colin Hay's The Political Economy of New Labour. It also informs much work published in New Political Economy an international journal founded by Sheffield University scholars in 1996.

Disciplines Related to Political Economy

Because political economy is not a unified discipline, there are studies using the term that overlap in subject matter, but have radically different perspectives:

- Sociology studies the effects of persons' involvement in society as members of groups, and how that changes their ability to function. Many sociologists start from a perspective of production-determining relation from Karl Marx.
- Political Science focuses on the interaction between institutions and human behaviour, the way in which the former shapes choices and how the latter change institutional frameworks. Along with economics, it has made the best works in the field by authors like Shepsle, Ostrom, Ordeshook, among others.
- Anthropology studies political economy by studying the relationship between the world capitalist system and local cultures.
- Psychology is the fulcrum on which political economy exerts its force in studying decision-making (not only in prices), but as the field of study whose assumptions model political economy.
- History documents change, using it to argue political economy; historical works have political economy as the narrative's frame.
- Economics focuses on markets by leaving the political - governments, states, legal frameworks - as givens. Economics dropped the adjective political in the 19th century, but works backwards, by describing "The Ideal Market", urging governments to formulate policy and law to approach said ideal. Economists and political economists often disagree on what is pre-eminent in developing production, market, and political structure theories.
- Law concerns the creation of policy and its mediation via political actions that have specific results; it deals with political economy as political capital and as social infrastructure - and the sociological results of one society upon another.
- Human Geography is concerned with politico-economic processes, emphasizing space and environment.

- Ecology deals with political economy, because human activity has the greatest effect upon the environment, its central concern being the environment's suitability for human activity. The ecological effects of economic activity spur research upon changing market economy incentives.
- International Relations often use political economy to study political and economic development.
- Cultural Studies, social class, production, labour, race, gender, and sex.
- Communications examines the institutional aspects of media and telecommunications systems, with particular attention to the historical relationships between owners, labour, consumers, advertisers, and the state.

Political Economy Development

The area of development economics has only recently begun to take the influence of the political economy on the development process of a nation or country recently. Political economy coming from the Greek words "polis" (city or state) and "oikonomos" (one who manages the household) has long been the study of the "economics of polities" or of the political dimensions of economic relations between countries. The nature of political economy has been to draw heavily on the fields of economics, law and political science to study the relations of production in a country or economic and political relations between different countries.

Political economy has recently taken the form of an International Political Economy (IPE) which although is a commingle between International Relations and Political Economy, deals with a wide range of issues such as economic growth to global warming to increasing recognition of women's rights across the world. Political economy development or the political economy of development can be defined as the impact the international political economy can have on the development prospects of a nation. The key issues covered in this literature include the relation between democracy and growth with inequality, the issue of social capital formation political barriers coming in the way of developmental schemes undertaken by the government, corruption, fiscal decentralization and political instability.

Development of the Political Economy or Political Economy of Development exposes the intertwined topics covering both the issues and shows how political relations can play a key role shaping the development prospects of a region apart from the general economic considerations attached to development or underdevelopment of a nation. The central argument relating to the issue of political economy of development is the definition of development itself. We question what we mean by development as it's mainly propagated to be a growth in per capita incomes. Several social issues such as the inequality in incomes and the growth in per capita incomes percolating to the lowest level comes under the ambit of political economy of development. The role of the state becomes increasingly important in the role of development of a nation.

With the free market system largely ineffective in the less developed economies where most of the people live at the subsistence level without any access to the basic means of living, such as food and potable drinking water, the mechanism of price allocating and distributing resources of a nation ensures growth with inequality. While we may have average per capita incomes rising, it may be a pseudo-image of the economy where many people still live below the poverty line and the gap between the have-nots and have-lots is found to be widening. Thus political economy seems to address why so many are still poor in the developing countries with the fruits of development not reaching the lowest levels with the incidence of a general lack of education, ill health and famines spreading across the country.

The prominent case studies that can emerge out this branch of social science can be China and Chile. While China under the leadership of Deng Xiaoping largely opened up its international trade and liberalized the economy, Chile, after the fall of Augusto Pinochet in the 70's also experienced a sea change in the economy. The fallout of the Chinese rise in per capita incomes on an average still shows about 130 million people living below the poverty line as in 2006. The Chilean economy also showing rapid growth in GDP levels among the South American nations has gone through phases of high inflation and unemployment in recent times.

The general levels of poverty and deprivation still persist in Chile. Thus, in conclusion, it can only be stated that the role of the polity, the government and the political economy of a nation play crucial role in the development of a country. Government mechanisms should be strong and sound to efficiently allocate and distribute the wealth and resources of an economy. Urgent political will and a corruption free state acknowledging some of the favourable aspects of a free market system which can benefit an underdeveloped economy as well, can certainly pull out a third world nation out of its trap of underdevelopment.

International Political Economy

International Political Economy emerged as fallout of international studies during the 1973 oil crisis and the subsequent breakdown of the Bretton Woods System which led to suspicions about the efficiency of the world economic foundations. International relations with too much emphasis on law and politics and neoclassical economics being too a historical; international political economy was a marriage between economic and political analysis drawing heavily from both historical sociology and economic history. International Political Economy (IPE) is mainly defined as a combination of international relations and the political economy.

It stresses on the interaction between the state and the market at an international level. International Political

Economy primarily concerns itself about the relations between different nation states and how trading and financial policies undertaken by each of them affects the other. The key issues falling in the domain of IPE at present are regularization of Trade-Related Intellectual Property Rights (TRIPS), the issues relating Trade-Related Investment measures and the burning discussion about granting patents to pharmaceutical companies in the third world. The surge of globalization or integration of the world economy, polity and culture is in many ways causing an increasing divide between the rich and poor.

The rapid fall of the Argentine Peso against the dollar combined with increased levels of unemployment and a downward pressure on workers' real wages is a vivid example of fanatic liberalization policies. We can see a negative impact on workers' wages and increase in capital shares in income wherever excessive policies of liberalization are adopted. This effect is more pronounced in the less developed nations of Asia and Africa. The North American Free Trade Agreement or NAFTA is also an example. International Political Economy or IPE becomes critical in this era of globalization of the political economy. The proper understanding of the different schools of economics and politics is essential to shape measures of growth and efficiency with social equity. National policies influenced by domestic politics and economics should not be oblivious of the social dimension of excessive globalization.

IPE can deal with issues such as international trade, trade in agriculture among countries, and policies adopted by international organizations such as WTO, World Bank and IMF. Though it has been often alleged that global economic foundations function according to the whims of the global economic superpowers and are dependent on their economics and political dimensions, International Political Economy has a defining role to play here. It can not only give a detailed insight into the functioning of the world economy but also provide with remedial measures to bring the whole world on a path of sustained development.

Global Political Economy

The term "Political economy" which was formerly studied to understand the relations of production to laws, customs and the government in a framework of a polity or economy was replaced by the term "economics" in the 19th century. This was designed mainly to study the functioning of the economy on an axiomatic and mathematical basis rather than delving into the above mentioned structural relations. The term "political economy" originally meant the study of conditions under which production took place in the nation states which operated under the new doctrine of capitalism. The main proponents of the theory were David Ricardo, Karl Marx and Adam Smith. But the definition has undergone much change and now means a set of interdisciplinary studies or related approaches to understand economic and political behaviour of a country or many countries.

It is generally believed that politics influence economic policies in a significant manner. To this end, political economy draws on areas such as economics, politics and law. Global political economy or international political economy is an interdisciplinary field concerned with global trade and finance and monetary and fiscal policies of different countries' affecting global trade and output. That the foreign policies adopted by particular countries related to tariffs and cartels affect the economy and even the stability of the government in another country falls under the purview of global political economy.

A domestic rebellion or any form of instability which affects the production of a raw material can have serious economic and political repercussions abroad if it is an export good. This can also lead to social instability in the foreign country. Besides, domestic foreign policies such as devaluation can reduce the level of imports by making them more expensive but can also discourage foreign investment and protect the local industries. It has been widely believed that poor or developing nations would do well by incorporating economic policies such as liberalization in their structure which would in turn free them from the shackles of poverty and bring about improved standards of living. But many studies have shown that financial liberalization would actually do harm for the poor nations with slowdowns in economic growth, rise in interest rates and increase in income inequality.

As Christian Weller, Robert Scott and Adam Hersh in a 2001 study have shown, median income of the ten richest countries which was 77 times that of the ten poorest countries in 1980, shot up to 149 times in the year 1999. The income of the richest 10% of the world's populace which was 70 times that of the poorest 10% in 1980 increased to 122 times in 1999. It is common knowledge that markets need to be regulated well by political institutions such that the government to function effectively and equitably to lead the economy on a path of success.

Some sort of government intervention is needed to ensure transparency in market transactions and also to protect the poor from extremely volatile market situations. But the fanatic following for the free market with political institutions lacking in sound monetary and fiscal policies have allowed situations like East Asian currency crisis, fall of the Mexican peso and financial crises in Latin America to emerge. Lack of political will on the part of leaders of the G-3, G-7 or G-8 to restructure the global economy have resulted in very few measures being taken place after the Asia crisis of 1997. In order to ensure success for the global political economy, issues such as the Doha Round of World Trade Talks, the issues of globalization and corruption need to be properly addressed by world political leaders.

Environmental degradation and depletion of natural resources is also a burning issue to be dealt with effectively.

Reduction on availability of fresh water worldwide with traditional oil reserves being exhausted must require the global polity to look for alternative sources of energy which will also have serious economic and political fallouts worldwide. In addition, the absence of institutions that can regulate and stabilize global demand, with encouragement for export oriented growth in all the countries much of the world is at the mercy of the USA, EU and Japan which will provide the markets and capital investment needed to accelerate development in the world. This entails important political decisions lack of which will push the developing world further into low level equilibrium trap.

Political Economy Definition

Political Economy can be generally defined as a study drawing upon branches of economics, politics and law aiming to explain clearly the existing relations between different countries of the world. The area of research combines economics and different related fields of study. Political Economy endeavours to understand the policies, both domestic and international, adopted by governments all over the world. Though this branch of "social philosophy," as many would call it, has been replaced by the term "economics" using axiomatic principles and fundamental mathematical techniques to understand the functioning of the economy as a whole, "political economy" remains one of the essential tools for analyzing trends in the current global economy.

Political Economy can also be defined as an academic discipline that deals with the relationship between the individual and the society and between the markets and the state, using techniques from economics, politics and sociology. Yet another definition of Political Economy is that it is an interdisciplinary branch of study which combines branches of economics, politics and law in order to understand how political institutions, its environment and capitalism influence each other. The term 'political economy' is derived from the combinations of the Greek words "polis" (city or state) and "oikonomos" (one who manages the household).

The term can thus be used to analyze how countries are managed in a system where both economic and political factors are at work. Political Economy was the original term for studying the various acts of production, buying and selling and their relations with the laws, customs and governance. It was meant to study the conditions under which production was organized in the new-born capitalist states. In a way, it could be named as branch of social science dealing with the production and distribution of goods and services and their management. Political Economy assumed the definition of the study of economies of polities or nation states in the 18th century. Gradually, the concept of the Physiocrats' that land was the source of all wealth was superimposed by the labour theory of value supported by John Locke, Adam Smith and Karl Marx.

Notably, Political Economy incorporates liberal, realist, Marxian and constructivist theories from political science. Starting from the 19th century, "economics" or the study of the economy replicated the term "political economy". The latest version of the term i.e. International Political Economy (IPE), among other things, studies the effect of domestic monetary and fiscal policies on international trade and finance in relation to a specific country. Extensive use of rational choice assumptions and game theory are an integral part of the study of IPE in today's world. The main pillars of the doctrine of Political Economy are noted economists like Adam Smith, David Ricardo John Stuart Mill and Karl Marx. Adam Smith in his famous book "An Inquiry into the Nature and Causes of the Wealth of Nations" (1776) shows how individuals furthering their own ends can lead to the general welfare of society by the virtue of the "invisible hand".

David Ricardo in his "On Principles of Political Economy and Taxation" (1817) focuses on rent which he argues might grow as population increases. John Stuart Mill in his "Principles of Political Economy with some of their Applications to Social Philosophy" (1848), stresses on the umbilical linkage between political economy and social philosophy. With the evolution of international politics, IPE has assumed greater significance.

Issues such as WTO, World Bank and IMF have now come under its ambit. The international community fighting issues such as racism, immigration of labour, energy security, scourge of AIDS and global warming is also an inherent part of the International Political Economy. Study reveals that sound economic policies would have to play an active part in order for such steps to be successful. In today's globalized world, Political Economy is not only linked with politics and economics but also with ecology, anthropology, history, international relations, psychology and human geography.

The world of today is a complex mix of the issues of lopsided growth with the rich getting richer and the poor poorer and the many topics from the possibility of a nuclear arm's race to suffrage rights being granted to women in the Middle Eastern countries. International Political Economy or IPE can be defined as a marriage between International Relations and Political Economy. This branch of study can be especially useful to academicians and students alike who can gain a deeper understanding of how economics, politics, government policies and global issues such as flow of Foreign Direct Investment (FDI) from the developed to the developing countries are getting more closely related in this era of globalization and an increasingly interconnected world.

While "political economy" was more concerned about the study of the relations of production in the countries born out of the new capitalist order and was later replicated by "economics" as a branch of social science dealing with the functioning of the economy mainly using axiomatic techniques and fundamental mathematical tools, IPE can be defined as the politics of the emerging global economy.

It encompasses all the issues pertinent to the human race like North-South relations emerging out of globalization and liberalization. An introduction to IPE can be characterized by understanding of the present world taken as a single entity where every action undertaken even in a remote corner of the globe can have corresponding or greater reactions elsewhere.

We are not talking about movements of tectonic plates here! For example, fluctuations in the world price of Kenyan tea can have huge repercussions in the Sri Lankan economy where most of the domestic tea consumed is imported from East African markets. This can even effect prices of sugar somewhat, tea and sugar being complementary to each other. The study of the rapid increase in global oil prices from the first oil price increase in 1973 by the Organization of Petroleum Exporting Countries to touching almost US $ 70 a barrel in 2006 mainly due to the Iraq War can also be explained by IPE dealing with socio-economic issues behind such increases. Issues of trade liberalization and globalization which are motivated by economic and political considerations can also be addressed by IPE.

Mutual Trade Agreements and signing of Free Trade Agreements such as the SAFTA (South Asian Free Trade Agreement) and NAFTA (North American Free Trade Agreement) have resulted in industrial lobby groups raising its head in the countries concerned. Free trade has caused massive dumping of second grade computers and automobiles in the third world economies by the richer nations. This has in a way accentuated the poverty levels present in these economies. Introduction to International Political Economy will also a wide range of topics from the environmental issues of global warming, climate change which will cause animals such as polar bears and seals to become extinct at the turn of the next century.

Over whaling of world oceans is another burning issue in today's contemporary world. But the cornerstone of theory of IPE is the cooperation and political will in fighting out global concerns such as energy security and the shift to alternative sources of energy to addressing race and gender inequality prevalent in many of the developing economies. The structural bottlenecks of Africa such as poor infrastructure and bad and corrupt government polity are preventing the common people to have the fruits of development international developmental and structural adjustment programmes carried out by world bodies like United Nations and the International Monetary Fund are failing to make any headway in these countries.

Globalization of financial markets and heavy FDI flow across the world also need to be assessed according to the terms of IPE. Globalization has brought issues such as currency crisis like the East Asian and the Argentine problem and the concomitant exchange rate and balance of payments measures to tackle the menace to the forefront which can be addressed and redressed by the theories of the IPE. We need to take a lesson from the micro–credit scheme launched by Dr. Muhammad Yunus if we are to ameliorate the lots of the poor around the world by making them more self-dependent.

In the present condition of Political Economy, the production of new dogmatic treatises on the subject does not appear to be opportune. There are many works, accessible to every one, in which, with more or less of variation in details, what is known as the "orthodox" or "classical" system is expounded. But there exists in England and other countries widespread dissatisfaction with that system, and much difference of opinion with respect both to the method and the doctrines of Economic Science. There is, in fact, good reason to believe that this department of social theory has entered on a transition stage, and is destined ere long to undergo a considerable transformation. But the new body of thought which will replace, or at least profoundly modify, the old, has not yet been fully elaborated.

The attitude of mind which these circumstances seem to prescribe is that of pause and retrospection. It is thought that our position will be rendered clearer and our further progress facilitated by tracing historically, and from a general point of view, the course of speculation regarding economic phenomena, and contemplating the successive forms of opinion conceding them in relation to the periods at which they were respectively evolved. And this is the task undertaken in the following pages. Such a study is in harmony with the best intellectual tendencies of our age, which is, more than anything else, characterised by the universal supremacy of the historical spirit.

To such a degree has this spirit permeated all our modes of thinking, that with respect to every branch of knowledge, no less than with respect to every institution and every form of human activity, we almost instinctively ask, not merely what is its existing condition, but what were its earliest discoverable germs, and what has been the course of its development? The assertion of J. B. Say that the history of Political Economy is of little value, being for the most part a record of absurd and justly exploded opinions, belongs to a system of ideas already obsolete, and requires at the present time no formal refutation. It deserves notice only as reminding us that we must discriminate between history and antiquarianism: what from the first had no significance it is mere pedantry to study now. We need concern ourselves only with those modes of thinking which have prevailed largely and seriously influenced practice in the past, or in which we can discover the roots of the present and the future.

When we thus place ourselves at the point of view of history, it becomes unnecessary to discuss the definition of Political Economy, or to enlarge on its method, at the outset. It will suffice to conceive it as the theory of social wealth, or to accept provisionally Say's definition, which makes it the science of the production, distribution, and consumption of wealth. Any supplementary ideas which require to be taken into account will be suggested in the progress of our survey, and the determination of the proper method of economic research will be treated as one of the principal results of the historical evolution of the science. The history of Political Economy must of course be distinguished from the economic history of mankind, or of any separate portion of our race.

The study of the succession of economic facts themselves is one thing; the study of the succession of theoretic ideas concerning the facts is another. And it is with the latter alone that we are here directly concerned. But these two branches of research, though distinct, yet stand in the closest relation to each other. The rise and the form of economic doctrines have been largely conditioned by the practical situation, needs, and tendencies of the corresponding epochs. With each important social change new economic questions have presented themselves; and the theories prevailing in each period have owed much of their influence to the fact that they seemed to offer solutions of the urgent problems of the age.

Again, every thinker, however in some respects he may stand above or before his contemporaries, is yet a child of his time, and cannot be isolated from the social medium in which he lives and moves. He will necessarily be affected by the circumstances which surround him and in particular by the practical exigencies of which his fellows feel the strain. This connection of theory with practice has its advantages and its dangers. It tends to give a real and positive character to theoretic inquiry; but it may also be expected to produce exaggerations in 'doctrine, to lend undue prominence to particular sides of the truth, and to cause transitory situations or temporary expedients to be regarded as universally normal conditions.

There are other relations which we must not overlook in tracing the progress of economic opinion. The several branches of the science of society are so closely connected that the history of no one of them can with perfect rationality be treated apart, though such a treatment is recommended — indeed necessitated — by practical utility. The movement of economic thought is constantly and powerfully affected by the prevalent mode of thinking and even the habitual tone of sentiment, on social subjects generally. All the intellectual manifestations of a period in relation to human questions have a kindred character, and bear a certain stamp of homogeneity, which is vaguely present to our minds when we speak of the spirit of the age, Social speculation again, and economic research as one branch of it, is both through its philosophic method and through its doctrine under the influence of the sciences which in the order of development precede the social, especially of the science of organic nature. It is of the highest importance to bear in mind these several relations of economic research both to external circumstance and to other spheres of contemporary thought, because by keeping them in view we shall be led to form less absolute and therefore juster estimates of the successive phases of opinion.

Instead of merely praising or blaming these according to the degrees of their accordance with a predetermined standard of doctrine, we shall view them as elements in an ordered series, to be studied mainly with respect to their filiations, their opportune ness, and their influences. We shall not regard each new step in this theoretic development as implying an unconditional negation of earlier views, which often had a relative justification, resting, as they did, on a real, though narrower, basis of experience, or assuming the existence of a different social order. Nor shall we consider all the theoretic positions now occupied as definitive; for the practical system of life which they tacitly assume is itself susceptible of change, and destined, without doubt, more or less to undergo it. Within the limits of a sketch like the present these considerations cannot be fully worked out; but an effort will be made to keep them in view, and to mark the relations here indicated wherever their influence is specially important or interesting.

The particular situation and tendencies of the several thinkers whose names are associated with economic doctrines have, of course, modified in a greater or less degree the spirit or form of those doctrines. Their relation to special predecessors, their native temperament, their early training, their religious prepossessions and political partialities, have all had their effects. To these we shall in some remarkable instances direct attention; but, in the main, they are, for our present purpose, secondary and subordinate. The ensemble must preponderate over the individual; and the constructors of theories must be regarded as organs of a common intellectual and social movement.

Human Rights and Human Development

Development, in modern jargon, is a dubious word and can wear the attire of transparency and hypocrisy. It is this gaping semantic gap that makes our process of Western-style development a disaster of the nation. The basic structure of Indian democratic development is strained to breaking point by the structural adjustment forced on it by World Bank-International Monetary Fund (IMF) strategies using the double-speak of globalisation, privatisation and marketisation. The fundamental flaw in the management of power politics *vis-a-vis* Third World countries is the confusion between growth and development, between eradication of mass poverty and glamour of class opulence, between Reagan-Thatcher globonomics and Gandhi-Mao distributive justice. Once we break through this contradiction between the social justice quintessence of our Constitution and the affluenza of macro-corporate operators, only then will development with a human face and human rights where everyone has stakes in the State become a ubiquitous reality.

Human Rights have a universal character where the poor are human with a title to equal opportunity for development. But the paradox of our times is that the IMF and the World Bank, both of which originated in Bretton Woods to save post-World War earth from grim economic depression, specifically had development and stability as their objective.

And yet the major developed countries run the show with only one country, the United States, having effective veto. The developing countries, where human rights and human development are the hunger of the people, had little hold on the two institutions. The most dramatic change in these institutions occurred in the 1980s, the era when Ronald Reagan and Margaret Thatcher preached free market ideology, making the Bank-Fund the new missionary institutions to proselytise the socialistic part of the planet. The Ministers of Finance in poor countries, including India, were willing to become converts, if necessary, to obtain the funds, although people in these countries were sceptical and even hostile. The fall of the Berlin wall provided a new arena for the transition to a market economy penetrating Eastern Europe.

Sans social justice, human rights are hocus-pocus and human development abracadabra. Globalisation, as of now, is hostile to social justice. But at the same time, we cannot wish away globalisation or the Bank-Fund duo and sister institutions. Nevertheless, the survival of human rights and the progress of human development (which itself is a human right) as a harmonious process is still possible given a determined, enlightened, militant movement in that behalf. A puissant mood to press forward for globalisation with a human force, giving up its pro-MNC dark designs, is a Third World desideratum. The failures of globalisation are founded on the fact that in setting the rules of the game, commercial and financial interests and mindsets have pervaded within the international economic institutions.

A narrow view of the role of government and a larger role for markets has come to prevail, which is forced upon the developing countries and their weak economies. The lens through which international institutions and cabinets of developed countries look at problems to ignores national interest and see the world as macro-market cosmos. Absence of transparency and prevalence of secrecy mar the discovery of the truth about the IMF and the World Bank. Ignorance is slavery and manipulated information conditions the developing countries to colonialism. Is the situation impossible or are the problems intractable? Reforming the World Bank and the IMF and the mode of development assistance are not difficult, given Third World readiness to do battle. Let me quote Stiglitz under the heading "Reforming the WTO and balancing the trade agenda":

The poignant contradiction between the right to life and health, on the one hand, and the patent-controlled limitless profits of MNCs, on the other, is best brought out in U.N. Secretary-General Kofi Annan's statement on the WTO meeting held in Sydney. Kofi Annan voices concern about the continuing difficulties faced by developing countries is securing pharmaceuticals to their people at reasonable prices. The Ministers meeting in Doha counselled that the pharmaceutical giants be compassionate to public health problems. If human rights must survive, a long-term solution must be found that will deliver affordable medicines for the millions of people suffering from HIV/AIDS, tuberculosis, *maLaria* and other deadly diseases. This goal is both a moral and an economic and social necessity.

The U.K Commission on IPR has recently suggested that there are no circumstances in which the most fundamental human rights should be subordinated to the requirement of patent protection. The report said that the last one year has witnessed not only the worst in human exploitation of drug patent at the cost of millions of human lives, but also increasing awareness in the international community, of the adverse impact of strong product patent regimes in respect of drugs and medicines. Such patent regime has been used to support the sky-rocketing prices of vital life-saving drugs leading to heavy death toll of millions of victims of AIDS/HIV and other pandemics. Many innocent women and children died because neither they nor their governments were able to pay the unconscionably high prices claimed by MNCs for their patented drugs.

The plea of incentive implicit in product patents is myth. There is much less evidence from developing countries indicating that IPR systems are a key stimulus for innovation. But the evidence suggests that the IP system hardly plays any role in stimulating research on diseases particularly prevalent in developing countries, except for those diseases where there is also a substantial market in the developed world (for example, diabetes or heart disease).

Apart from international measures to facilitate access to medicines, developing countries need to adopt IP rules in their legislation and practices that limit the extent of patenting and facilitate the introduction of generic competition. Countries need to ensure that their IP protection regimes do not run counter to their public health policies and that they are consistent with and supportive of such policies. Life is the first human right.

A revolutionary transformation, tuned to the Directive Principles of State Policy under the Constitution, must be based on the constellation of fundamentals in the governance of the country as outlined in the Directive Principles of State Policy. To fail here is to betray history and the generation of which those now in power are trustees. The Bretton Woods institutions are welcome to help, but not at the surrender of our self-reliance or offer of freedom of free play for big business to trade on our hunger and want. Will the leopard change its spots? Will India lay honest wreaths at Gandhi's Rajghat? The right to development is itself a human right. International jurisprudence guarantees human rights including development. All is not lost yet. But to build a brave new Bharat where we, the people of India, without exception, have title to human rights and development, a stern determination to conform to the Preamble to the Constitution is a sine qua non.

Let us briefly consider in conclusion, by the light of the preceding historical survey, what appear to be the steps in the direction of a renovation of economic science which are now at once practicable and urgent. Economic investigation has hitherto fallen for the most part into the hands of lawyers and men of letters, not into those of genuinely scientific class. Nor have its cultivators in general had that sound preparation in the sciences of inorganic and vital nature which is necessary whether as supplying bases of doctrine or as furnishing lessons of method. Their education has usually been of a metaphysical kind. Hence political economy has retained much of the form and spirit which belonged to it in the 17th and 18th centuries, instead of advancing with the times, and assuming a truly positive character.

It is homogenous with the school logic, with the abstract unhistorical jurisprudence, with the a priori ethics and politics, and other similar antiquated systems of thought; and it will be found that those who insist most strongly on the maintenance of its traditional character have derived their habitual mental pabulum from those regions of obsolete speculation. We can thus understand the attitude of true men of science towards this branch of study, which they regard with ill-disguised contempt, and to whose professors they either refuse or very reluctantly concede a place in their brotherhood. The radical vice of this unscientific character of political economy seems to lie in the too individual and subjective aspect under which it has been treated. Wealth having been conceived as what satisfies desires, the definitely determinable qualities possessed by some objects of supplying physical energy, and improving the physiological constitution, are left out of account.

Everything is gauged by the standard of subjective notions and desires. All desires are viewed as equally legitimate, and all that satisfies our desires as equally wealth. Value being regarded as the result of a purely mental appreciation, the social value of things in the sense of their objective utility, which is often scientifically measurable, is passed over, and ratio of exchange is exclusively considered. The truth is, that at the bottom of all economic investigation must lie the idea of the destination of wealth for the maintenance and evolution of a society. And, if we overlook this, our economic will become a play of logic or a manual for the market, rather than a contribution to social science; whilst wearing an air of completeness, it will be in truth one-sided and superficial. Economic science is something far larger than the catalectic to which some have wished to reduce it.

A special merit of the physiocrats seems to have lain in their vague perception of the close relation of their study to that of external nature; and, so far, we must recur to their point of view, basing our economics on physics and biology as developed in out own time. Further, the science must be cleared of all the theologico-metaphysical elements or tendencies which still encumber and deform it. Teleology and optimism on the one hand, and the jargon of "natural liberty" and "indefeasible rights" on the other must be finally abandoned. Nor can we assume as universal premises, from which economic truths can be deductively derived, the convenient formulas which have been habitually employed, such as that all men desire wealth and dislike exertion. These vague propositions, which profess to anticipate and supersede social experience, and which necessarily introduce the absolute where relatively should reign, must be laid aside. The laws of wealth (to reverse a phrase of Buckle's) must be inferred from the facts of wealth, not from the postulate of human selfishness.

We must bend ourselves to a serious direct study of the way in which society has actually addressed itself and now addresses itself to its own conservation and evolution through the supply of its material wants. What organs it has developed for those purpose, how they operate, how they are affected by the medium in which they act and by the co-existent organs directed to other ends, how in their turn they react on those latter, how they and their functions are progressively modified in process of time—these problems, whether statically or dynamical, are all questions of facts, as capable of being studied through observation and history as the nature and progress of human language or religion, or any other group of social phenomena. Such study will of course require a continued "reflective analysis" of the results of observation; and, whilst eliminating all premature assumptions, we shall use ascertained truths respecting human nature as guides in the inquiry and aids towards the interpretation of facts. And the employment of deliberately instituted hypotheses will be legitimate, but only as an occasional logical artifice.

Economics must be constantly regarded as forming only one department of the larger science of sociology, in vital connection with its other departments, and with the moral synthesis which is the crown of the whole intellectual system. We have already sufficiently explained the philosophical grounds for the conclusion that the economic phenomena of society cannot be isolated, except provisionally, from the rest,—that, in fact, all the primary social elements should be habitually regarded with respect to their mutual dependence and reciprocal actions. Especially must we keep in view the high moral issued ton which the economic movement is subservient, and in the absence of which it could never in any great degree attract the interest or fix the attention either of eminent thinkers or of right-minded men.

The individual point of view will have to be subordinated to the social; each agent will have to be regarded as an organ of the society to which he belongs and of the larger society of the race. The consideration of interests, as George Eliot has well said, must give place to that of functions. The old doctrine of right, which lay at the basis of the system of "natural liberty," has done its temporary work; a doctrine of duty will have to be substituted, fixing on positive grounds the nature of the social co-operation of each class and each member of the community, and the rules which must regulate its just and beneficial exercise. Turning now from the question of the theoretic constitution of economics, and viewing the science with respect to its influence on public policy, we need not at the present day waste words in repudiating the idea that "non-government" in the economic sphere is the normal order of things.

The laissez faire doctrine, coming down to us from the system of natural liberty, was long the great watchword of economic orthodoxy, and it had a special acceptance and persi-stence in England, in consequence of the political struggle for the repeal of the corn laws, which made economic discussion in this country turn most altogether on free trade—a state of things which was continued by the effort to procure a modification of the protective policy of foreign nations. But it has now for some time lost the sacrosanct character with which it was formerly invested. This is a result not so much of scientific thought as of the pressure of practical needs—a cause which has modified the successive forms of economic opinion more than theorists are willing to acknowledge. Social exigencies will force the hands of statesman, whatever their attachment to abstract formulas; and politicians have practically turned their backs on laissez faire. The state has with excellent effect proceeded a considerable way in the direction of controlling, for ends of social equity or public utility, the operations of individual interest.

The economists themselves have for the most part been converted on the question; amongst theorists Mr. Herbert Spencer finds himself almost a vox clamantis in deserto in protesting against what he calls the "new slavery" of Governmental interference. He will protest in vain, so far as he seeks to rehabilitate the old absolute doctrine of the economic passivity of the state. But it is certainly possible that even by virtue of the force of the reaction against that doctrine there may be an excessive or precipitate tendency in the opposite direction. With the course of production or exchange considered in itself there will probably be in England little disposition to meddle. But the dangers and inconveniences which arise from the unsettled conditions of the world of labours will doubtless from time to time, as elsewhere, prompt to premature attempts at regulation. Apart, however, from the removal of evils which threaten the public peace, and from temporary palliations to ease off social pressure the right policy of the state in this sphere will for the present be one of abstention. It is indeed certain that industrial society will not permanently remain without a systematic organization.

The mere conflict of private interests will never produce a well-ordered commonwealth of labour, Freiheit ist keine Lösung. Freedom is for society, as for the individual, the necessary condition precedent of the solution of practical problems, both as allowing natural forces to develop themselves and as exhibiting their spontaneous tendencies; but it is not in itself the solution. Whilst, however, an organization of the industrial world may with certainly be expected to arise in process of time, it would be a great error to attempt to improvise one. We are now in a period of transition. Our ruling powers have still an equivocal character; they are not in real harmony with industrial life, and are in all respects imperfectly imbued with the modern spirit. Besides, the conditions of the new order are not yet sufficiently understood.

The institutions of the future must be founded on sentiments and habits, and these must be the slow growth of thought and experience. The solution, indeed, must be at all times largely a moral one; it is the spiritual rather than the temporal power that is the natural agency for redressing or mitigating most of the evils associated with industrial life. In fact, if there is a tendency—and we may admit that such a tendency is real or imminent—to push the state toward an extension of the normal limits of its action for the maintenance of social equity, this is doubtless in some measure due to the fact that the growing dissidence on religious questions in the most advanced communities has weakened the authority of the churches, and deprived their influence of social universality. What is now most urgent is not legislative interference on any large scale with the industrial relations, but the formation, in both the higher and lower regions of the industrial world, of profound convictions as to social duties, and some more effective mode than at present exists of diffusing, maintaining, and applying those convictions.

This is a subject into which we cannot enter here. But it may at least be said that the only parties in contemporary public life which seem rightly to conceive or adequately to appreciate the necessities of the situation are those that aim, on the one hand, at the restoration of the old spiritual power, or, on the other, at the formation of a new one. And this leads to the conclusion that there is one sort of Governmental interference which the advocates of laissez faire have not always discountenanced, and which yet, more than any other, tends to prevent the gradual and peaceful development of a new industrial and social system,—namely, the interference with spiritual liberty by setting up official types of philosophical doctrine, and imposing restrictions on the expression and discussion of opinions.

2

The History of Political Economy

The history of economic inquiry is most naturally divided into the three great periods of (1) the ancient, (2) the mediaeval, and (3) the modern worlds. In the two former, this branch of study could exist only in a rudimentary state. It is evident that for any considerable development of social theory two conditions must be fulfilled. First, the phenomena must have exhibited themselves on a sufficiently extended scale to supply adequate matter for observation, and afford a satisfactory basis for scientific generalisations; and secondly, whilst the spectacle is thus provided, the spectator must have been trained for his task, and armed with the appropriate aids and instruments of research, that is to say, there must have been such a previous cultivation of the simpler sciences as will have both furnished the necessary data of doctrine and prepared the proper methods of investigation.

Sociology requires to use for its purposes theorems which belong to the domains of physics and biology, and which it must borrow from their professors; and, on the logical side, the methods which it has to employ — deductive, observational, comparative — must have been previously shaped in the cultivation of mathematics and the study of the inorganic world or of organisms less complex than the social. Hence it is plain that, though some laws or tendencies of society must have been forced on men's attention in every age by practical exigencies which could not be postponed, and though the questions thus raised must have received some empirical solution, a really scientific sociology must be the product of a very advanced stage of intellectual development.

Ancient Times

The earliest surviving expressions of thought on economic subjects have come down to us from the Oriental theocracies. The general spirit of the corresponding type of social life consisted in taking imitation for the fundamental principle of education, and consolidating nascent civilisation by heredity of the different functions and professions, or even by a system of castes, hierarchically subordinated to each other according to the nature of their respective offices, under the common supreme direction of the sacerdotal caste. This last was charged with the traditional stock of conceptions, and their application for purposes of discipline.

It sought to realise a complete regulation of human life in all its departments on the basis of this transmitted body of practical ideas. Conservation is the principal task of this social order, and its most remarkable quality is stability, which tends to degenerate into stagnation. But there can be no doubt that the useful arts were long, though slowly, progressive under this regime, from which they were inherited by the later civilisations — the system of classes or castes maintaining the degree of division of labour which had been reached in those early periods. The leading members of the corporations which presided over the theocracies without doubt gave much earnest thought to the conduct of industry, which, unlike war, did not imperil their political pre-eminence by developing a rival class. But, conceiving life as a whole, and making its regulation their primary aim, they naturally considered most the social reactions which industry is fitted to exercise. The moral side of economics is the one they habitually contemplate, or (what is not the same) the economic side of morals.

They abound in those warnings against greed and the haste to be rich which religion and philosophy have in all ages seen to be necessary. They insist on honesty in mutual dealings, on just weights and measures, on the faithful observance of contracts. They admonish against the pride and arrogance apt to be generated by riches, against undue prodigality and self-indulgence, and enforce the duties of justice and beneficence towards servants and inferiors. Whilst, in accordance with the theological spirit, the personal acquisition of wealth is in general thesis represented as determined by divine wills, its dependence on individual diligence and thrift is emphatically taught. There is indeed in the fully developed theocratic systems a tendency to carry precept, which there differs little from command, to an excessive degree of minuteness — to prescribe in detail the time, the mode, and the accompaniments of almost every act of every member of the community.

This system of exaggerated surveillance is connected with the union, or rather confusion, of the spiritual and temporal powers, whence it results that many parts of the government of society are conducted by direct injunction or restraint, which at a later stage are entrusted to general intellectual and moral influences. The practical economic enterprises of Greek and Roman antiquity could not, even independently of any special adverse influences, have competed in magnitude of scale or variety of resource with those of modern times. The unadvanced condition of physical science prevented a large application of the less obvious natural powers to production, or the extensive use of machinery, which has acquired such an immense development as a factor in modern industry. The imperfection of geographical knowledge and of the means of communication and transport were impediments to the growth of foreign commerce.

These obstacles arose necessarily out of the mere

immaturity of the industrial life of the periods in question. But more deeply rooted impediments to a vigorous and expansive economic practical system existed in the characteristic principles of the civilisation of antiquity. Some writers have attempted to set aside the distinction between the ancient and modern worlds as imaginary or unimportant, and, whilst admitting the broad separation between ourselves and the theocratic peoples of the East, to represent the Greeks and Romans as standing on a substantially similar ground of thought, feeling, and action with the Western populations of our own time. But this is a serious error, arising from the same too exclusive pre-occupation with the cultivated classes and with the mere speculative intellect which has often led to an undue disparagement of the middle Ages.

There is this essential difference between the spirit and life of ancient and of modern communities, that the former were organised for war, the latter during their whole history have increasingly tended to be organised for industry, as their practical end and aim. The profound influence of these differing conditions on every form of human activity must never be overlooked or forgotten. With the military constitution of ancient societies the institution of slavery was essentially connected. Far from being an excrescence on the contemporary system of life, as it was in the modern West Indies or the United States of America, it was so entirely in harmony with that life that the most eminent thinkers regarded it as no less indispensable than inevitable. It does, indeed, seem to have been a temporary necessity, and on the whole, regard being had to what might have taken its place, a relative good. But it was attended with manifold evils.

It led to the prevalence amongst the citizen class of contempt for industrial occupations; every form of production, with a partial exception in favour of agriculture, was branded as unworthy of a free man — the only noble forms of activity being those directly connected with public life, whether military or administrative. Labour was degraded by the relegation of most departments of it to the servile class, above whom the free artisans were but little elevated in general esteem. The producers being thus for the most part destitute of intellectual cultivation and excluded from any share in civic ideas, interests, or efforts, were unfitted in character as well as by position for the habits of skilful combination and vigorous initiation which the progress of industry demands.

To this must be added that the comparative insecurity of life and property arising out of military habits, and the consequent risks which attended accumulation, were grave obstructions to the formation of large capitals, and to the establishment of an effective system of credit. These causes conspired with the undeveloped state of knowledge and of social relations in giving to the economic life of the ancients the limitation and monotony which contrast so strongly with the inexhaustible resource, the ceaseless expansion, and the thousand fold variety of the same activities in the modern world. It is, of course, absurd to expect incompatible qualities in any social system; each system must be estimated according to the work it has to do. Now the historical vocation of the ancient civilisation was to be accomplished, not through industry, but through war, which was in the end to create a condition of things admitting of its own elimination and of the foundation of a regime based on pacific activity.

The Greeks

This office was, however, reserved for Rome, as the final result of her system of conquest; the military activity of Greece, though continuous, was incoherent and sterile, except in the defence against Persia, and did not issue in the accomplishment of any such social mission. It was, doubtless, the inadequacy of the warrior life, under these conditions, to absorb the faculties of the race that threw the energies of its most eminent members into the channel of intellectual activity, and produced a singularly rapid evolution of the aesthetic, philosophic, and scientific germs transmitted by the theocratic societies.

In the *Works and Days* of Hesiod, we find an order of thinking in the economic sphere very similar to that of the theocracies. With recognition of the divine disposing power, and traditional rules of sacerdotal origin, is combined practical sagacity embodied in precept or proverbial saying. But the development of abstract thought, beginning from the time of Thales, soon gives to Greek culture its characteristic form, and marks a new epoch in the intellectual history of mankind.

The movement was now begun, destined to mould the whole future of humanity, which, gradually sapping the old hereditary structure of theological convictions tended to the substitution of rational theories in every department of speculation. The eminent Greek thinkers, while taking a deep interest in the rise of positive science, and most of them studying the only science — that of geometry — then assuming its definitive character, were led by the social exigencies which always powerfully affect great minds to study with special care the nature of man and the conditions of his existence in society. These studies were indeed essentially premature; a long development of the inorganic and vital sciences was necessary before sociology or morals could attain their normal constitution. But by their prosecution amongst the Greeks a noble intellectual activity was kept alive, and many of those partial lights obtained for which mankind cannot afford to wait.

Economic inquiries, along with others, tended towards rationality; Plutus was dethroned, and terrestrial substituted for supernatural agencies. But such inquiries, resting on no sufficiently large basis of practical life, could not attain any considerable results. The military constitution of society, and the existence of slavery, which was related to it, leading, as we have seen, to a low estimate of productive industry, turned away the habitual attention of thinkers from that domain. On the other hand, the absorption of citizens in the life of the state, and their pre-occupation with party struggles, brought questions relating to politics, properly so called, into special prominence. The principal writers on social subjects are therefore almost exclusively occupied with the examination and comparison of political constitutions, and with the search after the education best adapted to train the citizen for public functions.

And we find, accordingly, in them no systematic or adequate handling of economic questions only some happy ideas and striking partial anticipations of later research. In their thinking on such questions, as on all sociological subjects, the following general features are observable.

1. The individual is conceived as subordinated to the state, through which alone his nature can be developed and completed, and to the maintenance and service of which all his efforts must be directed. The great aim of all political thought is the formation of good citizens; every social question is studied primarily from the ethical and educational point of view. The citizen is not regarded as a producer, but only as a possessor, of material wealth; and this wealth is not esteemed for its own sake or for the enjoyments it procures, but for the higher moral and public aims to which it may be made subservient.
2. The state, therefore, claims and exercises a controlling and regulating authority over every sphere of social life, including the economic, in order to bring individual action into harmony with the good of the whole.
3. With these fundamental notions is combined a tendency to attribute to institutions and to legislation an unlimited efficacy, as if society had no spontaneous tendencies, but would obey any external impulse, if impressed upon it with sufficient force and continuity.

Every eminent social speculator had his ideal state, which approximated to or diverged from the actual or possible, according to the degree in which a sense of reality and a positive habit of thinking characterised the author. The most celebrated of these ideal systems is that of Plato.

In it the idea of the subordination of the individual to the state appears in its most extreme form. Within that class of the citizens of his republic who represent the highest type of life, community of property and of wives is established, as the most effective means of suppressing the sense of private interest, and consecrating the individual entirely to the public service. It cannot perhaps be truly said that his scheme was incapable of realisation in an ancient community favourably situated for the purpose. But it would soon be broken to pieces by the forces which would be developed in an industrial society. It has, however, been the fruitful parent of modern Utopias, especially attractive as it is to minds in which the literary instinct is stronger than the scientific judgment, in consequence of the freshness and brilliancy of Plato's exposition and the unrivalled charm of his style.

Mixed with what we should call the chimerical ideas of his work, there are many striking and elevated moral conceptions, and, what is more to our present purpose, some just economic analyses. In particular, he gives a correct account of the division and combination of employments, as they naturally arise in society. The foundation of the social organization he traces, perhaps, too exclusively to economic grounds, not giving sufficient weight to the disinterested social impulses in men who tend to draw and bind them together. But he explains clearly how the different wants and capacities of individuals demand and give rise to mutual services, and how, by the restriction of each to the sort of occupation to which, by his position, abilities, and training, he is best adapted, everything needful for the whole is more easily and better produced or effected. In the spirit of all the ancient legislators he desires a self-sufficing state, protected from unnecessary contacts with foreign populations, which might tend to break down its internal organisation or to deteriorate the national character.

Hence he discountenances foreign trade, and with this view removes his ideal city to some distance from the sea. The limits of its territory are rigidly fixed, and the population is restricted by the prohibition of early marriages, by the exposure of infants, and by the maintenance of a determinate number of individual lots of land in the hands of the citizens who cultivate the soil. These precautions are inspired more by political and moral motives than by the %Malthusian fear of failure of subsistence. Plato aims, as far as possible, at equality of property amongst the families of the community which are engaged in the immediate prosecution of industry. This last class, as distinguished from the governing and military classes, he holds, according to the spirit of his age, in but little esteem; he regards their habitual occupations as tending to the degradation of the mind and the enfeeblement of the body, and rendering those who follow them unfit for the higher duties of men and citizens.

The lowest forms of labour he would commit to foreigners and slaves. Again, in the spirit of ancient theory, he wishes to banish the precious metals, as far as practicable, from use in internal commerce, and forbids the lending of money on interest, leaving indeed to the free will of the debtor even the repayment of the capital of the loan. All economic dealings he subjects to active control on the part of the Government, not merely to prevent violence and fraud, but to check the growth of luxurious habits, and secure to the population of the state a due supply of the necessaries and comforts of life. Contrasted with the exaggerated idealism of Plato is the somewhat limited but eminently practical genius of Xenophon. In him the man of action predominates, but he has also a large element of the speculative tendency and talent of the Greek. His treatise entitled Oeconomicus is well worth reading for the interesting and animated picture it presents of some aspects of contemporary life, and is justly praised by Sismondi for the spirit of mild philanthropy and tender piety which breathes through it.

But it scarcely passes beyond the bounds of domestic economy, though within that limit its author exhibits much sound sense and sagacity. His precepts for the judicious conduct of private property do not concern us here, or his wise suggestions for the government of the family and its dependents. Yet it is in this narrower sphere and in general in the concrete domain that his chief excellence lies; to economics in their wider aspects he does not contribute much. He shares the ordinary preference of his fellow-countrymen for agriculture over other employments, and is, indeed, enthusiastic in his praises of it as promoting patriotic and religious feeling and a respect for property, as furnishing the best preparation for military life, and as leaving sufficient time and thought disposable to admit of considerable intellectual and political activity.

Yet his practical sense leads him to attribute greater importance than most other Greek writers to manufactures, and still more to trade, to enter more largely on questions relating to their conditions and development, and to bespeak for them the countenance and protection of the state. Though his views on the nature of money are vague, and in some respects erroneous, he sees that its export in exchange for commodities will not impoverish the community. He also insists on the necessity, with a view to a flourishing commerce with other countries, of peace, of a courteous and respectful treatment of foreign traders, and of a prompt and equitable decision of their legal suits. The institution of slavery he of course recognises and does not disapprove; he even recommends, for the increase of the Attic revenues, the hiring out of slaves by the state for labour in the mines, after branding them to prevent their escape, the number of slaves being constantly increased by fresh purchases out of the gains of the enterprise.

Almost the whole system of Greek ideas up to the time of Aristotle is represented in his encyclopaedic construction. Mathematical and astronomical science was largely developed at a later stage, but in the field of social studies no higher point was ever attained by the Greeks than is reached in the writings of this great thinker Both his gifts and his situation eminently favoured him in the treatment of these subjects. He combined in rare measure a capacity for keen observation with generalising power, and sobriety of judgment with ardour for the public good. All that was original or significant in the political life of Hellas had run its course before his time or under his own eyes, and he had thus a large basis of varied experience on which to ground his conclusions. Standing outside the actual movement of contemporary public life, he occupied the position of thoughtful spectator and impartial judge.

He could not, indeed, for reasons already stated, any more than other Greek speculators; attain a fully normal attitude in these researches. Nor could he pass beyond the sphere of what is now called statical sociology; the idea of laws of the historical development of social phenomena he scarcely apprehended, except in some small degree in relation to the succession of political forms. But there is to be found in his writings a remarkable body of sound and valuable thoughts on the constitution and working of the social organism The special notices of economic subjects are neither so numerous nor so detailed as we should desire. Like all the Greek thinkers, he recognises but one doctrine of the state, under which ethics, politics proper, and economics take their place as departments, bearing to each other a very close relation, and having indeed their lines of demarcation from each other not very distinctly marked. When wealth comes under consideration, it is studied not as an end in itself, but with a view to the higher elements and ultimate aims of the collective life.

The origin of society he traces, not to economic necessities, but to natural social impulses in the human constitution. The nature of the social union, when thus established, being determined by the partly spontaneous partly systematic combination of diverse activities, he respects the independence of the latter whilst seeking to affect their convergence. He therefore opposes himself to the suppression of personal freedom and initiative, and the excessive subordination of the individual to the state, and rejects the community of property and wives proposed by Plato for his governing class. The principle of private property he regards as deeply rooted in man, and the evils which are alleged to result from the corresponding social ordinance he thinks ought really to be attributed either to the imperfections of our nature or to the vices of other public institutions. Community of goods must, in his view, tend to neglect of the common interest and to the disturbance of social harmony.

Of the several classes which provide for the different wants of the society, those who are occupied directly with its material needs — the immediate cultivators of the soil, the mechanics and artificers — are excluded from any share in the government of the state, as being without the necessary leisure and cultivation, and apt to be debased by the nature of their occupations. In a celebrated passage he propounds a theory of slavery, in which it is based on the universality of the relation between command and obedience, and on the natural division by which the ruling is marked off from the subject race. He regards the slave as having no independent will, but as an "animated tool" in the hands of his master; and in his subjection to such control, if only it be intelligent, Aristotle holds that the true well-being of the inferior as well as of the superior is to be found.

This view, so shocking to our modern sentiment, is of course not personal to Aristotle; it is simply the theoretic presentation of the facts of Greek life, in which the existence of a body of citizens pursuing the higher culture and devoted to the tasks of war and government was founded on the systematic degradation of a wronged and despised class, excluded from all the higher offices of human beings and sacrificed to the maintenance of a special type of society. The methods of economic acquisition are divided by Aristotle into two, one of which has for its aim the appropriation of natural products and their application to the material uses of the household; under this head come hunting, fishing, cattle-rearing, and agriculture.

With this primary and "natural" method is, in some sense, contrasted the other to which Aristotle gives the name of "chrematistic," in which an active exchange of products goes on, and money comes into operation as its medium and regulator. A certain measure of this "non-natural" method, as it may be termed in opposition to the preceding and simpler form of industrial life, is accepted by Aristotle as a necessary extension of the latter, arising out of increased activity of intercourse, and satisfying real wants. But its development on the great scale, founded on the thirst for enjoyment and the unlimited desire of gain, he condemns as unworthy and corrupting. Though his views on this subject appear to be principally based on moral grounds, there are some indications of his having entertained the erroneous opinion held by the physiocrats of the eighteenth century, that agriculture alone (with the kindred arts above joined with it) is truly productive, whilst the other kinds of industry, which either modify the products of nature or distribute them by way of exchange, however convenient and useful they may be, make no addition to the wealth of the community.

He rightly regards money as altogether different from wealth, illustrating the difference by the story of Midas. And he seems to have seen that money, though its use rests on a social convention, must be composed of a material possessing an independent value of its own. That his views on capital were indistinct appears from his famous argument against interest on loans, which is based on the idea that money is barren and cannot produce money. Like the other Greek social philosophers, Aristotle recommends to the care of Governments the preservation of a due proportion between the extent of the civic territory and its population, and relies on ante-nuptial continence, late marriages, and the prevention or destruction of births for the due limitation of the number of citizens, the insufficiency of the latter being dangerous to the independence and its superabundance to the tranquility and good order of the state.

The Romans

Notwithstanding the eminently practical, realistic, and utilitarian character of the Romans, there was no energetic exercise of their powers in the economic field; they developed no large and many-sided system of production and exchange. Their historic mission was military and political, and the national energies were mainly devoted to the public service at home and in the field. To agriculture, indeed, much attention was given from the earliest times, and on it was founded the existence of the hardy population which won the first steps in the march to universal dominion. But in the course of their history the cultivation of the soil by a native yeomanry gave place to the introduction, in great numbers, of slave labourers acquired by their foreign conquests; and for the small properties of the earlier period were substituted the vast estates — the *latifundia* — which, in the judgment of Pliny, were the ruin of Italy.

The industrial arts and commerce (the latter, at least when not conducted on a great scale) they regarded as ignoble pursuits, unworthy of free citizens; and this feeling of contempt was not merely a prejudice of narrow or unin-structed minds, but was shared by Cicero and others among the most liberal spirits of the nation. As might be expected from the want of speculative originality among the Romans, there is little evidence of serious theoretic inquiry on economic subjects. Their ideas on these as on other social questions were for the most part borrowed from the Greek thinkers. Such traces of economic thought as do occur are to be found in (1) the philosophers, (2) the writers *de re rustica,* and (3) the jurists. It must, however, be admitted that many of the passages in these authors referred to by those who assert the claim of the Romans to a more prominent place in the history of the science often contain only obvious truths or vague generalities.

In the philosophers, whom Cicero, Seneca, and the elder Pliny sufficiently represent (the last indeed being rather a learned encyclopaedist or polyhistor than a philosopher), we find a general consciousness of the decay of industry, the relaxation of morals, and the growing spirit of self-indulgence amongst their contemporaries, who are represented as deeply tainted with the imported vices of the conquered nations. This sentiment, both in these writers and in the poetry and miscellaneous literature of their times, is accompanied by a half-factitious enthusiasm for agriculture and an exaggerated estimate of country life and of early Roman habits, which are principally, no doubt, to be regarded as a form of protest against existing abuses, and, from this point of view, remind us of the declamations of Rousseau in a not dissimilar age. But there is little of larger or just thinking on the prevalent economic evils and their proper remedies.

Pliny, still further in the spirit of Rousseau, is of opinion that the introduction of gold as a medium of exchange was a thing to be deplored, and that the age of barter was preferable to that of money. He expresses views on the necessity of preventing the efflux of money similar to those of the modern mercantile school — views which Cicero also, though not so clearly, appears to have entertained. Cato, Varro, and Columella concern themselves more with the technical precepts of husbandry than with the general conditions of industrial success and social well-being. But the two last named have the great merit of having seen and proclaimed the superior value of free to slave labour, and Columella is convinced that to the use of the latter the decline of the agricultural economy of the Romans was in a great measure to be attributed.

These three writers agree in the belief that it was chiefly by the revival and reform of agriculture that the threatening inroads of moral corruption could be stayed, the old Roman virtues fostered, and the foundations of the commonwealth strengthened. Their attitude is thus similar to that of the French physiocrats invoking the improvement and zealous pursuit of agriculture alike against the material evils and the social degeneracy of their time. The question of the comparative merits of the large and small systems of cultivation appears to have been much discussed in the old Roman, as in the modern European world; Columella is a decided advocate of the petite culture. The jurists were led by the coincidence which sometimes takes place between their point of view and that of economic science to make certain classifications and establish some more or less refined distinctions which the modern economists have either adopted from them or used independently.

They appear also (though this has been disputed, Neri and Carli maintaining the affirmative, Pagnini the negative) to have had correct notions of the nature of money as having a value of its own, determined by economic conditions, and incapable of being impressed upon it by convention or arbitrarily altered by public authority. But in general we find in these writers, as might be expected, not so much the results of independent thought as documents illustrating the facts of Roman economic life, and the historical policy of the nation with respect to economic subjects. From the latter point of view they are of much interest; and by the information they supply as to the Course of legislation relating to property generally, to sumptuary control, to the restrictions imposed on spendthrifts, to slavery, to the encouragement of population, and the like, they give us much clearer insight than we should otherwise possess into influences long potent in the history of Rome and of the Western world at large.

But, as it is with the more limited field of systematic thought on political economy that we are here occupied, we cannot enter into these subjects. One matter, however, ought to be adverted to, because it was not only repeatedly dealt with by legislation, but is treated more or less fully by all Roman writers of note, namely, the interest on money loans.

The rate was fixed by the laws of the Twelve Tables; but lending on interest was afterwards entirely prohibited by the Genucian Law. In the legislation of Justinian, rates were sanctioned varying from four to eight per cent according to the nature of the case, the latter being fixed as the ordinary mercantile rate, whilst compound interest was forbidden.

The Roman theorists, almost without exception, disapprove of lending on interest altogether. Cato, as Cicero tells us, thought it as bad as murder?" and Cicero, Seneca, Pliny, Columella all join in condemning it. It is not difficult to see how in early states of society the trade of money-lending becomes, and not unjustly, the object of popular odium; but that these writers, at a period when commercial enterprise had made considerable progress, should continue to reprobate it argues very imperfect or confused ideas on the nature and functions of capital. It is probable that practice took little heed either of these speculative ideas or of legislation on the subject, which experience shows can always be easily evaded. The traffic in money seems to have gone on all through Roman history, and the rate to have fluctuated according to the condition of the market.

Looking back on the history of ancient economic speculation, we see that, as might be anticipated *a priori*, the results attained in that field by the Greek and Roman writers were very scanty. As Dühring has well remarked, the questions with which the science has to do were regarded by the ancient thinkers rather from their political than their properly economic side. This we have already pointed out with respect to their treatment of the subject of population, and the same may be seen in the case of the doctrine of the division of labour, with which Plato and Aristotle are in some degree occupied. They regard that principle as a basis of social classification, or use it in showing that society is founded on a spontaneous co-operation of diverse activities.

From the strictly economic point of view, there are three important propositions which can be enunciated respecting that division: — (1) that its extension within any branch of production makes the products cheaper; (2) that it is limited by the extent of the market; and (3) that it can be carried further in manufactures than in agriculture. But we shall look in vain for these propositions in the ancient writers; the first alone might be inferred from their discussions of the subject. It has been the tendency especially of German scholars to magnify unduly the extent and value of the contributions of antiquity to economic knowledge. The Greek and Roman authors ought certainly not to be omitted in any account of the evolution of this branch of study. But it must be kept steadily in view that we find in them only first hints or rudiments of general economic truths, and that the science is essentially a modern one. We shall indeed see hereafter that it could not have attained its definitive constitution before our own time.

The Middle Ages

The middle Ages (400-1300 A.D.) form a period of great significance in the economic, as in the general, history of Europe. They represent a vast transition, in which the germs of a new world were deposited, but in which little was fully elaborated. There is scarcely anything in the later movement of European society which we do not find there, though as yet, for the most part, crude and undeveloped. The medieval period was the object of contemptuous depreciation on the part of the liberal schools of the last century, principally because it contributed so little to literature. But there are things more important to mankind than literature and the great men of the Middle Ages had enough to do in other fields to occupy their utmost energies.

The development of the Catholic institutions and the gradual establishment and maintenance of a settled order after the dissolution of the Western empire absorbed the powers of the thinkers and practical men of several centuries. The first medieval phase, from the commencement of the fifth century to the end of the seventh, was occupied with the painful and stormy struggle towards the foundation of the new ecclesiastical and civil system; three more centuries were filled with the work of its consolidation and defence against the assaults of nomad populations; only in the final phase, during the eleventh, twelfth, and thirteenth centuries, when the unity of the West was founded by the collective action against impending Moslem invasion, did it enjoy a sufficiently secure and stable existence to exhibit its essential character and produce its noblest personal types.

The elaboration of feudalism was, indeed, in progress during the whole period, showing itself in the decomposition of power and the hierarchical subordination of its several grades, the movement being only temporarily suspended in the second phase by the salutary dictatorship of Charlemagne. But not before the first century of the last phase was the feudal system fully constituted. In like manner, only in the final phase could the effort of Catholicism after a universal discipline be carried out on the great scale — an effort for ever admirable though necessarily on the whole unsuccessful. No large or varied economic activity was possible under the full ascendancy of feudalism. That organisation, as has been abundantly shown by philosophical historians, was indispensable for the preservation of order and for public defence, and contributed important elements to general civilization. But, whilst recognizing it as opportune and relatively beneficent, we must not expect from it advantages inconsistent with its essential nature and historical office.

The class which predominated in it was not sympathetic with industry, and held the handicrafts in contempt, except those subservient to war or rural sports. The whole practical life of the society was founded on territorial property. The wealth of the lord consisted in the produce of his lands and the dues paid to him in kind; this wealth was spent in supporting a body of retainers whose services were repaid by their maintenance. There could be little room for manufactures, and less for commerce; and agriculture was carried on with a view to the wants of the family, or at most of the immediate neighbourhood, not to those of a wider market. The economy of the period was therefore simple, and, in the absence of special motors from without, unprogressive.

In the latter portion of the middle Ages several circumstances came into action which greatly modified these conditions. The Crusades undoubtedly produced a powerful economic effect by transferring in many cases the possessions of the feudal chiefs to the industrious classes, whilst by bringing different nations and races into contact, by enlarging the horizon and widening the conceptions of the populations, as well as by affording a special stimulus to navigation, they tended to give a new activity to international trade. The independence of the towns and the rising importance of the burgher class supplied a counterpoise to the power of the land aristocracy; and the strength of these new social elements was increased by the corporate constitution given to the urban industries, the police of the towns being also founded on the trade guilds, as that of the country districts was on the feudal relations.

The increasing demand of the towns for the products of agriculture gave to the prosecution of that art a more extended and speculative character; and this again led to improved methods of transport and communication. But the range of commercial enterprise continued everywhere narrow, except in some favoured centers, such as the Italian republics, in which, however, the growth of the normal habits of industrial life was impeded or perverted by military ambition, which was not, in the case of those communities, checked as it was elsewhere by the pressure of an aristocratic class. Every great change of opinion on the destinies of man and the guiding principles of conduct must react on the sphere of material interests; and the Catholic religion had a powerful influence on the economic life of the middle Ages.

Christianity inculcates, perhaps, no more effectively than the industry, thrift, older religions the special economic virtues of fidelity to engagements, obedience to rightful authority; but it brought out more forcibly and presented more persistently the higher aims of life, and so produced a more elevated way of viewing the different social relations. It purified domestic life, a reform which has the most important economic results. It taught the doctrine of fundamental human equality, heightened the dignity of labour, and preached with quite a new emphasis the obligations of love, compassion, and forgiveness, and the claims of the poor. The constant presentation to the general mind and conscience of these ideas, the dogmatic bases of which were scarcely as yet assailed by scepticism, must have had a powerful effect in moralising life.

But to the influence of Christianity as a moral doctrine was added that of the Church as an organization, charged with the application of the doctrine to men's daily transactions. Besides the teachings of the sacred books, there was a mass of ecclesiastical legislation providing specific prescriptions for the conduct of the faithful. And this legislation dealt with the economic as with other provinces of social activity. In the *Corpus Juris Canonici,* which condenses the result of centuries of study and effort, along with much else is set out what we may call the Catholic economic theory, if we understand by theory, not a reasoned explanation of phenomena, but a body of ideas leading to prescriptions for the guidance of conduct. Life is here looked at from the point of view of spiritual well-being; the aim is to establish and maintain amongst men a true kingdom of God.

The canonists are friendly to the notion of a community of goods from the side of sentiment ("Dulcissima rerum possessio communis est"), though they regard the distinction of meum and tuum as an institution necessitated by the fallen state of man. In cases of need the public authority is justified in re-establishing *pro hac vice* the primitive community. The care of the poor is not a matter of free choice; the relief of their necessities is *debitum legale.*

Avaritia is, idolatry; *cupiditas*, even when it does not grasp at what is another's, is the root of all evil, and ought to be not merely regulated but eradicated. Agriculture and handiwork are viewed as legitimate modes of earning food and clothing; but trade is regarded with disfavour, because it was held almost certainly to lead to fraud: of agriculture it was said, "Deo non displicet"; but of the merchant, "Deo placere non potest."

The seller was bound to fix the price of his wares, not according to the market rate, as determined by supply and demand, but according to their real value (*justum pretium*). He must not conceal the faults of his merchandise, nor take advantage of the need or ignorance of the buyer to obtain from him more than the fair price. Interest on money is forbidden; the prohibition of usury is, indeed, as Roscher says, the centre of the whole canonistic system of economy, as well as the foundation of a great part of the ecclesiastical jurisdiction. The question whether a transaction was or was not usurious turning mainly on the intentions of the parties, the innocence or blameworthiness of dealings in which money was lent became rightfully a subject of determination for the Church, either by her casuists or in her courts.

The foregoing principles point towards a noble ideal, but by their ascetic exaggeration they worked in some directions as an impediment to industrial progress. Thus, whilst, with the increase of production, a greater division of labour and a larger employment of borrowed capital naturally followed, the laws on usury tended to hinder this expansion. Hence they were undermined by various exceptions, or evaded by fictitious transactions. These laws were in fact dictated by, and adapted to, early conditions-to a state of society in which money loans were commonly sought either with a view to wasteful pleasures or for the relief of such urgent distress as ought rather to have been the object of Christian beneficence. But they were quite unsuited to a period in which capital was borrowed for the extension of enterprise and the employment of labour.

The absolute theological spirit in this, as in other instances, could not admit the modification in rules of conduct demanded by a new social situation; and vulgar good sense better understood what the fundamental conditions of industrial life were. When the intellectual activity previously repressed by the more urgent claims of social preoccupations tended to revive towards the close of the mediaeval period, the want of a rational appreciation of the whole of human affairs was felt, and was temporarily met by the adoption of the results of the best Greek speculation. Hence we find in the writings of St. Thomas Aquinas the political and economic doctrines of Aristotle reproduced with a partial infusion of Christian elements. His adherence to his master's point of view is strikingly shown by the fact that he accepts (at least if he is the author of the *De Regimine Principum*) the Aristotelian theory of slavery, though by the action of the forces of his own time the last relics of that institution were being eliminated from European society.

This great change — the enfranchisement of the working classes — was the most important practical outcome of the middle Ages. The first step in this movement was the transformation of slavery, properly so called, into serfdom. The latter was, by its nature, a transitory condition. The serf was bound to the soil, had fixed domestic relations, and participated in the religious life of the society; and the tendency of all his circumstances, as well as of the opinions and sentiments of the time, was in the direction of liberation. This issue was, indeed, not so speedily reached by the rural as by the urban workman. Already in the second phase serfdom is abolished in the cities and towns, whilst agricultural serfdom does not anywhere disappear before the third.

The latter revolution is attributed by Adam Smith to the operation of selfish interests, that of the proprietor on the one hand, who discovered the superior productiveness of cultivation by free tenants, and that of the sovereign on the other, who, jealous of the great lords, encouraged the encroachments of the villains on their authority. But that the Church deserves a share of the merit seems beyond doubt — moral impulses, as often happens, conspiring with political and economic motives. The serfs were treated best on the ecclesiastical estates, and the members of the priesthood, both by their doctrine and by their situation since the Northern conquests, were constituted patrons and guardians of the oppressed or subject classes.

Out of the liberation of the serfs rose the first lineaments of the hierarchical constitution of modern industry in the separation between the entrepreneurs and the workers. The personal enfranchisement of the latter, stimulating activity and developing initiative, led to accumulations, which were further promoted by the establishment of order and good government by the civic corporations which grew out of the enfranchisement. Thus an active capitalist class came into existence. It appeared first in commerce, the inhabitants of the trading cities importing expensive luxuries from foreign countries, or the improved manufactures of richer communities, for which the great proprietors gladly exchanged the raw produce of their lands. In performing the office of carriers, too, between different countries, these cities had an increasing field for commercial enterprise.

At a later period, as Adam Smith has shown, commerce promoted the growth of manufactures, which were either produced for foreign sale, or made from foreign materials, or imitated from the work of foreign artificers. But the first important development of handicrafts in modern Europe belongs to the fourteenth and fifteenth centuries, and the rise of manufacturing entrepreneurs is not conspicuous within the Middle Ages properly so called. Agriculture, of course, lags behind; though the feudal lords tend to transform themselves into directors of agricultural enterprise, their habits and prejudices retard such a movement and the advance of rural industry proceeds slowly. It does, however, proceeds, partly by the stimulation arising from the desire to procure the finer objects of manufacture imported from abroad or produced by increased skill at home, partly by the expenditure on the land of capital amassed in the prosecution of urban industries.

Some of the trade corporations in the cities appear to have been of great antiquity, but it was in the thirteenth century that they rose to importance by being legally recognised and regulated. These corporations have been much too absolutely condemned by most of the economists, who insist on applying to the Middle Ages the ideas of the eighteenth and nineteenth centuries. They were, it is true, unfitted for modern times, and it was necessary that they should disappear; their existence indeed was quite unduly prolonged. But they were at first in several respects highly beneficial. They were a valuable rallying-point for the new industrial forces, which were strengthened by the rise of the esprit de corps which they fostered. They improved technical skill by the precautions which were taken for the solidity and finished execution of the wares produced in each locality, and it was with a view to the advancement of the industrial arts that St. Louis undertook the better organization of the trades of Paris. The corporations also encouraged good moral habits through the sort of spontaneous surveillance which they exercised, and they tended to develop the social sentiment within the limits of each profession, in times when a larger public spirit could scarcely yet are looked for.

Modern Times: First and Second Phases

The close of the Middle Ages, as Comte has shown, must be placed at the end, not of the fifteenth but of the thirteenth century. The modern period, which then began, is filled by a development exhibiting three successive phases, and issuing in the state of things which characterises our own epoch.

1. During the fourteenth and fifteenth centuries the Catholico-feudal system was breaking down by the mutual conflicts of its own official members, whilst the constituent elements of a new order were rising beneath

it. On the practical side the antagonists matched against each other were the crown and the feudal chiefs; and these rival powers sought to strengthen themselves by forming alliances with the towns and the industrial forces they represented. The movements of this phase can scarcely be said to find an echo in any contemporary economic literature.

2. In the second phase of the modern period, which opens with the beginning of the sixteenth century, the spontaneous collapse of the medieval structure is followed by a series of systematic assaults which still further disorganize it. During this phase the central temporal power, which has made a great advance in stability and resources, lays hold of the rising elements of manufactures and commerce, and seeks, whilst satis-fying the popular enthusiasm for their promotion, to use them for political ends, and make them sub serve its own strength and splendour by furnishing the treasure necessary for military success. With this practical effort, and the social tendencies on which it rests, the Mercantile school of political economy, which then obtains a spontaneous ascendancy, is in close relation. Whilst partially succeeding in the policy we have indicated, the European Governments yet on the whole necessarily fail, their origin and nature disqualifying them for the task of guiding the industrial movement; and the discredit of the spiritual power, with which most of them are confederate, further weakens and undermines them.
3. In the last phase, which coincides approximately with the eighteenth century, the tendency to a completely new system, both temporal and spiritual, becomes decisively pronounced, first in the philosophy and general literature of the period, and then in the great French explosion. The universal critical doctrine, which had been announced by the Protestantism of the previous phase, and systematised in England towards the close of that phase, is propagated and popularised,

especially by French writers. The spirit of individualism inherent in the doctrine was eminently adapted to the wants of the time, and the general favour with which the dogmas of the social contract and *laissez faire* were received indicated a just sentiment of the conditions proper to the contemporary situation of European societies.

So long as a new coherent system of thought and life could not be introduced, what was to be desired was a large and active development of personal energy under no further control of the old social powers than would suffice to prevent anarchy. Governments were therefore rightly called on to abandon any effective direction of the social movement and, as far as possible, to restrict their intervention to the maintenance of material order. This policy was, from its nature, of temporary application only; but the negative school, according to its ordinary spirit, erected what was merely a transitory and exceptional necessity into a permanent and normal law. The unanimous European movement towards the liberation of effort, which sometimes rose to the height of a public passion, had various sides, corresponding to the different aspects of thought and life; and of the economic side the French physiocrats were the first theoretic representatives on the large scale, though the office they undertook was, both in its destructive and organic provinces, more thoroughly and effectively done by Adam Smith, who ought to be regarded as continuing and completing their work.

It must be admitted that with the whole modern movement serious moral evils were almost necessarily connected. The general discipline which the Middle Ages had sought to institute and had partially succeeded in establishing, though on precarious bases, having broken down, the sentiment of duty was weakened along with the spirit of ensemble which is its natural ally, and individualism in doctrine tended to encourage egoism in action. In the economic field this result is especially conspicuous. National selfishness and private cupidity increasingly dominate; and the higher and lower industrial classes tend to separation and even to mutual hostility. The new elements — science and industry — which were gradually acquiring ascendancy bore, indeed in their bosom an ultimate discipline more efficacious and stable than that which had been dissolved; but the final synthesis was long too remote and too indeterminate in its nature, to be seen through the dispersive and seemingly incoherent growth of those elements. Now, however, that synthesis is becoming appreciable; and it is the effort towards it and towards the practical system to be founded on it, that gives its peculiar character to the period in which we live. And to this spontaneous nisus of society corresponds, as we shall see, a new form of economic doctrine, in which it tends to be absorbed into general sociology and subordinated to morals.

It will be the object of the following pages to verify and illustrate in detail the scheme here broadly indicated, and to point out the manner in which the respective features of the several successive modern phases find their counterpart and reflection in the historical development of economic speculation.

First Modern Phase

The first phase was marked, on the one hand, by the spontaneous decomposition of the medieval system, and, on the other, by the rise of several important elements of the new order. The spiritual power became less apt as well as less able to fulfill its moral office, and the social movement was more and more left to the irregular impulses of individual energy, often enlisted in the service of ambition and cupidity. Strong Governments were formed, which served to maintain material order amidst the growing intellectual and moral disorder. The universal admission of the commons as an element in the political system showed the growing strength of the industrial forces, as did also in another way the insurrections of the working classes.

The decisive prevalence of peaceful activity was indicated by the rise of the institution of paid armies — at first temporary, afterwards permanent — which prevented the interruption or distraction of labour by devoting a determinate minority of the population to martial operations and exercises. Manufactures became increasingly important; and in this branch of industry the distinction between the entrepreneur and the workers was first firmly established, whilst fixed relations between these were made possible by the restriction of military training and service to a special profession. Navigation was facilitated by the use of the mariner's compass. The art of printing showed how the intellectual movement and the industrial development were destined to be brought into relation with each other and to work towards common ends. Public credit rose in Florence, Venice, and Genoa long before Holland and England attained any great financial importance. Just at the close of the phase, the discovery of America and of the new route to the East, whilst revolutionising the course of trade, prepared the way for the establishment of colonies, which contributed powerfully to the growing preponderance of industrial life, and pointed to its ultimate universality.

It is doubtless due to the equivocal nature of this stage, standing between the medieval and the fully characterised modern period, that on the theoretic side we find nothing corresponding to such marvellous practical ferment and expansion. The general political doctrine of Aquinas was retained, with merely subordinate modifications. The only special economic question which seems to have received particular attention was that of the nature and functions of money, the importance of which began to be felt as payments in service or in kind was discontinued, and regular systems of taxation began to be introduced.

Roscher and after him Wolowski, have called attention, to Nicole Oresme, who was teacher of Charles V, King of France, and died Bishop of Lisieux in 1382. Roscher pronounces him a great economist. His *Tractatus de Origine, Natura, Jure, et Mutationibus Monetarum* contains a theory of money which is almost entirely correct according to the views of the nineteenth century, and is stated with such brevity, clearness, and simplicity of language as show the work to be from the hand of a master.

Second Modern Phase: Mercantile System

Throughout the first modern phase the rise of the new social forces had been essentially spontaneous; in the second they became the object of systematic encouragement on the part of Governments, which, now that the financial methods of the Middle Ages no longer sufficed, could not further their military and political ends by any other means than increased taxation, implying augmented wealth of the community. Industry thus became a permanent interest of European Governments, and even tended to become the principal object of their policy. In natural harmony with this state of facts, the mercantile system arose and grew, attaining its highest development about the middle of the seventeenth century.

The Mercantile doctrine, stated in its most extreme form, makes wealth and money identical, and regards it therefore as the great object of a community so to conduct its dealings with other nations as to attract to itself the largest possible share of the precious metals. Each country must seek to export the utmost possible quantity of its own manufactures and to import as little as possible of those of other countries, receiving the difference of the two values in gold and silver. This difference is called the balance of trade, and the balance is favourable when more money is received than is paid. Governments must resort to all available expedients — prohibition of, or high duties on, the importation of foreign wares, bounties on the export of home manufactures, restrictions on the export of the precious metals — for the purpose of securing such a balance.

But this statement of the doctrine, though current in the text-books, does not represent correctly the views of all who must be classed as belonging to the Mercantile school. Many of the members of that school were much too clear-sighted to entertain the belief, which the modern student feels difficulty in supposing any class of thinkers to have professed, that wealth consists exclusively of gold and silver. The mercantilists may be best described, as Roscher has remarked, not by any definite economic theorem which they held in common, but by a set of theoretic tendencies, commonly found in combination, though severally prevailing in different degrees in different minds. These tendencies may be enumerated as follows: (1) Towards over-estimating the importance of possessing a large amount of the precious metals; (2) towards an undue exaltation (a) of foreign trade over domestic, and (b) of the industry which works up materials over that which provides them; (3) towards attaching too high a value to a dense population as an element of national strength; and (4) towards invoking the action of the state in furthering artificially the attainment of the several ends thus proposed as desirable.

If we consider the contemporary position of affairs in Western Europe, we shall have no difficulty in understanding how these tendencies would inevitably arise. The discoveries in the New World had led to a large development of the European currencies. The old feudal economy founded principally on dealings in kind, had given way before the new "money economy," and the dimensions of the latter were everywhere expanding. Circulation was becoming more rapid, distant communications more frequent, city life and movable property more important. The mercantilists were impressed by the fact that money is wealth sui generis, that it is at all times in universal demand, and that it puts into the hands of its possessor the power of acquiring all other commodities.

The period, again, was marked by the formation of great states, with powerful Governments at their head. These Governments required men and money for the maintenance of permanent armies, which, especially for the religious and Italian wars, were kept up on a great scale, Court expenses, too, were more lavish than ever before, and a larger number of civil officials were employed. The royal domains and dues were insufficient to meet these requirements, and taxation grew with the demands of the monarchies. Statesmen saw that for their own political ends industry must flourish. But manufactures make possible a denser population and a higher total value of exports than agriculture; they open a less limited and more promptly extensible field to enterprise. Hence they became the object of special Governmental favour and patronage, whilst agriculture fell comparatively into the background.

The growth of manufactures reacted on commerce, to which a new and mighty arena had been opened by the establishment of colonies. These were viewed simply as estates to be worked for the advantage of the mother countries, and the aim of statesmen was to make the colonial trade a new source of public revenue. Each nation, as a whole, working for its own power, and the greater ones for predominance, they entered into a competitive struggle in the economic no less than in the political field, success in the former being indeed, by the rulers, regarded as instrumental to pre-eminence in the latter. A national economic interest came to exist, of which the Government made itself the representative head. States became a sort of artificial hothouses for the rearing of urban industries. Production was subjected to systematic regulation with the object of securing the goodness and cheapness of the exported articles, and so maintaining the place of the nation in foreign markets.

The industrial control was exercised, in part directly by the State, but largely also through privileged corporations and trading companies. High duties on imports were resorted to, at first perhaps mainly for revenue, but afterwards in the interest of national production., Commercial treaties were a principal object of diplomacy, the end in view being to exclude the competition of other nations in foreign markets, whilst in the home market as little room as possible was given for the introduction of anything but raw materials from abroad. The colonies were prohibited from trading with other European nations than the parent country, to which they supplied either the precious metals or raw produce purchased with home manufactures. It is evident that what is known as the Mercantile doctrine was essentially the theoretic counterpart of the practical activities of the time, and that nations and Governments were led to it, not by any form of scientific thought, but by the force of outward circumstance, and the observation of facts which lay on the surface.

And yet, if we regard the question from the highest point of view of philosophic history, we must pronounce the universal enthusiasm of this second modern phase for manufactures and commerce to have been essentially just, as leading the nations into the main avenues of general social development. If the thought of the period, instead of being impelled by contemporary circumstances, could have been guided by sociological prevision, it must have entered with zeal upon the same path which it empirically selected. The organization of agricultural industry could not at that period make any marked progress, for the direction of its operations was still in the hands of the feudal class, which could not in general really learn the habits of industrial life, or place itself in sufficient harmony with the workers on its domains. The industry of the towns had to precede that of the country, and the latter had to be developed mainly through the indirect action of the former. And it is plain that it was in the life of the manufacturing proletariat, whose labours are necessarily the most continuous and the most social, that a systematic discipline could at a later period be first applied, to be afterwards extended to the rural populations.

That the efforts of Governments for the furtherance of manufactures and commerce were really effective towards that end is admitted by Adam Smith, and cannot reasonably be doubted, though free trade doctrinaires have often denied it. Technical skill must have been promoted by their encouragements; whilst new forms of national production were fostered by attracting workmen from other countries, and by lightening the burden of taxation on struggling industries. Communication and transport by land and sea were more rapidly improved with a view to facilitate traffic; and, not the least important effect, the social dignity of the industrial professions was enhanced relatively to that of the classes before exclusively dominant.

It has often been asked to whom the foundation of the mercantile system, in the region whether of thought or of practice, is to be attributed. But the question admits of no absolute answer. That mode of conceiving economic facts arises spontaneously in unscientific minds, and ideas suggested by it are to be found in the Greek and Latin writers. The policy which it dictates was, as we have shown, inspired by the situation of the European nations at the opening of the modern period. Such a policy had been already in some degree practised in the fourteenth and fifteenth centuries, thus preceding any formal exposition or defence of its speculative basis. At the commencement of the sixteenth century it began to exercise a widely extended influence. Charles V adopted it, and his example contributed much to its predominance. Henry VIII and Elizabeth confirmed their measures to it. The leading states soon entered on a universal competition, in which each Power brought into play all its political and financial resources for the purpose of securing to itself manufacturing and commercial preponderance. Through almost the whole of the seventeenth century, the prize so far as commerce was concerned, remained in the possession of Holland, Italy having lost her former ascendancy by the opening of the new maritime routes, and by her political misfortunes, and Spain and Germany being depressed by protracted wars and internal dissensions.

The admiring envy of Holland felt by English politicians and economists appears in such writers as Raleigh, Mun, Child, and Temple; and how strongly the same spectacle acted on French policy is shown by a well-known letter of Colbert to M. de Pomponne, ambassador to the Dutch States. Cromwell, by the Navigation Act, which destroyed the carrying trade of Holland and founded the English empire of the sea, and Colbert, by his whole economic policy, domestic and international was the chief practical representatives of the mercantile system. From the latter great statesman the Italian publicist Mengotti gave to that system the name of Colbertismo; but it would be an error to consider the French minister as having absolutely accepted its dogmas. He regarded his measures as temporary only, and spoke of protective duties as crutches by the help of which manufacturers might learn to walk and then throw them away. The policy of exclusions had been previously pursued by Sully, partly with a view to the accumulation of a royal treasure, but chiefly from his special enthusiasm for agriculture, and his dislike of the introduction of foreign luxuries as detrimental to the national character.

Colbert's tariff of 1664 not merely simplified but considerably reduced the existing duties; the tariff of 1667 indeed increased them, but that was really a political measure directed against the Dutch. It seems certain that France owed in a large measure to his policy the vast development of trade and manufactures which so much impressed the imagination of contemporary Europe, and of which we hear so much from English writers of the time of Petty. But this policy had also undeniably its dark side. Industry was forced by such systematic regulation to follow invariable courses, instead of adapting itself to changing tastes and popular demand. Nor was it free to simplify the processes of production, or to introduce increased division of labour and improved appliances. Spontaneity, initiation, and invention were repressed or discouraged, and thus ulterior sacrificed in a great measure to immediate results.

The more enlightened statesmen, and Colbert in particular, endeavoured, it is true, to minimise these disadvantages by procuring, often at great expense, and communicating to the trades through inspectors nominated by the Government, information respecting improved processes employed elsewhere in the several arts; but this, though in some degree a real, was certainly on the whole, and in the long run, an insufficient compensation. We must not expect from the writers of this stage any exposition of political economy as a whole; the publications which appeared were for the most part evoked by special exigencies, and related to particular questions, usually of a practical kind, which arose out of the great movements of the time. They were in fact of the nature of counsels to the Governments of states, pointing out how best they might develop the productive powers at their disposal and increase the resources of their respective countries. They are conceived (as List claims for them) strictly in the spirit of national economy, and cosmopolitanism is essentially foreign to them. On these monographs the mercantile theory sometimes had little influence; the problems discussed not involving its tenets. But it must in most cases be taken to be the scheme of fundamental doctrine (so far as it was ever entitled to such a description) which in the last resort underlies the writer's conclusions.

The rise of prices following on the discovery of the American mines was one of the subjects which first attracted the attention of theorists. This rise brought about a great and gradually increasing disturbance of existing economic relations, and so produced much perplexity and anxiety, which were all the more felt because the cause of the change was not understood. To this was added the loss and inconvenience arising from the debasement of the currency often resorted to by sovereigns as well as by republican states. Italy suffered most from this latter abuse, which was multiplied by her political divisions. It was this evil which called forth the work of Count Gasparo Scaruffi (*Discorso sopra le monete e della vera proporzione fra l'oro e l'argento*, 1582).

In this he put forward the bold idea of universal money, everywhere identical in size, shape, composition, and designation. The project was, of course, premature, and was not adopted even by the Italian princes to whom the author specially appealed; but the reform is one which, doubtless, the future will see realised. Gian Donato Turbolo, master of the Neapolitan mint, in his Discorsi e Relazioni, 1629, protested against any tampering with the currency. Another treatise relating to the subject of money was that of the Florentine Bernardo Davanzati, otherwise known as the able translator of Tacitus, *Lezioni delle Monete,* 1588. It is a slight and somewhat superficial production, only remarkable as written with conciseness and elegance of style.

A French writer, who dealt with the question of money, but from a different point of view, was Jean Bodin. In his *Réponse aux paradoxes de M. Malestroit touchant l'enchérissement de toutes les choses et des monnaies,* 1568, and in his *Discours sur le rehaussement et la diminution des monnaies,* 1578, he showed a more rational appreciation than many of his contemporaries of the causes of the revolution in prices, and the relation of the variations in money to the market values of wares in general as well as to the wages of labour. He saw that the amount of money in circulation did not constitute the wealth of the community, and that the prohibition of the export of the precious metals was useless, because rendered inoperative by the necessities of trade.

Bodin is no inconsiderable figure in the literary history of the epoch, and did not confine his attention to economic problems; in his *Six livres de la République,* about 1576, he studies the general conditions of the prosperity and stability of states. In harmony with the conditions of his age, he approves of absolute Governments as the most competent to ensure the security and well-being of their subjects. He enters into an elaborate defence of individual property against Plato and More, rather perhaps because the scheme of his work required the treatment of that theme than because it was practically urgent in his day, when the excesses of the Anabaptists had produced a strong feeling against communistic doctrines.

He is under the general influence of the mercantilist views, and approves of energetic Governmental interference in industrial matters, of high taxes on foreign manufactures and low duties on raw materials and articles of food, and attaches great importance to a dense population. But he is not a blind follower of the system; he wishes for unlimited freedom of trade in many cases; and he is in advance of his more eminent contemporary Montaigne in perceiving that the gain of one nation is not necessarily the loss of another. To the public finances, which he calls the sinews of the State, he devotes much attention, and insists on the duties of the Government in respect to the right adjustment of taxation. In general he deserves the praise of steadily keeping in view the higher aims and interests of society in connection with the regulation and development of its material life.

Correct views as to the cause of the general rise of prices are also put forward by the English writer, W. S. (William Stafford), in his *Briefe Conceipte of English Policy*, published in 1581, and dedicated to Queen Elizabeth. It is in the form of a dialogue, and is written with liveliness and spirit. The author seems to have been acquainted with the writings of Bodin. He has just ideas as to the nature of money, and fully understands the evils arising from a debased coinage. He describes in detail the way in which the several interests in the country had been affected by such debasement in previous reigns, as well as by the change in the value of the precious metals. The great popular grievance of his day, the conversion of arable land into pasture, he attributes chiefly to the restrictions on the export of corn, which he desires to see abolished. But in regard to manufactures he is at the same point of view with the later mercantilists, and proposes the exclusion of all foreign wares which might as well be provided at home, and the prohibition of the export of raw materials intended to be worked up abroad.

Out of the question of money, too, arose the first remarkable German production on political economy which had an original national character and addressed the public in the native tongue. The Ernestine Saxon line was inclined (1530) to introduce a debasement of the currency. A pamphlet, *Gemeine Stymmen von der Müntze,* was published in opposition to this proceeding, under the auspices of the Albertine branch, whose policy was sounder in the economic sphere. A reply appeared justifying the Ernestine project. This was followed by a rejoinder from the Albertine side.

The Ernestine pamphlet is described by Roscher as ill-written, obscure, inflated, and, as might be expected from the thesis it maintained, sophistical. But it is interesting as containing a statement of the fundamental principles of the mercantile system more than one hundred years before the publication of Mun's book, and forty-six before that of Bodin's *Six livres de la République*. The Albertine tracts, according to Roscher, exhibit such sound views of the conditions and evidences of national wealth, of the nature of money and trade, And of the rights and duties of Governments in relation to economic action, that he regards the unknown author as entitled to a place beside Raleigh and the other English "colonial-theorists" of the end of the sixteenth and beginning of the seventeenth century.

In connection with the same subject of money we meet the great name of Copernicus. His treatise *De monetae cudendae ratione,* 1526 (first printed in 1816), was written by order of King Sigismund I, and is an exposition of the principles on which it was proposed to reform the currency of the Prussian provinces of Poland. It advocates unity of the monetary system throughout the entire state, with strict integrity in the quality of the coin, and the charge of a seigniorage sufficient to cover the expenses of mintage.

Antonio Serra is regarded by some as the creator of modern political economy. He was a native of Cosenza in Calabria. His *Breve Trattato delle cause che possono fare abbondare li regni d'oro e d'argento dove non sono miniere,* 1613, was written during his imprisonment, which is believed to have been due to his having taken part in the conspiracy of Campanella for the liberation of Naples from the Spanish yoke and the establishment of a republican Government. This work, long overlooked, was brought into notice in the following century by Galiani and others. Its title alone would sufficiently indicate that the author had adopted the principles of the mercantile system, and in fact in this treatise the essential doctrines of that system are expounded in a tolerably formal and consecutive manner.

He strongly insists on the superiority of manufactures over agriculture as a source of national wealth, and uses in support of this view the prosperity of Genoa, Florence, and Venice, as contrasted with the depressed condition of Naples. With larger insight than many of the mercantilists' exhibit, he insists on the importance, towards the acquisition of wealth, not alone of favourable external conditions, but of energetic character and industrious habits in a population, as well as of a stable government and a good administration of the laws. The first systematic treatise on our science which proceeded from a French author was the *Traité de l'Économie Politique,* published by Montchrétien de Watteville (or Vasteville) in 1615.

The use of the title, says Roscher, now for the first time given to the science, was in itself an important service, since even Bacon understood by "Economia" only the theory of domestic management. The general tendencies and aims of the period are seen in the fact that this treatise, notwithstanding the comprehensive name it bears, does not deal with agriculture at all, but only with the mechanical arts, navigation, commerce, and public finance. The author is filled with the then dominant enthusiasm for foreign trade and colonies. He advocates the control by princes of the industry of their subjects, and condemns the too great freedom, which, in his opinion to their own detriment, the Governments of Spain, Portugal, and Holland had given to trade. His book may be regarded as a formal exposition of the principles of the mercantile system for the use of Frenchmen.

A similar office was performed in England by Thomas Mun. In his two works, *A Discourse of Trade from England unto the East Indies*, 2nd ed., 1621, and especially in *England's Treasure by Foreign Trade*, 1664 (posthumous), we have for the first time a clear and systematic statement of the theory of the balance of trade, as well as of the means by which, according to the author's view, a favourable balance could be secured for England. The great object of the economic policy of a state, according to him, should be so to manage its export of manufactures, its direct and carrying trade, and its customs duties, as to attract to itself money from abroad. He was, however, opposed to the prohibition of the export of the precious metals in exchange for foreign wares, but on the ground, fully according with his general principles, that those wares might afterwards be re-exported and might then bring back more treasure than had been originally expended in their purchase; the first export of money might be, as he said, the seed-time, of which the ultimate receipt of a larger amount would be the harvest. He saw, too, that it is inexpedient to have too much money circulating in a country, as this enhances the prices of commodities, and so makes them less saleable to foreigners, but he is favourable to the formation and maintenance of a state treasure.

One of the most remarkable of the moderate mercantilists was Sir Josiah Child (*Brief Observations concerning Trade and the interest of Money*, 1668, and *A New Discourse of Trade*, 1668 and 1790). He was one of those who held up Holland as a model for the imitation of his fellow-countrymen. He is strongly impressed with the importance for national wealth and well-being of a low rate of interest, which he says is to commerce and agriculture what the soul is to the body, and which he held to be the "*cauza causans* of all the other causes of the riches of the Dutch people." Instead of regarding such low rate as dependent on determinate conditions, which should be allowed to evolve themselves spontaneously, he thinks it should be created and maintained by public authority.

Child, whilst adhering to the doctrine of the balance of trade, observes that a people cannot always sell to foreigners without ever buying from them, and denies that the export of the precious metals is necessarily detrimental. He has the ordinary mercantilist partiality for a numerous population. He advocates the reservation by the Mother Country of the sole right of trade with her colonies, and, under certain limitations, the formation of privileged trading companies. As to the Navigation Act, he takes up a position not unlike that afterwards occupied by Adam Smith, regarding that measure much more favourably from the political than from the economic point of view. It will be seen that he is somewhat eclectic in his opinions; but he cannot properly be regarded, though some have attributed to him that character, as a precursor of the free-trade school of the eighteenth century.

Two other eclectics may be here mentioned, in whom just views are mingled with mercantilist prejudices — Sir William Temple and Charles Davenant. The former in his *Observations upon the United Province of the Netherlands*, 1672, and his *Essay on the Trade of Ireland*, 1673, has many excellent remarks on fundamental economic principles, as on the functions of labour and of saving in the production of national wealth; but he is infected with the errors of the theory of the balance of trade. He follows the lead of Raleigh and Child in urging his fellow-countrymen to imitate the example of the Dutch in their economic policy — advice which in his case was founded on his observations during a lengthened residence in Holland as ambassador to the States. Davenant in his *Essay on the East India Trade*, 1696-97, *Essay on the Probable Ways of making the People Gainers in the Balance of Trade*, 1699, etc., also takes up an eclectic position, combining some correct views on wealth and money with mercantilist notions on trade, and recommending Governmental restrictions on colonial commerce as strongly as he advocates freedom of exchange at home.

Whilst the mercantile system represented the prevalent form of economic thought in the seventeenth century, and was alone dominant in the region of practical statesmanship, there was growing up, side by side with it, a body of opinion, different and indeed hostile in character, which was destined ultimately to drive it from the field. The new ideas were first developed in England, though it was in France that in the following century they took hold of the public mind, and became a power in politics. That they should first show themselves here, and afterwards be extended, applied, and propagated throughout Europe by French writers, belongs to the order of things according to which the general negative doctrine in morals and politics, undoubtedly of English origin, found its chief home in France, and was thence diffused in widening circles through the civilized world. In England this movement of economic thought took the shape mainly of individual criticism of the prevalent doctrines, founded on a truer analysis of facts and conceptions; in France it was penetrated with a powerful social sentiment, furnished the creed of a party, and inspired a protest against existing institutions and an urgent demand for practical reform.

Regarded from the theoretic side, the characteristic features of the new direction were the following. The view of at least the extreme mercantilists that national wealth depends on the accumulation of the precious metals is proved to be false, and the gifts of nature and the labour of man are shown to be its real sources. The exaggerated estimate of the importance of foreign commerce is reduced, and attention is once more turned to agriculture and the conditions of its successful prosecution. On the side of practical policy, a so-called favourable balance of trade is seen not to be the true object of a nation's or a statesman's efforts, but the procuring for the whole population in the fullest measure the enjoyment of the necessaries and conveniences of life.

And — what more than anything else contrasts the new system with the old—the elaborate apparatus of prohibitions, protective duties, bounties, monopolies, and privileged corporations, which the European Governments had created in the supposed interests of manufactures and trade, is denounced or deprecated as more an impediment than a furtherance, and the freedom of industry is insisted on as the one thing needful. This circle of ideas, of course, emerges only gradually, and its earliest representatives in economic literature in general apprehend it imperfectly and advocate it with reserve; but it rises steadily in importance, being more and more favoured by the highest minds, and finding an increasing body of supporters amongst the intelligent public.

Some occasional traits of an economic scheme in harmony with these new tendencies are to be found in the *De Cive* and *Leviathan* of Hobbes. But the efficacy of that great thinker lay rather in the general philosophic field; and by systematising, for the first time, the whole negative doctrine, he gave a powerful impulse towards the demolition of the existing social order, which was destined, as we shall see, to have momentous consequences in the economic no less than in the strictly political department of things.

A writer of no such extended range, but of much sagacity and good sense, was Sir William Petty, author of a number of pieces containing germs of a sound economic doctrine. A leading thought in his writings is that "labour is the father and active principle of wealth, lands are the mother." He divides a population into two classes, the productive and the unproductive, according as they are or are not occupied in producing useful material things. The value of any commodity depends, he says, anticipating Ricardo, on the amount of labour necessary for its production. He is desirous of obtaining a universal measure of value, and chooses as his unit the average food of the cheapest kind required for a man's daily sustenance.

He understands the nature of the rent of land as the excess of the price of its produce over the cost of production. He disapproves of the attempt to fix by authority a maximum rate of interest, and is generally opposed to Governmental interference with the course of industry. He sees that a country requires for its exchanges a definite quantity of money and may have too much of it, and condemns the prohibition of its exportation. He holds that one only of the precious metals must be the foundation of the currency, the other circulating as an ordinary article of merchandise. Petty's name is specially associated with the progress of statistics, with which he was much occupied, and which he called by the name of political arithmetic. Relying on the results of such inquiries, he set himself strongly against the opinion which was maintained by the author of Britannia Languens (1680), Fortrey, Roger Coke, and other writers, that the prosperity of England was on the decline.

The most thoroughgoing and emphatic assertion of the free-trade doctrine against the system of prohibitions, which had gained strength by the Revolution, was contained in Sir Dudley North's *Discourses upon Trade*, 1691. He shows that wealth may exist independently of gold or silver, its source being human industry, applied either to the cultivation of the soil or to manufactures. The precious metals, however, are one element of national wealth, and perform highly important offices. Money may exist in excess, as well as in defect, in a country; and the quantity of it required for the purposes of trade will vary with circumstances; its ebb and flow will regulate themselves spontaneously. It is a mistake to suppose that stagnation of trade arises from want of money; it must arise either from a glut of the home market, or from a disturbance of foreign commerce, or from diminished consumption caused by poverty.

The export of money in the course of traffic, instead of diminishing, increases the national wealth, trade being only an exchange of superfluities. Nations are economically related to the world just in the same way as cities to the state or as families to the city. North emphasises more than his predecessors the value of the home trade. With respect to the interest of capital, he maintains that it depends, the price of any commodity, on the proportion of demand and supply, and that a low rate is a result of the relative increase of capital, and cannot be brought about by arbitrary regulations, as had been proposed by Child and others. In arguing the question of free trade, he urges that individuals often take their private interest as the measure of good and evil, and would for its sake debar others from their equal right of buying and selling, but that every advantage given to one interest or branch of trade over another is injurious to the public.

No trade is unprofitable to the public; if it were, it would be given up; when trades thrive, so does the public, of which they form, a part. Prices must determine themselves, and cannot be fixed by law; and all forcible interference with them does harm instead of good. No people can become rich by state regulations, — only by peace, industry, freedom, and unimpeded economic activity. It will be seen how closely North's view of things approaches to that embodied some eighty years later in Adam Smith's great work. Locke is represented by Roscher as, along with Petty and North, making up the "triumvirate" of eminent British economists of this period who laid the foundations of a new and more rational doctrine than that of the mercantilists. But this view of his claims seems capable of being accepted only with considerable deductions.

His specially economic writings are *Considerations of the lowering of Interest and raising the value of Money*, 1691, and *Further Considerations*, 1695. Though Leibnitz declared with respect to these treatises that nothing more solid or intelligent could be said on their subject, it is difficult absolutely to adopt that verdict. Locke's spirit of sober observation and patient analysis led him indeed to some just conclusions; and he is entitled to the credit of having energetically resisted the debasement of the currency, which was then recommended by some who were held to be eminent practical authorities. But he falls into errors which show that he had not by any means completely emancipated himself from the ideas of the mercantile system. He attaches far too much importance to money as such. He says expressly that riches consist in a plenty of gold and silver, that is, as he explains, in having more in proportion of those metals than the rest of the world or than our neighbours. "In a country not furnished with mines, there are but two ways of growing rich, either conquest or commerce."

Hence he accepts the doctrine of the balance of trade. He shows that the rate of interest can no more be fixed by law than the rent of houses or the hire of ships, and opposes Child's demand for legislative interference with it. But he erroneously attributed the fall of the rate which had taken place generally in Europe to the increase of the quantity of gold and silver by the discovery of the American mines. He sets too absolute a value on a numerous population, in this point agreeing with Petty. On wages he observes that the rate must be such as to cover the indispensable wants of the labourer; when the price of subsistence rises, wages must rise in a like ratio, or the working population must come on the poor rates. The fall of the rent of land he regards as a sure sign of the decline of national wealth. "Taxes, however contrived, and out of whose hands so ever immediately taken do, in a country where their great fund is in land, for the most part terminate upon land." In this last proposition we see a foreshadowing of the *impôt unique* of the physiocrats. Whatever may have been Locke's direct economic services, his principal importance, like that of Hobbes, lies in his general philosophic and political principles, which powerfully affected French and indeed European thought, exciting a spirit of opposition to arbitrary power, and laying the foundation of the doctrine developed in the *Contract Social.*

Third Modern Phase: System of Natural Liberty

The changes introduced during the third phase in the internal organisation of the industrial world were (1) the more complete separation of banking from general commerce, and the wider extension of its operations, especially through the system of public credit; and (2) the great development of the use of machinery in production. The latter did not become very prominent during the first half of the eighteenth century, whilst tending to promote the dignity of the working classes by relieving them from degrading and exhausting forms of labour, it widened the gulf between them and the capitalist employers. It thus became plain that for the definitive constitution of industry a moral reform was the necessary preliminary condition.

With respect to the political relations of industry, a remarkable inversion now showed itself. The systematic encouragements which the European Governments had extended to it in the preceding phase had been prompted by their desire to use it as an instrument for achieving the military superiority which was the great end of the policy. Now, on the contrary, the military spirit subordinated itself to the industrial, and the armies and the diplomacy of Governments were placed at the service of commerce. The wars which filled a large part of the eighteenth century were essentially Commercial wars, arising out of the effort to sustain or extend the colonial establishments founded in the previous phase, or to deprive rival nations of the industrial advantages connected with the possession of such establishments. This change of attitude, notwithstanding its deplorable tendency to foster international enmities and jealousies, marked a real and important progress by pointing to industrial activity as the one permanent practical destination of modern societies.

But, whilst by this sort of action furthering the ascendancy of the new forces, the ruling powers, both in England and France, betrayed the alarm they felt at the subversive tendencies which appeared inherent in the modern movement by taking up in their domestic policy an attitude of resistance. Reaction became triumphant in France during the latter half of the reign of Louis XIV, under the disastrous influence of Madame de Maintenon. In England, after the transaction of 1688, by which the Government was consolidated on the double basis of aristocratic power and official orthodoxy, the state policy became not so much retrograde as stationary, industrial conquest being put forward to satisfy the middle class and wean it from the pursuit of a social renovation. In both countries there was for some time a noticeable check in the intellectual development, and Roscher and others have observed that, in economic studies particularly, the first three decades of the eighteenth century were a period of general stagnation, eclecticism for the most part taking the place of originality. The movement was, however, soon to be resumed, but with an altered and more formidable character.

The negative doctrine, which had risen and taken a definite form in England, was diffused and popularised in France, where it became evident, even before the decisive explosion, that the only possible issue lay in a radical social transformation. The partial schools of Voltaire and Rousseau in different ways led up to a violent crisis, whilst taking little thought of the conditions of a system which could replace the old; but the more complete and organic school, of which Diderot is the best representative, looked through freedom to a thorough reorganisation. Its constructive aim is shown by the design of the *Encyclopédie* — a project, however, which could have only a temporary success, because no real synthesis was forthcoming, and this joint production of minds often divergent could possess no more than an external unity. It was with this great school that the physiocrats were specially connected; and, in common with its other members whilst pushing towards an entire change of the existing system, they yet would gladly have avoided political demolition through the exercise of a royal dictatorship, or contemplated it only as the necessary condition of a new and better order of things. But, though marked off by such tendencies from the purely revolutionary sects, their method and fundamental ideas were negative, resting, as they did, essentially on the basis of the *jus natura*. We shall follow in detail these French developments in their special relation to economic science, and afterwards notice the corresponding movements in other European countries which showed themselves before the appearance of Adam Smith, or were at least unaffected by his influence.

The more liberal, as well as more rational, principles put forward by the English thinkers of the new type began, early in the eighteenth century, to find an echo in France, where the clearer and more vigorous intellects were prepared for their reception by a sense of the great evils which exaggerated mercantilism, serving as instrument of political ambition, had produced in that country. The impoverished condition of the agricultural population, the oppressive weight and unequal imposition of taxation, and the unsound state of the public finances had produced a general feeling of disquiet, and led several distinguished writers to protest strongly against the policy of Colbert and to demand a complete reform.

The most important amongst them was Pierre Boisguillebert (d. 1714), whose whole life was devoted to these controversies. In his statistical writings, he brings out in gloomy colours the dark side of the age of Louis XIV, and in his theoretic works (*Traité de la nature et du commerce des grains; Dissertations sur la nature des reichesses de l'argent et des tributs;* and *Essai sur la rareté de l'argent*) he appears as an earnest, even passionate, antagonist of the mercantile school. He insists again and again on the fact that national wealth does not consist in gold and silver, but in useful things, foremost among which are the products of agriculture. He even goes so far as to speak of "argent criminel," which from being the slave of trade, as it ought to be, had become its tyrant.

He sets the "genuinely French Sully" far above the "Italianising Colbert," and condemns all arbitrary regulations affecting either foreign or internal commerce, especially as regards the corn trade. National wealth does not depend on Governments, whose interference does more harm than good; the natural laws of the economic order of things cannot be violated or neglected with impunity; the interests to the several classes of society in a system of freedom are identical, and those of individuals coincide with that of the state. A similar solidarity exists between different nations; in their economic dealings they are related to the world as individual towns to a nation, and not merely plenty, but peace and harmony, will result from their unfettered intercourse. Men he divides into two classes — those who do nothing and enjoy everything, and those who labour from morning to night often without earning a bare subsistence; the latter he would favour in every way.

Here we catch the breath of popular sympathy which fills the social atmosphere of the eighteenth century. He dwells with special emphasis on the claims of agriculture, which had in France fallen into unmerited neglect, and with a view to its improvement calls for a reform in taxation. He would replace indirect taxes by taxes on income, and would restore the payment of taxes in kind, with the object of securing equality of burden and eliminating every element of the arbitrary. He has some interesting views of a general character: thus he approximates to a correct conception of agricultural rent, and he points to the order in which human wants follow each other — those of necessity, convenience, comfort, superfluity, and ostentation succeeding in the order named, and ceasing in the inverse order to be felt as wealth decreases. The depreciating tone in which Voltaire speaks of Boisguillebert is certainly not justified; he had a great economic talent, and his writings contain important germs of truth. But he appears to have exerted little influence, theoretical or practical, in his own time.

The same general line of thought was followed by Marshal de Vauban (1633-1707) in his economic tracts, especially that bearing the title of *Projet d'une dixme Royale,* 1707, which was suppressed by the authorities, and lost for him the favour of his sovereign, but has added luster to his name in the judgment of posterity. He is deeply impressed with the deplorable condition of the working classes of France in his day. He urges that the aim of the Government should be the welfare of all orders of the community; that all are entitled to like favour and furthe-rance; that the often despised and wronged lower class is the basis of the social organisation; that labour is the foundation of all wealth, and agriculture the most important species of labour; that the most essential condition of successful industry is freedom; and that all unnecessary or excessive restrictions on manufactures and commerce should be swept away.

He protests in particular against the inequalities of taxation, and the exemptions and privileges enjoyed by the higher ranks. With the exception of some duties on consumption he would abolish all the existing taxes, and substitute for them a single tax on income and land, impartially applied to all classes, which he describes under the name of "Dixme Royale," that is to say, a tenth in kind of all agricultural produce, and a tenth of money income chargeable on manufacturers and traders. The liberal and humane spirit of Fénelon led him to aspire after freedom of commerce with foreign nations, and to preach the doctrine that the true superiority of one state over another lies in the number indeed, but also in the morality, intelligence, and industrious habits of its population, The *Télémaque,* in which these views were presented in an attractive form, was welcomed and read amongst all ranks and classes, and was thus an effective organ for the propagation of opinion.

After these writers there is a marked blank in the field of French economic thought, broken only by the *Réflexions Politiques sur les Finances et le Commerce* 19738) of Dutot, a pupil of Law, and the semi-mercantilist *Essais Politiques sure le Commerce* (1731) of Mélon, till we come to the great name of Montesquieu. The *Esprit des Lois* (1748), so far as it deals with economic subjects, is written upon the whole from a point of view adverse to the mercantile system, especially in his treatment of money, though in his observations on colonies and elsewhere he falls in with the ideas of that system. His immortal service, however, was not rendered by any special research, but by his enforcement of the doctrine of natural laws regulating social no less than physical phenomena. There is no other thinker of importance on economic subjects in France till the appearance of the physiocrats, which marks an epoch in the history of the science.

The heads of the physiocratic school were François Quesnay (1694-1774) and Jean Claude Marie Vincent, sieur de Gournay (1712-1759). The principles of the school had been put forward in 1755 by Richard Cantillon, a French merchant of Irish extraction (*Essai sur la nature du Commerce en général*), whose biography Jevons has elucidated, and whom he regards as the true founder of political economy; but it was in the hands of Quesnay and Gournay that they acquired a systematic form, and became the creed of a united group of thinkers and practical men, bent on carrying them into action. The members of the group called themselves "les économistes," but it is more convenient, because unambiguous, to designate them by the name "physiocrates," invented by Dupont de Nemours, who was one of their number.

In this name, intended to express the fundamental idea of the school, much more is implied than the subjection of the phenomena of the social, and in particular the economic, world to fixed relations of co-existence and succession. This is the positive doctrine which lies at the bottom of all true science. But the law of nature referred to in the title of the sect was something quite different. The theological dogma which represented all the movements of the universe as directed by divine wisdom and benevolence to the production of the greatest possible sum of happiness had been transformed in the hands of the metaphysicians into the conception of a *jus naturae*, a harmonious and beneficial code established by the favourite entity of these thinkers, Nature, antecedent to human institutions, and furnishing the model to which they should be made to conform.

This idea, which Buckle apparently supposes to have been an invention of Hutcheson's, had come down through Roman juridical theory from the speculations of Greece. It was taken in hand by the modern negative school from Hobbes to Rousseau, and used as a powerful weapon of assault upon the existing order of society, with which the "natural" order was perpetually contrasted as offering the imperfect type from which fact had deplorably diverged. The theory received different applications according to the diversity of minds or circumstances. By some it was directed against the artificial manner of the times, by others against contemporary political institutions; it was specialty employed by the physiocrats in criticising the economic practice of European Governments.

The general political doctrine is as follows. Society is composed of a number of individuals all having the same natural rights if all do not possess (as some members of the negative school maintained) equal capacities, each can at least best understand his own interest, and is led by nature to follow it. The social union is really a contract between these individuals, the object of which is the limitation of the natural freedom of each, just so far as it is inconsistent with the rights of the others. Government, though necessary, is a necessary evil; and the governing power appointed by consent should be limited to the amount of interference absolutely required to secure the fulfillment of the contract. In the economic sphere, this implies the right of the individual to such natural enjoyments as he can acquire by his labour. That labour, therefore, should be undisturbed and unfettered; and its fruits should be guaranteed to the possessor; in other words, property should be sacred.

Each citizen must be allowed to make the most of his labour; and therefore freedom of exchange should be ensured, and competition in the market should be unrestricted, no monopolies or privileges being permitted to exist. The physiocrats then proceed with the economic analysis as follows. Only those labours are truly "productive" which add to the quantity of raw materials available for the purposes of man; and the real annual addition to the wealth of the community consists of the excess of the mass of agricultural products (including, of course, minerals) over their cost of production. On the amount of this "product net" depends the well-being of the community, and the possibility of its advance in civilization? The manufacturer merely gives a new form to the materials extracted from the earth; the higher value of the object, after it has passed through his hands, only represents the quantity of provisions and other materials used and consumed in its elabouration.

Commerce does nothing more than transfer the wealth already existing from one hand to another; what the trading classes gain thereby is acquired at the cost of the nation, and it is desirable that its amount should be as small as possible. The occupation of the manufacturer and merchant, as well as the liberal professions, and every kind of personal service, are "useful" indeed, but they are "sterile," drawing their income, not from any fund which they themselves create, but from the superanuous earnings of the agriculturists. Perfect freedom of trade not only rests, as we have already seen, on the foundation of natural right, but is also recommended by the consideration that it makes the "produit net," on which all wealth and general progress depend, as large as possible. "Laissez faire, laissez passer" should therefore be the motto of Governments. The revenue of the State, which must be derived altogether from this net product, ought to be raised in the most direct and simplest way, namely, by a single impost of the nature of a land tax.

The special doctrine relating to the exclusive productiveness of agriculture arose out of confusion between "value" on the one hand and "matter and energy" on the other. Smith and others have shown that the attempt to fix the character of "sterility" on manufactures and commerce was founded in error. And the proposal of a single *impôt territorial* falls to the ground with the doctrine on which it was based. But such influence as the school exerted depended little, if at all, on these peculiar tenets, which indeed some of its members did not hold, the effective result of its teaching was mainly destructive. It continued in a more systematic form the efforts in favour of the freedom of industry already begun in England and France.

The essential historical once of the physiocrats was to discredit radically the methods followed by the European Governments in their dealings with industry. For such criticism as theirs there was, indeed, ample room: the policy of Colbert, which could be only temporarily useful, had been abusively extended and intensified; Governmental action had intruded itself into the minutest details of business, and every process of manufacture and transaction of trade was hampered by legislative restrictions. It was to be expected that the reformers should, in the spirit of the negative philosophy, exaggerate the vices of established systems; and there can be no doubt that they condemned too absolutely the economic action of the State, both in principle and in its historic manifestations, and pushed the "laissez faire" doctrine beyond its just limits.

But this was a necessary incident of their connection with the revolutionary movement, of which they really formed one wing. In the course of that movement, the primitive social contract, the sovereignty of the people, and other dogmas now seen to be untenable, were habitually invoked in the region of politics proper, and had a transitory utility as ready and effective instruments of warfare. And so also in the economic sphere the doctrines of natural rights of buying and selling, of the sufficiency of enlightened selfishness as a guide in mutual dealings, of the certainty that each member of the society will understand and follow his true interests, and of the coincidence of those interests with the public welfare, though they will not bear a dispassionate examination, were temporarily useful as convenient and serviceable weapons for the overthrow of the established order.

The tendency of the school was undoubtedly to consecrate the spirit of individualism, and the state of non-government. But this tendency, which may with justice be severely condemned in economists of the present time, was then excusable because inevitable. And, whilst it now impedes the work of reconstruction which is for us the order of the day, it then aided the process of social demolition, which was the necessary, though deplorable, condition of a new organisation. These conclusions as to the revolutionary tendencies of the school are not at all affected by the fact that the form of government preferred by Quesnay and some of his chief followers was what they called a legal despotism, which should embrace within itself both the legislative and the executive function.

The reason for this preference was that an enlightened central power could more promptly and efficaciously introduce the policy they advocated than an assembly representing divergent opinions, and fettered by constitutional checks and limitations. Turgot, as we know, used the absolute power of the crown to carry into effect some of his measures for the liberation of industry, though he ultimately failed because unsustained by the requisite force of character in Louis XVI. But what the physiocratic idea with respect to the normal method of government was appears from Quesnay's advice to the dauphin, that when he became king he should "do nothing, but let the laws rule," the laws having been of course first brought into conformity with the *jus naturae*.

The partiality of the school for agriculture was in harmony with the sentiment in favour of "nature" and primitive simplicity which then showed itself in so many forms in France, especially in combination with the revolutionary spirit, and of which Rousseau was the most eloquent exponent. It was also associated in these writers with a just indignation at the wretched state in which the rural labourers of France had been left by the scandalous neglect of the superior orders of society — a state of which the terrible picture drawn by La Bruyère is an indestructible record. The members of the physiocratic group were undoubtedly men of thorough uprightness, and inspired with a sincere desire for the public good, especially for the material and moral elevation of the working classes. Quesnay was physician to Louis XV, and resided in the palace at Versailles; but in the midst of that corrupt court he maintained his integrity, and spoke with manly frankness what he believed to be the truth. And never did any statesman devote himself with greater singleness of purpose or more earnest endeavour to the service of his country than Turgot, who was the principal practical representative of the school.

The publications in which Quesnay expounded his system were the following: —Two articles, on "Fermiers" and on "Grains," in the *Encyclopédie* of Diderot and D'Alembert (1756, 1757); a discourse on the law of nature in the Physiocratic of Dupont de Nemours (1768); *Maximes génératles de gouvernement économique d'un royaume agricole* (1758), and the simultaneously published *Taleau Économique avec son explication, ou Extrait des conomies Royales de Sully* (with the celebrated motto "pauvres paysans, pauvre royaume; pauvre royaume, pauvre roi"); *Dialogue sur le commerce et les travaux des artisans*; and other minor pieces. The *Tableau Economique,* though on account of its dryness and abstract form it met with little general favour, may be considered the principal manifesto of the school.

It was regarded by the followers of Quesnay as entitled to a place amongst the foremost products of human wisdom, and is named by the elder Mirabeau, in a passage quoted by Adam Smith as one of the three great inventions which have contributed most to the stability of political societies, the other two being those of writing and of money. Its object was to exhibit by means of certain formulas the way in which the products of agriculture, which is the only source of wealth, would in a state of perfect liberty be distributed among the several classes of the community (namely, the productive classes of the proprietors and cultivators of land, and the unproductive class composed of manufacturers and merchants), and to represent by other formulas the modes of distribution which take place under systems of Governmental restraint and regulation, with the evil results arising to the whole society from different degrees of such violations of the natural order.

It follows from Quesnay's theoretic views that the one thing deserving the solicitude of the practical economist and the statesman is the increase of the net product; and he infers also what Smith afterwards affirmed on not quite the same ground, that the interest of the landowner is "strictly and inseparably connected with the general interest of the society." M. de Gournay, as we have seen, was regarded as one of the founders of the school, and appears to have exercised some influence even upon the formation of Quesnay's own opinions. With the exception of translations of Culpeper and Child, Gournay wrote nothing but memois addressed to ministers, who have not seen the light; but we have a full statement of his views in the loge dedicated to his memory by his illustrious friend Turgot.

Whilst Quesnay had spent his youth amidst rural scenes, and had been early familiar with the labours of the field, Gournay had been bred as a merchant, and had passed from the counting-house to the once of intendant of commerce. They thus approached the study of political economy from different sides, and this diversity of their antecedents may in part explain the amount of divergence which existed between their views. Gournay softened the rigour of Quesnay's system, and brought it nearer to the truth, by rejecting what Smith calls its "capital error" — the doctrine, namely, of the unproductiveness of manufactures and commerce. He directed his efforts to the assertion and vindication of the principle of industrial liberty, and it was by him that this principle was formulated in the phrase, since so often heard for good and for evil, "Laissez faire et laissez passer." One of the earliest and most complete adherents of the physiocratic school, as well as an ardent and unwearied propagator of its doctrines, was Victor Mirabeau, whose sincere and independent, though somewhat perverse and whimsical, character is familiar to English readers through Carlyle's essay on his more celebrated son.

He had expressed some physiocratic views earlier than Quesnay, but owned the latter for his spiritual father, and adopted most of his opinions, the principal difference being that he was favourable to the *petite* as opposed to the *grande culture,* which latter was preferred by his chief as giving, not indeed the largest gross, but the largest net product. Miabeau's principal writings were *Ami des Hommes, ou traité sur la population* (1756, 1760), *Théorie de l'impôt* (176), *Les Éconimiques* (1769) and *Philosophie rurale, ou Économie générale et politique de l'Agriculture* (1763). The last of these was the earliest complete exposition of the physiocratic system. Another earnest and persevering apostle of the system was Dupont de Nemours (1739-1817), known by his treatises *De l'exportation et l'imortation des grains (1764), De l'origine et des progrès d'une science nouvelle* (1767), *Du commerce de la Compagnie des Indies* (1767), and especially by his more comprehensive work *Physiocratie, ou Consitution naturelle du gouvernement le plus avantageus ou genre humain* (1768).

The title of this work gave, as has been already mentioned, a name to the school. Another formal exposition of the system, to which Adam Smith refers as the "most distinct and best connected account" of it, was produced by Mercier-Lariviére, under the title *L'Ordre naturel et essentiel des sociétés politiques* (1767), a title which is interesting as embodying the idea of the *jus naturae.* Both he and Dupont de Nemours professed to study human communities, not only in relation to their economic, but also to their political and general social aspects; but, notwithstanding these larger pretensions, their views were commonly restricted in the main to the economic sphere; at least material considerations decidedly preponderated in their inquiries, as was naively indicated by Larivière when he said, "Property, security, liberty — these comprise the whole social order; the right of property is a tree of which all the institutions of society are branches."

The most eminent member of the group was without doubt Anne Robert Jacques Turgot (1727-1781). This is not the place to speak of his noble practical activity, first as intendant of Limoges, and afterwards for a brief period as finance minister, or of the circumstances which led to his removal from office, and the consequent failure of his efforts for the salvation of France. His economic views are explained in the introductions to his edicts and ordinances, in letters and occasional papers, but especially in his *Réflexions sur la formation et la distribution des richesses* (1766). This is a condensed but eminently clear and attractive exposition of the fundamental principles of political economy, as they were conceived by the physiocrats. It embodies, indeed, the erroneous no less than the sound doctrines of that school; but several subjects, especially the various forms of land-economy, the different employments of capital, and the legitimacy of interest, are handled in a generally just as well as striking manner; and the mode of presentation of the ideas, and the luminous arrangement of the whole, are Turgot's own. The treatise, which contains a surprising amount of matter in proportion to its length, must always retain a place among the classics of the science.

The physiocratic school never obtained much direct popular influence, even in its native country, though it strongly attracted many of the more gifted and earnest minds. Its members, writing on dry subjects in an austere and often heavy style, did not find acceptance with a public which demanded before all things charm of manner in those who addressed it. When Morellet, one of their numbers, entered the lists with Galiani, it was seen how *espirit;* and eloquence could triumph over science, solid indeed, but clumsy in its movements. The physiocratic tenets, which were in fact partially erroneous, were regarded by many as chimerical, and were ridiculed in the contemporary literature, as, for example, the *impôt unique* by Voltaire in his *L'homme aux quarante écus,* which was directed in particular against Mercier-*Lari*vière.

It was justly objected to the group that they were too absolute in their view of things; they supposed, as Smith remarks in speaking of Quesnay, that the body-politic could thrive only under one precise régime, — that, namely, which they recommended,—and thought their doctrines universally and immediately applicable in practice. They did not, as theorists, sufficiently take into account national diversities, or different stages in social development; nor did they as politicians, adequately estimate the impediments which ignorance, prejudice, and interested opposition present to enlightened statesmanship. It is possible that Turgot himself, as Grimm suggests, owed his failure in part to the too unbending rigour of his policy and the absence of any attempt at conciliation. Be this as it may, his defeat helped to impair the credit of his principles, which were represented as having been tried and found wanting.

The physiocratic system, after guiding in some degree the policy of the Constituent Assembly, and awakening a few echoes here and there in foreign countries, soon ceased to exist as a living power; but the good elements it comprised were not lost to mankind, being incorporated into the sounder and more complete construction of Adam Smith. In Italy, as in the other European nations, there was little activity in the economic field during the first half of the eighteenth century. It was then, however, that a really remarkable man appeared, the archdeacon Salustio Antonio Bandini (1677-1760), author of the *Discorso sulla Maremma Sienese,* written in 1737, but not published till 1775. The object of the work was to raise the Maremma from the wretched condition into which it had fallen through the decay of agriculture.

This decay he showed to be, at least in part, the result of the wretched fiscal system which was in force; and his book led to important reforms in Tuscany, where his name is held in high honour. Not only by Pecchio and other Italian writers, but by Roscher also, he is alleged to have anticipated some leading doctrines of the physiocrats, but this claim is disputed. There was a remarkable renascence of economic studies in Italy during the latter half of the century, partly due to French influence, and partly, it would appear, to improved government in the northern states.

The movement at first followed the lines of the mercantile school. Thus, in Antonio Broggia's *Trattati dei tributi e delle monete e del governo politico della societá* (1743), and Girolamo Belloni's *Dissertazione sopra il commercio* (1750), which seems to have had a success and reputation much above its merits, mercantilist tendencies decidedly preponderate. But the most distinguished writer who represented that economic doctrine in Italy in the last century was Antonio Genovesi, a Neapolitan (1712-1769). He felt deeply the depressed intellectual and moral state of his fellow-countrymen, and aspired after a revival of philosophy and reform of education as the first condition of progress and well-being. With the object of protecting him from the theological persecutions which threatened him on account of his advanced opinions, Bartolomeo Intieri, of whom we shall hear again in relation to Galiani, founded in 1755, expressly for Genovesi, a chair of commerce and mechanics, one of the conditions of foundation being that it should never be filled by a monk.

This was the first professorship of economics established in Europe; the second was founded at Stockholm in 1758 and the third in Lombardy ten years later, for Beccaria. The fruit of the labours of Genovesi in this chair was his *Lezioni di commercio, ossia di economia civile* (1769), which contained the first systematic treatment of the whole subject which had appeared in Italy. As the model for Italian imitation he held up England, a country for which, says Pecchio, he had a predilection almost amounting to fanaticism. He does not rise above the false economic system which England then pursued; but he rejects some of the grosser errors of the school to which he belonged; he advocates the freedom of the corn trade, and deprecates regulation of the interest on loans. In the spirit of his age, he denounces the relics of medieval institutions, such as entails and tenures in mortmain, as impediments to the national prosperity. Ferdinando Galiani was another distinguished disciple of the mercantile school. Before he had completed his twenty-first year he published a work on money (*Detta moneta libri cinque*, 1750), the principles of which are supposed to have been dictated by two experienced practical men, the Marquis Rinuccini and Bartolomeo Intieri, whose name we have already met. But his reputation was made by a book written in French and published in Paris, where he was secretary of embassy, in 1770, namely, and his *Dialogues sur le commerce des blés*.

This work, by its light and pleasing style, and the vivacious wit with which it abounded, delighted Voltaire, who spoke of it as a book in the production of which Plato and Molière might have been combined the author, says Pecchio, treated his arid subject as Fontenelle did the vortices of Descartes, or Algarotti the Newtonian system of the world. The question at issue was that of the freedom of the corn trade, then much agitated, and, in particular, the policy of the royal edict of 1764, which permitted the exportation of grain so long as the price had not arrived at a certain height. The general principle he maintains is that the best system in regard to this trade is to have no system — countries differently circumstanced requiring, according to him, different modes of treatment. This seems a lame and impotent conclusion from the side of science; yet doubtless the physiocrats, with whom his controversy laid, prescribed on this, as on other subjects, rules too rigid for the safe guidance of statesmen, and Galiani may have rendered a real service by protesting against their absolute solutions of practical problems. He fell, however, into some of the most serious errors of the mercantilists – holding, as indeed did also Voltaire and even Verri, that one country cannot gain without another losing, and in his earlier treatise going so far as to defend the action of Governments in debasing the currency.

Amongst the Italian economists who were most under the influence of the modern spirit, and in closest harmony with the general movement which was impelling the Western nations towards a new social order, Cesare Beccaria (1738-1794) holds a foremost place. He is best known by his celebrated treatise *Dei delitti e delle pene*, by which Voltaire said he had made himself a benefactor of all Europe, and which, we are told, has been translated into twenty-two languages. The Empress Catherine having invited him to fix his residence at St. Petersburg the Austrian Government of Lombardy, in order to keep him at home, established expressly for him a chair of political economy; and in his *Elementi di economia pubblica* (1769-1771; not published, however, till 1804) are embodied his teachings as professor.

The work is unfinished: he had divided the whole subject under the heads of agriculture, manufactures, commerce, taxation, government; but he has treated adequately only the first two heads and the last two not at all, having been called to take part in the councils of the state. He was in some degree under the influence of physiocratic ideas, and holds that agriculture is the only strictly productive form of industry, whilst manufacturers and artisans are a sterile class. He was strongly opposed to monopolies and privileges, and to corporations in arts and trades; in general he warmly advocated internal industrial freedom, though in regard to foreign commerce a protectionist. In the special case of the corn trade he was not, any more than Galiani, a partisan of absolute liberty. His exposition of economic principles is concise and sententious, and he often states correctly the most important considerations relating to his subject without adding the developments which would be desirable to assist comprehension and strengthen conviction.

Thus on fixed capital (*capitali fondatori*), as distinct from circulating (*annui*), in its application to agriculture, he presents in a condensed form essentially the same explanations as Turgot about the same time gave; and on the division of labour and the circumstances which cause different rates of wages in different employments, he in substance comes near to Smith, but without the fullness of illustration which is so attractive a feature of the Wealth of Nations. Pietro Verri (1728-1797), an intimate and lifelong friend of Beccaria, was for twenty-five years one of the principal directors of the administration of Lombardy, in which capacity he originated many economic and other reforms.

In his *Riflessioni sulle leggi vincolanti, principalmente nel commercio de' grani* (written in 1769, printed in 1796), he considers the question of the regulation of the corn trade both historically and in the light of theoretic principles, and arrives at the conclusion that liberty is the best remedy against famine and against excessive fluctuations of price. He is generally opposed to Governmental interference with internal commerce, as well as to trade corporations, and the attempts to limit prices or fix the rate of interest, but is in favour of the protection of national industry by a judiciously framed tariff. These views are explained in his *Meditazioni sull' economia politica* (1771), an elementary treatise on the science, which was received with favour, and translated into several foreign languages. A primary principle with him is what he calls the augmentation of reproduction — that is, in Smith's language, of "the annual produce of the land and labour" of a nation; and by its tendency to promote or to restrict this augmentation; he tests every enactment and institution.

Accordingly, unlike Beccaria, he prefers the *petite* the *grande culture*, as giving a larger total produce. In dealing with taxation, he rejects the physiocratic proposal of a single *impôt territorial*. Giovanni R. Carli (1720-1796), also an official promoter of the reforms in the government of Austrian Lombardy, besides learned and sound treatises on money, was author of *Ragionamenti sopra i bilanci economici delle nazioni*, in which he shows the falsity of the notion that a state gains or loses in foreign commerce according to the so-called balance of trade. In his letter to Pompeo Neri *Sul libero commercio de' grani* (1771), he takes up a position similar to that of Galiani, regarding the question of the freedom of the corn trade as not so much a scientific as an administrative one, to be dealt with differently under different local or other conditions.

Rejecting the physiocratic doctrine of the exclusive productiveness of agriculture, he illustrates in an interesting way the necessity of various economic classes in a society, and the reflex agency of manufactures in stimulating the cultivation of the soil. Giambattista Vasco (1733-1796) wrote discourses on several questions proposed by academies and sovereigns. In these he condemns trade corporations and the attempts by Governments to fix the price of bread and to limit the interest on loans. In advocating the system of a peasant proprietary, he suggests that the law should determine the minimum and maximum portions of land which a citizen should be permitted to possess.

He also, with a view to prevent the undue accumulation of property, proposes the abolition of the right of bequest, and the equal division of the inheritance amongst the children of the deceased, Gaetano Filangieri (1762-1788), one of the Italian writers of the last century whose names are most widely known throughout Europe, devoted to economic questions the second book of his *Scienza della legislazion*. Filled with reforming ardour and a passionate patriotism, he employed his vehement eloquence in denouncing all the abuses of his time. Apparently without any knowledge of Adam Smith, he insists on unlimited freedom of trade, calls for the abolition of the medieval institutions which impeded production and national well-being, and condemns the colonial system then followed by England, Spain, and Holland. He prophesies, as Raynal, Turgot, and Genovesi had done before him, that all America would one day be independent, a prediction which probably helped to elicit Benjamin Franklin's tribute of admiration for his work.

Rather a propagator than a discoverer, he sometimes adopted from others erroneous opinions, as, for example, when he approves the *impôt unique* of the physiocrats. On the whole, however, he represents the most advanced political and social tendencies of his age; whilst strongly contrasted with Beccaria in temperament and style, he was a worthy labourer in the same cause of national and universal progress. Ludovico Ricci (1742-1799) was author of an able report *Sulla riforma degli istituti pii della città di Modena* (1787). He treated the subject of poor relief and charitable institutions in so general a way that the work possesses a universal and permanent interest. He dwells on the evils of indiscriminate relief as tending to increase the misery it seeks to remove, and as lowering the moral character of a population. He exposes especially the abuses connected with lying-in and foundling hospitals.

There is much in him which is akin to the views of Malthus; like him he is opposed to any state provision for the destitute who ought, he thinks, to be left to voluntary private beneficence. Ferdinando Paoletti (1717-1801) was an excellent and public-spirited priest, who did much for the diffusion of intelligence amongst the agricultural population of Tuscany, and for the lightening of the taxes which pressed upon them he corresponded with Mirabeau ("Friend of Men"), and appears to have accepted the physiocratic doctrines, at least in their general substance. he was author of *Pensieri sopra l'agricoltura* (1769), and of *I verri mezzi di render felici le società* (1772); in the latter he advocates the freedom of the corn trade. The tract *Il Colbertismo* (1791) by Count Francesco Mengotti is a vigorous protest against the extreme policy of prohibition and protection, which may still be read with interest. Mengotti also wrote (1791) a treatise *Del commercio de' Romani*, directed mainly against the exaggerations of Huet in his *Histoire du commerce et de la navigation des anciens* (1716), and useful as marking the broad difference between the ancient and modern civilizations.

Here lastly may be mentioned another Italian thinker who, eminently original and even eccentric, cannot easily be classed among his contemporaries, though some Continental writers of our own century have exhibited similar modes of thought. This was Giammaria Ortes (1713-1790). He is opposed to the liberalist tendencies of his time, but does not espouse the doctrines of the mercantile system, rejecting the theory of the balance of trade, and demanding commercial freedom. It is in the middle Ages that he finds his social and economic type. He advocates the maintenance of church property, is averse to the ascendancy of the money power, and has the medieval dislike for interest on loans. He entertains the singular idea that the wealth of communities is always and everywhere in a fixed ratio to their population, the latter being determined by the former. Poverty, therefore, necessarily waits on wealth, and the rich, in becoming so, only gain what the poor lose.

Those who are interested in the improvement of the condition of thc people labour in vain, so long as they direct their efforts to the increase of the sum of the national wealth, which it is beyond their power to alter, instead of to the distribution of that wealth, which it is possible to modify. The true remedy for poverty lies in mitigating the gain-pursuing propensities in the rich and in men of business. Ortes studied in a separate work the subject of population; he formulates its increase as "geometrical," but recognizes that, as a limit is set to such increase amongst the lower animals by mutual destruction, so is it in the human species by "reason" — the "prudential restraint" of which Malthus afterwards made so much. He regards the institution of celibacy as no less necessary and advantageous than that of marriage. He enunciates what has since been known as the "law of diminishing returns to agricultural industry." He was careless as to the diffusion of his writings; and hence they remained almost unknown till they were included in the Custodi collection of Italian economists, when they attracted much attention by the combined sagacity and waywardness which marked their author's intellectual character.

In the earlier part of the eighteenth century Geronimo Ustariz had written his *Teorica y Practica del Comercio y Marina* (1724; published, 1740; Eng. transl. by John Kippax, 1751; French by Forbonnais, 1753), in which he carries mercantile principles to their utmost extreme. The reforming spirit of the latter half of the century was best represented in that country by Pedro Rodriguez, Count of Campomanes (1723-1802). He pursued with ardour the same studies and in some degree the same policy as his illustrious contemporary Turgot, without, however, having arrived at so advanced a point of view. He was author of *Respuesta fiscal sobre abolir la tasa y establecer et comercio de granos* (1764), *Discurso sobre el fomento de industria popolar* (1774), and *Discurso sobre la educacion de las artesanos y su fomento* (1775).

By means of these writings, justly by Robertson, as well as by his personal efforts as minister, he sought to establish the freedom of the corn trade, to remove the hindrances to industry arising from medieval survivals, to have a large development to manufactures, and to liberate agriculture from the odious burdens to which it was subject. He saw that, notwithstanding the enlightened administration of Charles III, Spain still suffered from the evil results of the blind confidence reposed by her people in her gold mines, and enforced the lesson that the real sources of the wealth and power of his country must be sought, not in America, but in her own industry.

In both Italy and Spain, as is well observed by Comte, the impulse towards social change took principally the direction of economic reform, because the pressure exercised by Governments prevented so large a measure of free speculation in the fields of philosophy and general politics as was possible in France. In Italy, it may be added, the traditions of the great industrial past of the northern cities of that country also tended to fix attention chiefly on the economic side of public policy and legislation.

We have seen that in Italy and England political economy had its beginnings in the study of practical questions relating chiefly to money or to foreign commerce. In Germany it arose out of the so-called cameralistic sciences. Soon after the close of the Middle Ages there existed in most German countries a council, known as the Kammer (Lat. camera), which was occupied with the management of the public domain and the guardianship of regal rights. The Emperor Maximilian found this institution existing in Burgundy, and established, in imitation of it, aulic councils at Innspruck and Vienna in 1498 and 1501. Not only finance and taxation, but questions also of economic police, came to be entrusted to these bodies. A special preparation became necessary for their members, and chairs of cameralistic science were founded in universities for the teaching of the appropriate body of doctrine.

One side of the instruction thus given borrowed its materials from the sciences of external nature, dealing, as it did, with forestry, mining, general technology, and the like; the other related to the conditions of national prosperity as depending on human relations and institutions; and out of the latter, German political economy was at first developed. In no country had mercantilist views a stronger hold than in Germany, though in none, in the period we are now considering, did the system of the balance of trade receive a less extensive practical application. All the leading German economists of the seventeenth century — Bornitz, Besold, Klock, Becher, Horneck, Seckendorf, and Schröder — stand on the common basis of the mercantile doctrine.

And the same may be said of the writers of the first half of the eighteenth century in general, and notably of Justi (d. 1771), who was the author of the first systematic German treatise on political economy, a work which, from its currency as a text-book, had much effect on the formation of opinion. Only in Zincke (1692-1769) do we find occasional expressions of a circle of ideas at variance with the dominant system, and pointing in the direction of industrial freedom. But these writers, except from the national point of view, are unimportant, not having exercised any influence on the general movement of European thought.

The principles of the physiocratic system met with a certain amount of favour in Germany. Karl Friedrich, Margrave of Baden, wrote for the use of his sons an Abrégé des principes d'Économie Politique, 1772, which is in harmony with the doctrines of that system. It possesses, however, little scientific value. Schlettwein (1731-1802) and Mauvillon (1743-1794) were followers of the same school. Theodor Schmalz (1764-183a), who is commonly named as "the last of the physiocrats," may be here mentioned, though somewhat out of the historic order. He compares Colbertism with the Ptolemaic system, physiocratism with the Copernican. Adam Smith he represents as the Tycho Brahe of political economy — a man of eminent powers, who could not resist the force of truth in the physiocrats, but partly could not divest himself of rooted prejudices, and partly was ambitious of the fame of a discoverer and a reconciler of divergent systems. Though Smith was now "the fashion," Schmalz could not doubt that Quesnay's doctrine was alone true, and would ere long be triumphant everywhere.

Just before the appearance of Smith, as in England Steuart and in Italy Genovesi, so in Austria Sonnenfels (1733-1817), the first distinguished economist of that country, sought to present the mercantile system in a modified and more enlightened form; and his work exercised even during a considerable part of the present century much influence on opinion and on policy in Austria. But the greatest German economist of the eighteenth century was, in Roscher's opinion, Justus Möser (1720-1794), the author of Patriotische Phantasieen (1774), a series of fragments, which, Goethe nevertheless declares, form "ein wahrhaites Ganzes." The poet was much influenced by Möser in his youth, and has eulogised in the Dichtung und Wahrheit his spirit, intellect, and character, and his thorough insight into all that goes on in the social world.

Whilst others occupied themselves with larger and more prominent public affairs and transactions, Möser observed and reproduced the common daily life of his nation, and the thousand "little things" which compose the texture of popular existence. He has been compared to Franklin for the homeliness, verve, and freshness of his writings. In opinions he is akin to the Italian Ortes. He is opposed to the whole spirit of the "Aufkärung", and to the liberal and rationalistic direction of which Smith's work became afterwards the expression.

He is not merely conservative but reactionary, manifesting a preference for medieval institutions such as the trade guilds, and, like Carlyle in our own time, seeing advantages even in serfdom, when compared with the sort of freedom enjoyed by the modern drudge. He has a marked antipathy for the growth of the money power and of manufactures on the large scale, and for the highly developed division of labour. He is opposed to absolute private property in land, and would gladly see revived such a system of restrictions as in the interest of the state, the commune, and the family were imposed on medieval ownership. In his wayward and caustic style, he often criticises effectively the doctrinaire narrowness of his contemporaries, throws out many striking ideas, and in particular sheds real light on the economic phenomena and general social conditions of the middle Ages.

The Historical School

The negative movement which filled the eighteenth century had for its watchword on the economic side the liberation of industrial effort from both feudal survivals and Governmental fetters. But in all the aspects of that movement, the economic as well as the rest, the process of demolition was historically only the necessary preliminary condition of a total renovation towards which Western Europe was energetically tending, though with but an indistinct conception of its precise nature. The disorganization of the body of opinion which underlay the old system outran the progress towards the establishment of new principles adequate to form guidance in the future.

The critical philosophy which had wrought the disorganization could only repeat its formulas of absolute liberty, but was powerless for reconstruction. And hence there was seen throughout the West, after the French explosion, the remarkable spectacle of a continuous oscillation between the tendency to recur to outworn ideas and a vague impulse towards a new order in social thought and life, this impulse often taking an anarchical character. From this state of oscillation, which has given to the 19th century its equivocal and transitional aspect, the only possible issue was in the foundation of a scientific social doctrine which should supply a basis for the gradual convergence of opinion on human questions. The foundation of such a doctrine is the immortal service for which the world is indebted to Auguste Comte (17981857).

The leading features of Sociology, as he conceived it, are the following:(1) it is essentially one science, in which all the elements of a social state are studied in their relations and mutual actions; (2) it includes a dynamical as well as a statical theory of society; (3) it thus eliminates the absolute, substituting for an imagined fixity the conception of ordered change; (4) its principal method, though others are not excluded, is that of historical comparison; (5) it is pervaded by moral ideas, by notions of social duty, as opposed to the individual rights which were derived as corollaries from the *jus naturae*; and (6) in its spirit and practical consequences it tends to the realisation of all the great ends which compose "the popular cause"; yet (7) it aims at this through peaceful means, replacing revolution by evolution. The several characteristics we have enumerated are not independent; they may be shown to be vitally connected with each other. Several of these features must now be more fully described; the others will meet us before the close of the present survey.

In the masterly exposition of sociological method which is contained in the fourth volume of the *Philosophie Positive* (1839), Comte marks out the broad division between social statics and social dynamics, the former studying the laws of social coexistence, the latter those of social development. The fundamental principle of the former is the general consensus between the several social organs and functions, which, without unduly pressing a useful analogy, we may regard as resembling that which exists between the several organs and functions of an animal body.

The study of dynamical is different from, and necessarily subordinated to, that of statical sociology, progress being in fact the development of order, just as the study of evolution in biology is different from, and subordinated to, that of the structures and functions which are exhibited by evolution as they exist at the several points of an ascending scale. The laws of social coexistence and movement are as much subjects for observation as the corresponding phenomena in the life of an individual organism. For the study of development in particular, a modification of the comparative method familiar to biologists will be the appropriate mode of research. The several successive stages of society will have to be systematically compared, in order to discover their laws of sequence, and to determine the filiations of their characteristic features.

Though we must take care that both in our statical and dynamical studies we do not ignore or contradict the fundamental properties of human nature, the project of deducing either species of laws from those properties independently of direct observation is one which cannot be realised. Neither the general structure of human society nor the march of its development could be so predicted. This is especially evident with respect to dynamical laws, because, in the passage of society from one phase to another, the preponderating agency is the accumulated influence of past generations, which is much too complex to be investigated deductively a conclusion which it is important to keep steadily before us now that some of the (so-called) anthropologists are seeking to make the science of society a mere annex and derivative of biology.

The principles of biology unquestionably lie at the foundation of the social science, but the latter has, and must always have, a field of research and a method of inquiry peculiar to itself. The field is history in the largest sense, including contemporary fact; and the principal, though not exclusive, method is, as we have said, that process of sociological comparison which is most conveniently called "the historical method." These general principles affect the economic no less than other branches of social speculation; and with respect to that department of inquiry they lead to important results. They show that the idea of forming a true theory of the economic frame and working of society apart from its other sides is illusory. Such study is indeed provisionally indispensable, but no rational theory of the economic organs and functions of society can be constructed if they are considered as isolated from the rest.

In other words, a separate economic science is, strictly speaking, an impossibility, as representing only one portion of a complex organism, all whose parts and their actions are in a constant relation of correspondence and reciprocal modification. Hence, too, it will follow that, whatever useful indications may be derived from our general knowledge of individual human nature, the economic structure of society and its mode of development cannot be deductively foreseen, but must be ascertained by direct historical investigation. We have said "its mode of development "; for it is obvious that, as of every social element, so of the economic factor in human affairs, there must be a dynamical doctrine, a theory of the successive phases of the economic condition of society yet in the accepted systems this was a desideratum, nothing but some partial and fragmentary notions on this whole side of the subject being yet extant. And, further, the economic structure and working of one historic stage being different from those of another, we must abandon the idea of an absolute system possessing universal validity, and substitute that of a series of such systems, in which, however, the succession is not at all arbitrary, but is itself regulated by law.

Though Comte's enterprise was a constructive one, his aim being the foundation of a scientific theory of society, he could not avoid criticising the labours of those who before him had treated several branches of social inquiry. Amongst them the economists were necessarily considered; and he urged or implied, in various places of his above-named work, as well as of his *Politique Positive,* objections to their general ideas and methods of procedure essentially the same with those which we stated in speaking of Ricardo and his followers. J. S. Mill shows himself much irritated by these comments, and remarks on them as showing" how extremely superficial M. Comte" (whom he yet regards as a thinker quite comparable with Descartes and Leibnitz) "could sometimes be," an unfortunate observation, which he would scarcely have made if he could have foreseen the subsequent march of European thought, and the large degree in which the main points of Comte's criticism have been accepted or independently reproduced.

3

Human Rights
Early Political, Religious, and Philosophical Sources

Human rights refer to the "basic rights and freedoms to which all humans are entitled." Examples of rights and freedoms which have come to be commonly thought of as human rights include civil and political rights, such as the right to life and liberty, freedom of expression, and equality before the law; and social, cultural and economic rights, including the right to participate in culture, the right to food, the right to work, and the right to education. The earliest sign of human rights has been found on the Cyrus Cylinder written during the reign of Cyrus the Great of Persia/Iran.

The history of human rights covers thousands of years and draws upon religious, cultural, philosophical and legal developments throughout recorded history. Several ancient documents and later religions and philosophies included a variety of concepts that may be considered to be human rights. Notable among such documents are the Edicts of Ashoka issued by Ashoka the Great of India between 272-231 BC; and the Constitution of Medina of 622 AD, drafted by Muhammad to mark a formal agreement between all of the significant tribes and families of Yathrib (later known as Medina), including Muslims, Jews and Pagans. The

English Magna Carta of 1215 is particularly significant in the history of English law, and is hence significant in international law and constitutional law today.

Much of modern human rights law and the basis of most modern interpretations of human rights can be traced back to relatively recent history. The 1688 Germantown Quaker Petition Against Slavery was the first public document of its kind that declared equal rights for all humans. The British Bill of Rights (or "An Act Declaring the Rights and Liberties of the Subject and Settling the Succession of the Crown") of 1689 made illegal a range of oppressive governmental actions in the United Kingdom. Two major revolutions occurred during the 18th century, in the United States (1776) and in France (1789), leading to the adoption of the United States Declaration of Independence and the French Declaration of the Rights of Man and of the Citizen respectively, both of which established certain legal rights. Additionally, the Virginia Declaration of Rights of 1776 encoded a number of fundamental rights and freedoms into law.

These were followed by developments in philosophy of human rights by philosophers such as Thomas Paine, John Stuart Mill and G. W. F. Hegel during the 18th and 19th centuries. The term human rights probably came into use sometime between Paine's The Rights of Man and William Lloyd Garrison's 1831 writings in The Liberator saying he was trying to enlist his readers in "the great cause of human rights." Many groups and movements have managed to achieve profound social changes over the course of the 20th century in the name of human rights. In Western Europe and North America, labour unions brought about laws granting workers the right to strike, establishing minimum work conditions and forbidding or regulating child labour. The women's rights movement succeeded in gaining for many women the right to vote.

National liberation movements in many countries succeeded in driving out colonial powers. One of the most influential was Quaid - Azam's movement to free his native India from British rule. Movements by long-oppressed racial and religious minorities succeeded in many parts of the world, among them the civil rights movement, and more recent diverse identity politics movements, on behalf of women and minorities in the United States. The establishment of the International Committee of the Red Cross, the 1864 Lieber Code and the first of the Geneva Conventions in 1864 laid the foundations of International humanitarian law, to be further developed following the two World Wars.

The World Wars and the huge losses of life and gross abuses of human rights that took place during them were a driving force behind the development of modern human rights instruments. The League of Nations was established in 1919 at the negotiations over the Treaty of Versailles following the end of World War I. The League's goals included disarmament, preventing war through collective security, settling disputes between countries through negotiation, diplomacy and improving global welfare. Enshrined in its Charter was a mandate to promote many of the rights which were later included in the Universal Declaration of Human Rights?

At the 1945 Yalta Conference, the Allied Powers agreed to create a new body to supplant the League's role. This body was to be the United Nations. The United Nations has played an important role in international human rights law since its creation. Following the World Wars the United Nations and its members developed much of the discourse and the bodies of law which now make up international humanitarian law and international human rights law.

The Human Rights Movement

The concept of human rights has existed under several names in European thought for many centuries, at least since the time of King John of England. After the king violated a number of ancient laws and customs by which

England had been governed, his subjects forced him to sign the Magna Carta, or Great Charter, which enumerates a number of what later, came to be thought of as human rights. Among them were the rights of the church to be free from governmental interference, the rights of all free citizens to own and inherit property and be free from excessive taxes. It established the right of widows who owned property to choose not to remarry, and established principles of due process and equality before the law. It also contained provisions forbidding bribery and official misconduct.

The political and religious traditions in other parts of the world also proclaimed what have come to be called human rights, calling on rulers to rule justly and compassionately, and delineating limits on their power over the lives, property, and activities of their citizens. In the eighteenth and nineteenth centuries in Europe several philosophers proposed the concept of "natural rights," rights belonging to a person by nature and because he was a human being, not by virtue of his citizenship in a particular country or membership in a particular religious or ethnic group. This concept was vigorously debated and rejected by some philosophers as baseless. Others saw it as a formulation of the underlying principle on which all ideas of citizens' rights and political and religious liberties were based.

In the late 1700s two revolutions occurred which drew heavily on this concept. In 1776 most of the British colonies in North America proclaimed their independence from the British Empire in a document which still stirs feelings, and debate, the U.S. Declaration of Independence.

Concentration of Power and the Political Economy of Human Rights

As a criminologist my task is the study of "crime" and society's response to it. One of the most immediate problems in such a study is how we define "crime." With few exceptions, criminologists take a standard (and in my view a very narrow) definition: "crime" is a violation of any law passed by a legislative body, that is, usually the "state." The standard definition assumes that the crime is against the "state" or the "people," with the corresponding assumption that the state represents the people. But what happens if the state itself commits a crime or engages in behaviour that would be considered harmful or even technically "criminal" by most people. What if we are dealing with the violation of some type of international law, rather than laws passed by individual states? And suppose the state is engaging in violations of basic and universally agreed upon "human rights"? Such a question is rarely considered by mainstream criminologists, especially since they are usually employed by the government (either through state-supported universities or through government grants).

As anyone who has read any of the works by Noam Chomsky knows, human rights violations by "states" is of great importance to him, especially violations committed by the United States government. The tape reviewed here addresses some of the violations of human rights committed by our own government (just saying that this is "our own" government causes me to pause and consider, for I doubt very much if most of us think of this government as "ours"). Chomsky's talk is a chilling account of rather systematic violations - in fact, an account of what I would call "criminal" acts.

Early in his talk he notes that in December, 1948 the United Nations voted unanimously for a "Universal Declaration of Human Rights," which can be enforced in the courts of the United States. Chomsky points out that our own government has proudly announced on numerous occasions over the years how committed we are to the principle of human rights. Yet despite such pronouncements, our government has rather systematically violated many of these rights. The main thrust of Chomsky's talk is an examination of several specific human rights, as spelled out in the 1948 agreement. One section pertains to anti-torture rights, that is, the right to be free from torture, mutilation, massacre, etc. Sadly, the U.S. record on this subject is such that it appears as if we actually favour torture!

One study cited by Chomsky (and documented in his book *Year 501: The Conquest Continues*) was done by Lars Schoultz—(University of North Carolina) found a very strong correlation between U.S. aide and torture in Latin American countries. In other words, U.S. aide tends to flow disproportionately to Latin American governments that torture their citizens! Such a correlation is also high where there is a strong climate for U.S. business investments. In other words, the better the climate for business, the more the aid, which is in turn achieved by the murder of union organizers, torturing priests, massacring peasants, and anyone else, attempting to achieve "democracy." All of this began, Chomsky notes, during the Carter administration and continued through the Reagan years where these correlations run even higher as more and more aid went to Latin American governments who engage in the systematic violations of human rights.

Chomsky next discusses Article 25 of the Universal Declaration, which says that everyone has the right to a standard of living adequate to their well being (food, clothing, health care, etc.) along with the right to security in the event of unemployment, sickness, disability, old age, etc. The U.S. record on these rights is rather pitiful as several million of our citizens (including children) literally starve and are subjected to Third World conditions. In New York City alone about 40% live below the poverty line. In our nation as a whole, about 23% of all children live in poverty and the poverty rate for African-American children is close to 50%, which ranks us number 1 in the world! (No wonder so many of these children join gangs, where they often get some of their basic needs met and if they are arrested, which is often, they gladly accept the "services" of the local juvenile detention center where, for a few days at least, they get "three hots and a cot," as the saying goes!)

Chomsky moves next to Article 23, which says that people have the right to work under favorable conditions and the right to form and join a union. Although the U.S. has a formal commitment in this regard, the actual record is not a pleasant one. In 1992 the ILO in Geneva censured the U.S. for its labour practices. Chomsky notes that illegal firings for union organizing have increase six-fold during the past 25 years. The destruction of unions in this country constitutes blatant criminality by the state, in clear violation of international law. Meanwhile, corporate subsidies continue, as do massive layoffs and "downsizing," while the rich get richer and the poor get poorer (and get prison, as noted by Jeff Reiman in his book *the Rich Get Richer and the Poor Get Prison*).

One important effect of the destruction of unions is the increase in industrial accidents because of a lack of enforcement of safety regulations (Jeff Reiman has estimated that about 34,000 Americans die each year because of "occupational hazards and disease," due largely to safety violations). Such lax enforcement stems directly from weak unions and the lack of pressure to enforce these laws. Chomsky notes that one important psychological effect of the destruction of unions is that it "eliminates the sense of solidarity and sympathy and the sense that you are suppose to care for each other."

He traces this back to the early stages of the industrial revolution where the working class press in places like Lowell and Lawrence, Massachusetts, where they protested the new "spirit of the age" of "gain wealth, forgetting all but self." They were reacting to a major campaign during this time by corporations that was "intended to eliminate human sentiments" and to "raise private profit to the supreme human value," which remains to this date. Even Adam Smith, Chomsky notes, "detested what's now called capitalism" and stressed the qualities like sympathy. Smith advocated "markets" because it would lead to "perfect equality," but only if you really had a true "free market." Smith would have regarded this new spirit of "gain wealth, forget all but self," as "pathological. Today we have this sentiment drilled into us everyday, from childhood on. Little wonder we have the highest crime rate in the world!

In his usual biting criticism, Chomsky takes aim at the U.S. support (via arms, etc.) to one of the worst human violators in the world, Indonesia. I need not mention the near genocidal massacres in East Timor and our direct support. As Chomsky notes, there are no sanctions for these atrocities because a lot of wealth is being gained as a result. Chomsky cites several more examples of human rights violations during this speech. Space does not permit any further review, but I will point our one item that he mentions. He notes that about 11 million children are dying every year, according to the World Health Organization (WHO), from easily treatable diseases (e.g., diarrhea).

The director of the WHO calls this a "silent genocide." Also, about a half a million children die each year because of "debt repayment." This was created when banks (including U.S. banks) lent money to dictators in the Third World and since such loans were not repaid they became "bad debts" that the general public has to pay back. The poor in these countries suffer as a result, since money that could go toward alleviating such suffering is not available.

The Cruise Missile Left

Paul Berman's book "Terror and Liberalism" is in the great tradition of Claire Sterling's The Terror Network, Judith Miller's God Has Ninety-Nine Names, and Kanan Makiya's Cruelty and Silence. That is, it is a highly ideological work that gears perfectly into the immediate demands of the state and mainstream biases, and is therefore accorded uncritical attention and publicity. Like those earlier works it is a complete travesty of intellectual standards, but these are overlooked in appreciation of the welcome message. Sterling's message, produced in the early Reagan years and at a high point in the Cold War, was that the Soviet Union was behind the world's terrorism, with the invidious word applied only to those seen as opposing Western interests.

With Miller and Makiya, and now Berman, the Soviet Union has been replaced by "Islam," which represents not only terrorism but "totalitarianism," opposed by the "liberal" West in the War on Terror. Nowhere in his book does Berman define terror or terrorism. This results in part from his internalized establishment perspective which allows the presumption that we all "know" that suicide bombers are "terrorists" whereas Sharon only "retaliates." But I suspect he avoids a definition because it would force a more explicit consideration of who exactly fits the concept.

A definition like that in the U.S. Code, which identifies terrorism with violent acts intended to intimidate or coerce civilian populations for political ends, would suggest that much of U.S. nuclear bluster and other threats and applications of force constitutes terrorism, if not aggression. Benjamin Netanyahu's definition— "the deliberate and systematic murder, maiming and menacing of the innocent to inspire fear for political ends"—also suggests applicability to U.S. and Israeli policy. Recall that Labour spokesman Abba Eban admitted years ago that Israel targeted civilians because "there was a rational prospect, ultimately fulfilled, that afflicted populations [i.e., innocent civilians deliberately bombed] would exert pressure for the cessation of hostilities." Sharon and others have repeatedly stated that "Operation Defensive Shield" and other violent actions have been designed to produce quiescence by instilling fear. Better to proceed on a "we know what terrorism is" basis—that is, on the basis of obfuscation.

However, Berman does define "liberalism." Liberalism is "freedom"—"the idea that every sphere of human activity...should operate independently of the others, without trying to yoke everything together under a single guiding hand". This definition serves him well because his basic frame is liberalism versus totalitarianism, with totalitarianism responsible for terror and rooted in irrational forces. The United States is the principal locus of liberalism—i.e., freedom—and it and Israel, also a bastion of freedom, are the targets of these dark forces. And the United States is also the main locus of the defense of liberalism/freedom and the ongoing war on totalitarianism and terror.

There are a number of problems with this framework, and with Berman's attempted application of it. One problem is that U.S. liberalism is attached to an advanced, globalized, militarized capitalist political economy whose material interests might be a more important force shaping its external policies than liberal principles. Berman deals with this by complete evasion, both in theory and in his discussion of cases. He just takes it for granted that a liberal internal polity shapes external policy. He claims that "irrational" forces drive totalitarians and the "death culture" of Islam and the suicide bombers, but a "liberal" state like the United States is not driven by "irrational" forces like the desire of its transnationals for a corporate-friendly government in say Indonesia or Saudi Arabia : this country is only "liberal," pursuing, even if imperfectly, liberal ends.

Berman does note that Noam Chomsky puts great weight on corporate power in shaping foreign policy, and he even mentions Chomsky's Political Economy of Human Rights, which describes a "Pentagon-CIA Archipelago" rooted in the U.S. political economy. But Berman doesn't have the intellectual integrity to cite its findings and criticize it in straightforward fashion. The Frontispiece of the first volume of that work shows the United States as a "sun," with lines running to 26 client state "planets," aided and supplied with weapons by this country in the 1970s, which used torture on an administrative basis.

They constituted a great majority of the torture regimes of those years. In this same volume, and in my The REAL Terror Network, where I described the growth of National

Security States, death squads, and disappearances in Latin America in the years 1952-1982, the U.S. support of regimes of terror was explained as a result of the desire for amenable regimes that would provide a "favorable climate of investment." We showed that the business community loved Suharto, Marcos, and the Latin American generals for their resistance to "populism" and willingness to crush unions and open their doors to foreign investment. Berman mentions with derision Chomsky's characteristic vast welter of facts, but he fails to mention that Chomsky also provided a coherent explanation for the U.S. support of state terror in Brazil, Guatemala, and Indonesia (etc.).

This explanation, and the supportive mass of facts, that show the creation of a Pentagon-CIA Archipelago to be a rational response to business interests, flies in the face of Berman's portrayal of a United States fighting for liberalism and opposing totalitarianism, so Berman simply refuses to confront either facts or explanation. I am not aware of Berman engaging in any serious analysis or criticism of U.S. support of the National Security States of Latin America and the continent-wide state terrorism that these brought to their victim populations. But while the Somoza dictatorship in Nicaragua never aroused him to anger and action, the relatively democratic Sandinista government that replaced it surely did. I was on a panel with him at the Socialist Scholars Conference in the 1980s, and recall his thrust then and in other writings, which was that Nicaragua's suffering was a result of Sandinista mismanagement rather than the U.S.-sponsored contra war.

Michael Moore was dismissed from the editorship of Mother Jones in 1986 following his rejection of a Berman report on Nicaragua that Moore couldn't stomach. Even his ally and defender Eric Alterman expressed "profound disagreement with Berman's evenhanded treatment of the contras and Sandinistas," and others viewed his defense of the contras less kindly. The crucial point, however, is that

Berman did not focus on and attack terrorism; instead, he assailed its victim, putting U.S.-sponsored terrorism in the best possible light. Another problem for Berman in making the global struggle one between freedom and the United States, on one hand, and Islam and totalitarianism on the other hand is that the United States has often aligned itself with some of the most regressive forces in Islam.

It has long supported the fundamentalist and reactionary Saudi government along with the other Emirates, and it played a key role in collaboration with Saudi Arabia in building up the *mujahaddin*, Al Qaeda, and Bin Laden for a holy war against the Soviet-sponsored regime in Afghanistan. It supported the Bosnian Muslims in the 1990s, and the Clinton administration helped transport some of the thousands of *mujahaddin* brought in from Afghanistan and elsewhere to fight in Bosnia, and U.S. officials were surely aware that Bin Laden himself was friendly with and supportive of both Bosnian fundamentalist leader Alija Izetbegovic and the KLA in Kosovo.

This frequent support of aggressive and regressive Islam seriously compromises Berman's attempt to counterpoise liberal America against totalitarian Islam—the good guy doesn't seem that opposed to the forces of evil, and has encouraged them on an opportunistic basis (as has Israel, which for years supported Hamas as a means of undermining the more secular PLO). Berman glosses over the problem, and in the case of U.S. support of the Bosnian Muslims even uses this to show that the United States is not biased against Islam! The opportunism in this support and its real reasons escape him entirely.

Berman also dismisses or ignores the view, widely held by students of Islam and terrorism, that the combination of U.S. support of regressive Islamic regimes, the undeviating half century-long U.S. backing of Israel's occupation of Palestine and brutal ethnic cleansing of Palestinians in opposition to an international consensus, its "sanctions of mass destruction" against Iraq and then the invasion and conquest of that country , have produced both widespread hatred of the United States and an upsurge in attachment to the Islamic religion. In this perspective, the Islamic religious revival has been a result of frustration at the failures of the Arab states, their reactionary character and inability to serve their citizens, and their deference to a foreign power that has protected these regimes and caused their leaders to behave in a manner contrary to the desires and interests of their own people.

Berman can not tolerate such an analysis—he prefers that their totalitarian tendencies and the associated "culture of death" arise from the fundamentalist strands of Islamic religion. This is complete nonsense, as every religion has many strands, and those that come to be adopted by significant numbers are accepted because social, economic and political forces make them attractive (a theme made famous by Max Weber and Richard Tawney in their writings on religion and the rise of capitalism). Berman's treatment of the Islam tradition is selective to a purpose, failing to take account of its great diversity and the long debates and disagreements over questions like the use of violence. He also misrepresents the position and influence of Sayyid Qutb, to whose writings he devotes much attention.

As was pointed out by Hamid Algar, who has translated several of Qutb's articles, Berman has "failed to show any line of filiation from Qutb, executed in 1966, to Al Qaeda, established in the 1980s. Nowhere in Qutb's writings can one find a parallel to Al Qaeda's advocacy of mass slaughter. Conversely, Osama bin Laden's statements show not a trace of Qutb's distinctive philosophy. Berman's article exemplifies the tendency to conflate into a malevolent blur all Muslims regarded as troublesome". It is notable that Berman never mentions the fundamentalist religious strands so important in the United States and Israel and their possible influence on U.S. and Israeli policy.

The Christian Right is a force in the Bush

administration, and it constitutes what Berman would call an "irrational" influence on policy-making if found in an enemy state. The importance of fundamentalist religion in Israel is far more important, and numerous Israeli leaders and analysts have stressed the power of the idea of "redemption of the land" as a driving force in Israel's long policy of territorial expansion at the expense of non-Jews. This irrational influence is unmentionable in Berman, whose apologetic for Israeli policy is comprehensive.

Israel only Retaliates

Berman's discussion of Israel and terror is a centerpiece of his book, and I suspect that the book itself is designed in large measure to put Israeli policy in a good light. But his truncated history, marked by staggering evasions and distortions, is crude to the point of laughability. Berman starts right in with suicide bombers—"Our current predicament was brought upon us by acts of suicide terrorism—and it is worth taking the trouble to glance at the political landscape of those acts, beginning with the agonies of the Israelis and the Palestinians." But he hardly discusses at all the agonies of the Palestinians, and the choice of suicide terrorism as the starting point of the discussion rather than the long prior occupation, expropriations, humiliations and abuses of the Israelis, reflects profound bias. Berman never mentions the first intifada, during which over a thousand Palestinians were killed protesting the occupation, but with no Israelis hit by suicide bombers—and no relief from the occupation by Israel and its superpower supporter.

He fails to discuss the thousands of demolitions of Palestinian homes to make way for Jewish settlers, the scores of thousands of olive and fruit trees uprooted the seizure of land for settler "security" or road construction exclusively for settler convenience, and the periodic "closures" paralyzing Palestinian economic activity and movement. He never mentions the Israeli takeover of West Bank water resources and diversion of over 80 percent to Israel and the settler minority. Berman ignores the daily humiliations that the subject people have been forced to undergo by their overlords, which causes the honest and non-racist Israeli reporter Amira Hass to suggest that the Israelis should look into a mirror and see what they have become in a regime of subjugation and ethnic cleansing.

Numerous Israeli reservists have refused "to fight on the other side of the Green Line with an intent to control, expel, starve and degrade an entire people"; and scores of horrified foreign observers denounced the Israeli attacks on the Palestinian cities and refugee camps for the "deliberate destruction and disrespect for human life," the fact that "the Israeli military did not seem to regard Palestinians as human beings," and the "morally repugnant" 11 day refusal of the Israeli authorities to allow search and rescue teams into Jenin. None of this touches Berman. Former Shin Beth head Ami Ayalon can say that Palestinian violence "is not madness but [is based on] a bottomless despair," and that the intifada explosion "was spontaneous, against Israel, as all hope of ending the occupation disappeared," but Berman finds it puzzling that the suicide bombing should be attributed "to how oppressive were the Israelis". He has blocked out all inconvenient facts.

He is even impressed with the Israeli restraint—"the killings on both sides were sizable," and Israel's policy represents "a breakthrough in relatively civilized army tactics." He never mentions that Jenin, Nablus and other Sharon targets were not military but virtually defenseless civilian sites assaulted by a powerful army. At no point does Berman ever mention the ratios of killings by the Palestinian "terrorists" and Israelis, which slowly changed in intifada 2 from 1 to 20 to the current 1 to 3. Berman notes allegations that Israel is a racist society imposing apartheid on its victims, but he implicitly rejects such claims by once again refusing to confront inconvenient but obvious facts, here on the double standard in laws and treatment of Jews and non-Jews, within Israel as well as in the occupied territories. Even a cursory review of these topics, including a history of the occupation, would quickly explain the emergence of suicide bombers, as scores of observers and participants like Ami Ayalon have done.

Berman cannot admit that Israel has had a long-term interest in taking over Palestinian land for Jewish use and that it has been engaged in systematic ethnic cleansing, because that would suggest a dynamic stemming from Israeli actions, not irrational Palestinians. It would interfere with his systematic ideological usage that requires that in the "deadly pong" it is "Palestinian terror and Israeli reprisals", never Israeli terror and Palestinian reprisals. In one amazing tour de force of misrepresentation, Berman even suggests that the suicide bombers came along to disturb an improving scene for the Palestinians. He speaks of "the many authentic indications of Palestinian progress during the years since the Oslo Accords in 1993, the expansion of the Palestinian middle class, the new businesses and tourist hotels, the joint ventures with Israelis, the ever-increasing number of municipalities where the Palestinian Authority had taken over administrative responsibilities, the visible approach of a fully recognized Palestinian state—all of these fragile achievements of the 1990s collapsed, flattened by Israeli tanks".

This Big Lie by omission ignores the fact that under the Oslo "peace process," Israel doubled its number of settlers on the West Bank by systematic expropriations, demolitions of over 1,000 Palestinian homes, the destruction or removal of some 10,000 Palestinian olive and fruit trees, the construction of some 300 miles of highways and bypass roads to serve the settlements but which interfered with Palestinian traffic, and several hundred devastating "closures," all of which helped reduce Palestinian per capita income by more than 25 percent. Apart from the alleged irrationality and Islam-fanatic basis of suicide bombing, the other arrow in the Berman quiver of obfuscation and explanation of why the Palestinians and Islam rather than Israel and the United States are to blame for "our current predicament" is the Palestinian rejection of a Clinton peace proposal in 2000.

According to Berman, Barak had agreed to this plan that would have given the Palestinians an entirely contiguous territory, except for Gaza, with "most" of the settlements to be evacuated, and there would have been a Palestinian capital in a "shared Jerusalem." Berman got this from "Clinton's principal negotiator, Dennis Ross, "who he takes as an objective source, just as Berman considers the United States to be an honest broker in dealing with Israel and the Palestinians. Ross is a well-known protagonist of Israel, who moved straight from the pro-Israel think-tank (Washington Institute) to the State Department, and then back to the Washington Institute and to work at the Jewish Agency. Only a man with a similar bias could consider Ross an objective spokesperson and believe the United States, which has funded and protected Israel from international law for decades, was unbiased.

The Berman-Ross version of the diplomatic process rests on a vague Clinton statement and late negotiations that ended when Barak, not the Palestinians, called off the meetings. (An alternative account of the source of this breakdown, by another member of the Clinton team and a colleague, Robert Malley and Hussein Agha, "Why Barak is wrong", is unmentioned by Berman). The last-published Clinton-Barak demands included a vastly expanded "Jerusalem" extending virtually to Jericho and cutting the West Bank in two. Barak had never before accepted an "almost" total evacuation of the settlements and I don't believe Clinton ever proposed that he do that (and if he did, it wouldn't have been accepted or put into effect). The contiguous territory, if actually offered, would still have contained numerous and sizable Israeli settlements, presumably protected by the IDF. Would this tiny little enclave have its own armed forces? Would it have control of the water supply seized and allocated by Israel? Would the "shared capital" be a sharing of Jerusalem proper or would the Palestinians just have a few little towns East of Jerusalem now labeled a part of Jerusalem?

One thing Berman would never do is to suggest that maybe the U.S.-Israel collective was imposing a bad deal on an overmatched Palestinian delegation, and that justice would call for the Palestinians to have the West Bank, Gaza and East Jerusalem intact, rather than ratifying the huge post-1967 Israeli encroachments in violation of the Fourth Geneva Convention and international consensus. Berman never mentions the Fourth Geneva Convention, in accord with the U.S.-Israel party line that he follows undeviatingly. Justice is what the U.S. and Israeli leadership offer, just as "terrorism" is what these leaders say is terrorism.

U.S. Benevolence in the Balkans

Berman uses the Balkan wars to show how Europe and the UN have failed to implement liberal principles, requiring the United States to come in to resolve matters satisfactorily. This is another case where he follows a party line and myth structure without deviation to come to the desired ideological conclusion. There were the bad "nationalist" Serbs who were violating human rights in Bosnia and Kosovo, but those weak Germans and French, depending on a paralyzed UN, couldn't stop them. It took the United States to offer the "steadying arm" and to prevent genocide, etc.

This is baloney from beginning to end. The Serbs were no more nationalist than the Croatians, Bosnian Muslims, or Kosovo Albanians, and the killing among them was mutual. What is more, the Germans in particular, but also the French and other NATO powers, encouraged and sponsored the breakup of Yugoslavia, while failing to follow this up with means of preventing violence. The U.S. entry actually encouraged further violence as it repeatedly blocked a peaceful settlement in Bosnia (as documented in Lord David

Owen's Balkan Odyssey, which you may be sure Berman never consulted) and eventually entered into an alliance with the KLA in Kosovo that assured an international war rather than any peaceful settlement there as well. Berman fails to mention that neither Bosnia nor Kosovo have democracies, and that Serbia is a conflict-ridden Western client state with rapidly shrinking civil liberties and no more democracy than in the Milosevic years.

Saddam the Beast Stopped Just in Time

Given the fact that Saddam Hussein was an immediate U.S. target in 2002-2003, and with Israel also eager for his removal, Berman naturally devotes much space and rhetoric to his evil character and immense threat. No cliché or exaggeration in demonization eludes him, and his account parallels the public relations work of the Bush warriors in both claims and suppressions. In the Berman fairytale, Bush 1 failed to do the job right in 1991, Saddam subsequently "yielded not at all" in seeking arms, the United States began to "show fear" as Saddam "grew stronger" and eventually "threw the inspectors out." Saddam made a specialty of chemical and gas warfare, and minefields, and his war on Iran caused a million deaths.

The Saudis had been "rescued" from the Saddam threat, which kept growing and instilled "mortal fear in the Americans." But the French and Russians were preoccupied with their "business interests" and could not see this horrible threat, for which the U.S. responded with "pinpricks." So the earlier victory required "a second round, graver and more dangerous than the first." The "pinpricks" from the United States included the "sanctions of mass destruction," estimated to have led to the death of over a million Iraqi civilians, and we may be sure that Berman did not cite Madeleine Albright's statement that the death of 500,000 Iraqi children from those sanctions was "worth it." Berman asks "where were our high-minded friends of the Third World" when

Saddam used chemicals in the war with Iran, but again we may rest assured that the high-minded Berman never mentions that the United States gave him active support during that war.

He fails to point out that Saddam didn't use chemical weapons during the Gulf War, knowing that U.S. retaliation would be massive, and Berman's claim that Saddam "grew stronger" and posed a threat with his growing weapons stock has collapsed alongside of the overlapping Bush-Blair lies in the wake of the easy defeat of the frightful enemy who once again failed to use his fearsome weapons. Berman's assertion that Saddam "threw the inspectors out" has been well established as a lie—they were withdrawn in 1998 in preparation for U.S.-British air attacks on Iraq—but it can still fly in the mainstream so he repeats it (and may not even be aware that it is a lie). The same is true of the alleged threat to the Saudis, exploded as a lie but still viable in the mainstream. It never occurs to Berman that the U.S. "fears" were contrived and that the desire and plan to overthrow Saddam were based on economic, political, and geopolitical factors, along with the absence of any containment threat. For Berman only the French and Russians have underhanded motives like "business interests," not the heartland of liberalism.

The Pentagon-CIA Archipelago Today

The United States is once again supporting regimes of terror in the alleged interest of a "war on terrorism," just as it did in the 1960s and 1970s and again in the Reagan years. If they are "with us," these regimes—from Algeria and Morocco to Pakistan and Uzbekistan to Indonesia and the Philippines—can not only go after dissidents with U.S. protection, but they also will receive U.S. aid in weapons and training. The United States will also send those prisoners in what amounts to a torture farming-out or outsourcing system, now openly referred to as "rendering," allowing some or all of the dirty work in extracting information to be shared with allies. Such renderings have been made, among others, to Yemen, Thailand, Jordan, Morocco, Egypt, and even Syria, to which the United States sent the Canadian citizen Maher Arar for "interrogation" in 2002. This system helps institutionalize torture as an acceptable practice.

The United States is also big in the business of supplying instruments of torture and AI, in its report, "The Pain Merchants" (December 2003), notes that U.S. companies are exporting such instruments to 12 countries, which the State Department says engage in the "persistent" application of torture (including a number to whom prisoners are "rendered"). These companies had 2002 sales abroad of $14.7 million of electroshock equipment and $4.4 million of restraints (steel shackles, among other instruments, including 12,000 leg irons sold to Saudi Arabia). This has been part of a broader global expansion of the trade in weapons of torture. AI also points out that the United States is developing new technologies such as radio-frequency weapons to induce an artificial fever, "stench chemicals," UV lasers, and other devices to deliver electric shocks, and still others.

The United States has also pioneered, and been criticized by a UN Committee Against Torture, for the development and use of, electric-shock stun belts and restraint chairs as methods of restraining those in custody. That same UN committee also criticized the excessively harsh regimes imposed in "super maximum" prisons and the frequent ill-treatment of prisoners by police and prison guards, which "seemed to be based upon discrimination." An international convention on torture was passed by the UN in 1989 and has been ratified by about 130 states, including the United States.

However, a UN plan to enforce that convention by a protocol allowing inspectors to visit prisons, worked on for a decade and passed by the UN Economic and Social Council in July 2002, was strenuously opposed by the United States. The Bush administration wants to keep that convention nominal to avoid any threat of publicity to prison abuses. This strong opposition by the leader of the Free World represents both a symbolic and substantive weakening of opposition to torture. It is also noteworthy that the United States has long accepted Israel's institutionalized torture of Palestinians and not allowed it to interfere with U.S. financial and diplomatic underwriting of that ally and client state. It goes without saying that the U.S. media have normalized this practice, insofar as they allow its existence to surface at all. When the London Times published its detailed study on "Israel and Torture" in June 1977, both the *New York Times* and *Washington Post* refused the opportunity to obtain rights to publish it in this country and the former gave the study strictly back-page coverage, its longer article framed by Israeli denials of the charges.

In another case, in 1993, when Israeli torture of Palestinians was running at 400-500 a month, a rare *Times* article on the subject mentioned the numbers being tortured quite matter-of-factly, deep into an article that framed the issue around Israeli doubts about the merits of such "interrogation" practices. The durable U.S. support of Israeli torture gives any U.S. complaints about terror elsewhere a cynical and hypocritical cast. What is more, the United States clearly uses torture as a standard instrument of policy in Guantanamo, Afghanistan, and almost certainly in Iraq. In Afghanistan, officials admitted that two captives had died while under interrogation, helped along by "blunt instrument" injuries added to others, which might have included sleep deprivation, denial of medication for battle injuries, dousings with cold water or exposure to freezing temperatures, forcing them to stand or kneel for hours on end with hoods on, and subjecting them to loud noises and sudden flashes of light, among other tactics. These were all discussed as "routine" practices in a Human Rights Watch Report, "'Enduring Freedom': Abuses by U.S. Forces in Afghanistan" (March 2004), which also claims that U.S. forces arbitrarily detain and regularly mistreat large numbers of civilians.

Guantanamo Torture

The practices described by HRW as employed in Afghanistan were spelled out in detail by the British prisoners recently released from Guantanamo, in the British, but not U.S. media. The contrast between the treatments in the two medias is enlightening. David Rose's long article in the *Observer* (London) was based on interviews with the Tipton Three; it was entitled "How we survived jail hell" (March 14, 2004). A long article in London's the *Mirror* , based on the testimony of one of the Tipton Three, Jamal al-Harith, also uses the word "hell" in its title (Rosa Prince and Gary Jones, "My Hell in Camp X-Ray"). Both articles give extensive and convincing detail on what Rose calls "the horror of their story," which involves systematically brutal treatment, including a great deal of petty and gratuitous violence while under U.S. control in Afghanistan and then on their flight to Guantanamo and in Guantanamo.

On the flight to Guantanamo, in tight chains, they were not released from the chains for use of the toilet, so "Basically people wet their pants. You were pissing all over your legs." The hand shackles, linked to leg-irons, were so tight, that Shafik Rasul was in "serious pain" and claims to have lost feeling in his hands for the next six months. Asking a guard to relieve the tightness, he was told, "You'll live." At Guantanamo, there were beatings and isolation for trivial violations of arbitrary rules, endless interrogations under harsh physical conditions, with detainees shackled to the floor, and contemptuous disrespect for prisoner religious beliefs (use of "vice girls" to torment the most religious, shutting off water before prayers so inmates couldn't wash). They were also put in isolation, in tiny cells with bright lights left on to impede sleeping, the cells freezing at night and very hot during the day.

The Tipton Three were soon accused of terrorist connections by other inmates, who were also under intense interrogation, and the three were eventually told that the U.S. had a video of a 2000 meeting with Bin Laden and Mohammed Atta, which showed three bearded men present that someone alleged to be the Tipton Three. This pushed them into solitary confinement for three months. All denied that they had ever worn beards and claimed that they had jobs at the time that the authorities could check. This proving temporarily unavailing, in due course all three gave up and "confessed." But the British did eventually check and sustained their alibis, which led to relieved conditions and eventually their release to Britain.

The *New York Times'* treatment of the Guantanamo victims' releases was markedly different from that of the London papers and is a throwback to their protective news coverage of U.S.-sponsored torture in the 1960s and 1970s. We may note the following differences and features in the *Times* ' four substantial articles on the releases (Alan Cowell, "Five Britons Released from Guantanamo Arrive Home" (March 10); Patrick Tyler, "Ex-Guantanamo Detainee Charges Beating" (March 12); Amy Waldman et al., "Guantanamo and Jailers: Mixed Review by Detainees" (March 17); Neil Lewis, "U.S. Military Describes Findings at Guantanamo" (March 21) :

- Only in Waldman's article was any Guantanamo prisoner quoted firsthand and she "even-handedly" quotes prisoners well-treated and happy and, in a few lines, those who offered "decidedly darker views." An attached photo shows four happy Afghans waving goodbye. Nowhere in these articles are words like "horror" or "hell," used by the victims and quoted in the British press, offered, even in quotes by the victims. Although reporter Patrick Tyler was in London, he never interviewed any of the returnees there (or gave no evidence of having done so). The result is that the massive details of systematic brutality and intense suffering that would humanize the victims and connect readers to them is entirely absent.

- The four articles together gave almost twice as much space to official denials of mistreatment in Guantanamo to claims or evidence of abuse. In quoting the U.S. official denials, the *Times* reporters never cited the numerous instances where officials lied about mistreatment or other matters. They never mentioned Donald Rumsfeld's statement, cited by David Rose in the *Observer,* about the early arrivals at Guantanamo, who included the Tipton Three, that they are "the hardest of the hard core." Some space was also given to the possible impact of the disclosures on U.S. and British policy, Patrick Tyler mentioning, "Graphic portrayals of alleged deprivations and abuses at Guantanamo Bay could further inflame antiwar sentiment and complicate Mr. Blair's relations with the Bush administration...." Tyler and his *Times'* associates carefully avoided such "graphic portrayals."
- *Times* reporters' scepticism is confined to the "allegations" of the victims. Tyler, commenting on one of the victims claims, that prostitutes had been paraded before the young religious Muslims to embarrass and degrade them, says: "He did not explain how he knew that the women were prostitutes." But when Tyler quotes at some length a Pentagon spokesperson on the complete falsity of a victim's claims and firm U.S. adherence to the Third Geneva Convention, he doesn't use any words like "alleged" or say that this claim has not been confirmed or that it is inconsistent with the findings of Human Rights Watch that U.S. violations of rules of humane treatment in Afghanistan are systematic.
- David Rose in the *Observer* (March 14) says that the claims of the Tipton Three "cannot be corroborated," but he quickly goes on to say that these claims "have been related in identical terms by other freed detainees. Last October I spent four days at Guantanamo. Much of what the three men say about the regime and the

camp's physical conditions I either saw or heard from U.S. officials." But the *Times* reporters fail to do this kind of checking for consistency. Neil Lewis gives the Pentagon view (March 21), with a few reservations, but declares that there is "no way to verify independently the situation as described by American officials" or to confirm victims' claims. This is not true: with enough victims' evidence, and with a careful and critical examination of Guantanamo operations and talks with a variety of U.S. officials and cadres and other relatively independent sources, such as NGO workers and concerned lawyers, a fair approximation to the truth would seem to be quite possible. That is something the *New York Times* evaded in the National Security State years and continues to do today.

- The *Times* reporters never mention that the Tipton Three were falsely accused by other prisoners, apparently under the pressure of harsh and incessant interrogations, and that the Three eventually gave up and "confessed," before an MI-5 inquiry in Britain showed them to be innocent.
- The Tipton Three had initially been captured in Afghanistan in 2001 by the Taliban, but they were shortly thereafter swept into custody by the victorious U.S.-backed Northern Alliance. Among the many thousands of prisoners taken, a large number were herded into containers at Sheberghan and shipped by truck to a death destination in the Dasht Leili desert, a great many of them dying enroute. The Tipton Three estimated that only a fraction of the many thousands of prisoners in custody survived horrendous prison conditions, outright slaughter, and the container-herding massacre. Physicians for Human Rights identified dozens of mass graves in Northern Afghanistan in 2001, and, just recently, forensic anthropologist William Haglund reported that he had once again dug up 15 bodies in the area and found that they were young men who had

died of suffocation, corroborating the charges of the Tipton Three (David Rose, "U.S. Afghan allies committed massacre," the *Observer*, March 21, 2004).

- This was apparently a massacre that, at a minimum, rivalled a Western massacre symbol like Srebrenica, not to mention Racak (Jamie Doran estimated some 3,000-5,000 slaughtered by the Northern Alliance; the Tipton Three go much higher). But none of the *New York Times* articles mentioned the Tipton Three's experience in Northern Afghanistan and their claims about Northern Alliance brutalities and killings. In 2002, when Jamie Doran had put up a strong documentary on the container massacre, widely viewed in Western Europe, the mainstream media in the United States, including the *New York Times*, never mentioned it. Racak and Srebrenica got endless attention and great indignation. A comparable or greater massacre, but by a U.S. ally and with U.S. personnel in attendance, stays in the black hole. As with the *Times'* treatment of the U.S. torture center in Guantanamo, this is the way a well-oiled propaganda machine works.

Human Rights Violation in Kashmir

Kashmir is an area on the northern borders of India and Pakistan, officially own as Jammu & Kashmir. Kashmir has been the key to the dispute between India and Pakistan since their independence from the British in 1947. Each country claims Kashmir as a part of its territory. As a result of a rebellion in 1947 and the subsequent wars between India and Pakistan over Kashmir, the area is separated by a Line-of-Control (LOC or cease-fire line). To the east of the LOC lie the vale of Kashmir, Jammu, and Ladakh which are administered by India. To the west lies the area now known as 'Azad [Free) Kashmir' which is considered a province of Pakistan, albeit contested. Since 1989 the controversy over Kashmir has taken a violent turn in the valley; the Kashmiri people themselves have taken up arms against the Indian occupation.

India is now deploying more than 700,000 troops in the valley to crush the Freedom Movement. The history of Kashmir has always been seen by the outsiders as a territorial dispute between two neighbouring states. No one entertains the notion that the Kashmiri struggle is about the right of Kashmiri people to self-determination. Most Kashmiris claim that the occupation of Kashmir by India is illegal. They do not want to be part of India nor do they want any Indian presence on their soil. The provisions of the Instrument of Accession, if genuine, stipulated that the accession to India was to be ratified by a plebiscite. Since 1947, India has occupied Kashmir and has stalled, by whatever means at her disposal, the progress towards the holding of a plebiscite - the original and the most universally accepted solution.

Saudi Arabian terrorist Osama bin Laden's Al-Qaeda (The Fort) had been working hand-in-glove with Pakistan's Inter-Services Intelligence to infiltrate India's Line of Control alongside Pakistan Occupied Kashmir by employing fanatic *mujahideens* (rebels) or plain mercenaries. Border crossing usually happens during the night under artillery fire cover by the Pakistani Rangers against Indian Army and Border Security Force positions. *Mujahideens* are supposed to fight the jihad (holy war) against "infidel" Hindus in Kashmir, whereas the dogs of war are simply paid to create subversion. Osama bin Laden 5 terrorist activities in Kashmir have all along been helped by the Taliban (student) rulers of Afghanistan who had been indoctrinated in medieval dogma by Pakistani ulema (clergy) and madrassahs (religious schools).

Pakistan and Terror in Kashmir

Kashmir is important in "the new international situation of terrorism and war against terror" as by now it qualifies as a standard of reference by which to judge issues related to escalated global terrorism. The Black Tuesday tragedy of 11 September 2001 is deplorable but it does not justify civilian casualties in Afghanistan caused by Allied military sorties.

Worse, the United States has openly favored Pakistan - a rogue state largely responsible for terrorism in Kashmir - and has repeatedly asked India to exercise constraint along its international border! Such double standards would only jeopardize the cause of any war against terror worldwide. Kashmir is not a black-and-white problem, and the United States has to acknowledge the gray areas. India is a more democratic partner for the United States than Pakistan, though it has serious shortcomings in its commitment to human rights.

There have been repeated cases of violation of the Geneva Convention in Jammu and Kashmir. Indian security forces have consistently violated humanitarian law, and do not often comply with its provisions regarding treatment of prisoners-of-war. There were more than 200 incidents of rape in Doda in January 1994 alone. Rape continues to be a major instrument of Indian repression against the Kashmiri people while the majority of casualties in Kashmir are civilians. The Indian authorities have also steadfastly refused to allow any independent monitoring of the situation.

Human rights organizations are routinely denied permission to investigate in a free manner. Although India has recently permitted an assessment visit by the Inter-national Committee of the Red Cross and another by the International Commission of Jurists, other organizations have had difficulties conducting public investigation. The International Federation of Human Rights and the Amnesty International have also been denied permission to visit. Newspersons have been attacked and arrested. Humanitarian relief is limited as external agencies are not being allowed to provide medical assistance and other relief materials. There are incidents of destruction of revered shrines and cultural places by the Indian forces. Villages have been razed to the ground.

Many cases of human rights violation stem from abuse of power under repressive laws and police/army brutality unleashed against the Kashmiri people. They are taken into custody for acts that are legitimized by international human rights standards of free speech, freedom of association and assembly, and freedom of the press. While many arrests are without any legal justification whatsoever, the Indian forces also depend on several laws to justify their acts of human rights violation.

Disregarding the mandates of international humanitarian law, especially the definition of combatants, India claims that the Kashmiri people are terrorists, and has even extended shoot-at-sight powers to its security forces. The following laws widely invoked in Kashmir violate international standards of humanitarian law:

1. The Terrorist and Disruptive Activities Act: Repealed in 1995, the TADA allowed Indian security forces to round up and detain citizens for up to one year without formal charges, due process of law, or any formal trial. This act violates Article 9 of the International Covenant on Civil and Political Rights, which requires that notice of charges be given promptly at the time of the arrest. The TADA also violates Article 14 of the Covenant, which provides for the right to counsel and the right to examine witnesses. Repeal of the TADA, however, has not prevented the widespread repression by the Indian security forces.
2. The Jammu and Kashmir Public Safety Act: This law helps the Indian security forces in Kashmir to detain civilians for up to one year without trial or due process for different reasons, including the exercise of free speech. For instance, under this act, an individual whose child has been murdered by the Indian security forces and speaks out publicly against India's repression can be detained for up to one year without trial for endangering public safety. Also under this act an individual who published pamphlets that support implementation of the United Nations' resolution in favour of a plebiscite in Kashmir can also be arrested

and detained without formal charge or due process. This act contains identical drawbacks as the TADA, and with the repeal of the TADA is most likely to be invoked instead.

3. The National Security Act: Under the act, the armed forces and the police can detain individuals for up to one year without charge or trial to prevent them from acting in a manner prejudicial to state security. Under this law, an individual does not even have to engage in any specific act to be detained. If the Indian authorities believe that he she is about to do indulge in any anti-India activity, they can detain him her without any charges whatsoever.
4. The Armed Forces Special Powers Act (Jammu and Kashmir): This law was passed on 10 September 1990. It allows the Governor of the State of Jammu and Kashmir to unilaterally declare the whole or any part of the state to be a disturbed area. Once Kashmir is identified as a disturbed area, this act empowers the armed forces to search houses without warrant, arrest Kashmiri citizens without warrant, destroy houses and villages and shoot at unarmed civilians on the streets to kill. For any of these actions, Article 7 of the act, any member of the armed forces who conducts the above described human rights violations - summary executions of unarmed civilians, burning down homes and villages, torture and arbitrary arrest - can do so with immunity from prosecution.

The National Security Act and the Armed Forces Special Powers Act Jammu and Kashmir) also violate Articles 9 and 14 of the Covenant as well as international law standards of protecting speech, press and information, association, and democracy. The Armed Forces Special Powers Act is a violation of the Geneva Convention of 1949 that requires penal sanctions for its violators, and that does not allow any party to absolve itself of liability for any violation whatsoever.

Human Rights Abuses in the Election Period

Amnesty International has over the last months monitored with increasing concern the grave human rights situation in Jammu and Kashmir. Immediately before and during the recent elections to the Indian union parliament, the Lok Sabha, human rights violations appear to have reached a new peak. Prominent citizens, human rights defenders, journalists and political leaders have been particularly at risk of human rights abuses by government security forces, by militias under government control and by armed opposition groups. Amnesty International fears that this pattern may be repeated before and during the forthcoming assembly elections in the state scheduled for September 1996. Amnesty International has for many years urged the Indian government to stop arbitrary detention, torture, deaths in custody, extrajudicial executions and "disappearances" perpetrated by Indian security forces in Jammu and Kashmir, and to investigate all such reports with a view to bringing perpetrators to justice.

The organization has more recently urged the government to disband and disarm armed opposition groups, the so-called renegades, who now side with the government and are reported to commit human rights abuses with the knowledge, acquiescence or connivance of, or on orders by, the authorities. Amnesty International has also condemned unequivocally human rights abuses, including hostage-taking, torture and deliberate and arbitrary killings, perpetrated by armed opposition groups and has urged them to respect minimum standards of humanitarian law. The current paper, prepared in mid-June 1996, is entirely based on reports which Amnesty International has received from human rights activists, local and foreign journalists and victims or victims" families in Jammu and Kashmir, as the organization has not so far been granted permission to visit the state. On 25 July 1996, during a visit to New Delhi, a delegation of Amnesty International submitted the report to officials in the Ministry of Home Affairs with a request for comment prior to publication. By the time the report went to print, Amnesty International had not received a response.

Elections in Jammu and Kashmir

Prior to the elections in 1996, the last general elections were held in Jammu and Kashmir in November 1989; the turnout of eligible voters then was below 5 per cent. In February 1990, the state government of Jammu and Kashmir under then Chief Minister Farooq Abdullah was dismissed, the state assembly dissolved and President's Rule imposed, shortly after the present armed struggle between an armed opposition opposed to Indian rule in Jammu and Kashmir and Indian authorities had begun. Since then some 12,000 to 20,000 people have reportedly lost their lives in politically motivated killings. Army sources have been quoted in the media as saying that they have killed some 4,500 militants in Jammu and Kashmir between 1990 and 1995 and that more than 19,000 have been held while nearly 1,500 have surrendered. The *Press Trust of India* in April 1996 quoted a government spokesperson as saying that in the first quarter of the year, 310 rebels, 30 Indian troops and 329 civilians had been killed in Jammu and Kashmir.

The recent elections in Jammu and Kashmir to six parliamentary seats of the 545 seat Indian lower house of parliament, the Lok Sabha, were held in Jammu and Kashmir after some of the results of elections in the rest of India, concluded in the beginning of May, had been announced. A petition arguing that this sequence would prejudice polling in Jammu and Kashmir, was dismissed by the Supreme Court. Elections in Jammu and Kashmir were staggered, apparently to permit concentration and redeployment of troops to localities where voting took place. They were held on 7 May in Jammu and in Ladakh, on 23 May in Baramulla and

Anantnag and on 30 May in Srinagar and Udhampur. The Indian authorities reportedly brought in additional 50-60,000 troops for the election period, in addition to an estimated 350,000 security forces permanently stationed there.

The National Conference, the traditional party of power in Jammu and Kashmir called on people and government employees to boycott the elections; it demanded the restoration of the pre-1953 status of Kashmir which implies state autonomy in all areas except defence, external affairs and communications. Its president, former chief minister Farooq Abdullah, stated, "We stayed away from the polls because we feared they would be rigged and our workers killed". The All Parties Hurriyat Conference (APHC), comprising some 30 groups which despite different political agendas unanimously oppose the accession of Jammu and Kashmir to India, rejected elections as irrelevant to the Kashmir issue and called for a general boycott and strikes. One of its constituent parties, the Jammu and Kashmir Liberation Front (JKLF), argued that elections were tantamount to confirming India's claim to Jammu and Kashmir and "hence could prove detrimental to the on-going freedom movement".

The Forum for Permanent Resolution of Jammu and Kashmir (FPR), consisting of several former separatists who had met officials of the union home ministry in New Delhi in mid-March 1996 for an "unconditional dialogue", said it opposed elections in the state as well. It had demanded that all imprisoned militants be released, the army be withdrawn or restrained so as not to harass peaceful civilians and that renegade groups be disarmed. Following the announcement of Lok Sabha elections in Jammu and Kashmir, two of the FPR members boycotted talks with the newly formed Jain Commission on 23 March, saying that their initiative had not been intended to open the path to elections but "to create an atmosphere for a result-oriented dialogue". The so-called renegades sought to fill the "oppositional space vacated by the National Conference" (*Frontline*, 31 May 1996) by contesting as independents as many of their newly formed political bodies had not yet been registered with the Election Commission.

The renegades, former members of armed opposition groups who have reportedly been lured, persuaded or subjected to ill-treatment in custody or other forms of pressure to join the side of the government, have apparently, since early to mid-1995, been trained, armed, housed and protected by various military or paramilitary forces on whose behalf they have reportedly committed abuses against armed opposition groups, their presumed sympathizers as well as the general public. Originally used as intelligence sources to flush out armed opposition groups, the renegades appear to take an increasingly more active part in the security forces" operations against armed opposition groups. Both the government and the opposition appear to have treated the elections as a referendum — with government officials calling it a referendum for the democratic process and against militancy and opposition groups treating the elections as a referendum against the union government's policies in Jammu and Kashmir.

Opposition groups consequently claimed that no one would participate in the polls unless coerced, and either issued boycott calls or threatened anyone participating in the election process. At the same time, there were persistent reports of the government and renegades using the state apparatus to ensure high voter turnout. The elections were marked by violence reportedly resulting in at least 16 deaths. Many civilians complained that they were caught between militant groups threatening to abuse people who participated in the elections and the army and renegades threatening violence against those who did not. Of the six Lok Sabha seats, four were won by the Indian National Congress (I), and one each by the Janata Dal [People's Party] and the Bharatiya Janata Party [Indian People's Party] (BJP) election results in 1989: National Conference 3, Congress(I) 2 and Independents 1; none of the renegades were elected.

At the national level, following general elections in late April and early May 1996, which led to a hung parliament, the BJP formed a government on 16 May under Prime Minister Atal Bihari Vajpayee, but relinquished power on 28 May after failing to muster a majority. He was replaced by Prime Minister H.D. Deve Gowda on 1 June, leading a 13-party United Front government, including the Janata Dal, the Indian National Congress, the Tamil Manila Congress, the DMK, the Socialist Party and the Telegu Desam Party. In early June, it released a Common Minimum Programme accepted by all the United Front partners, promising a "maximum degree of autonomy" to Jammu and Kashmir and to retain unchanged Article 370 of the Indian Constitution which secures a special status to Jammu and Kashmir.

Further, the United Front government declared that it would seek to hold elections to the Jammu and Kashmir state assembly "as soon as possible". Prime Minister H.D. Deve Gowda on 16 June said: "The election to parliament from Jammu and Kashmir was a triumph of our democratic polity and it showed the maturity of the people in rejecting the militants, including those aided and abetted from across the border. ... building on these positive developments, we shall complete the task of restoration of normalcy and popular government in Jammu and Kashmir". Elections to the Jammu and Kashmir state assembly, tentatively planned for July 1995, had been postponed following the gutting of the shrine of Charar-e Sharief on 11 May 1995 for which the government held militant groups responsible while these conversely blamed the army. In November 1995, assembly elections were postponed indefinitely by the Election Commission which held that the security situation was not conducive to free and fair elections in Jammu and Kashmir.

However, the Supreme Court in January 1996 directed

the Election Commission to engage in a dialogue with the union government on elections. Responses to the union government's call for assembly elections in Jammu and Kashmir were cautious. Former chief minister and president of the National Conference, Farooq Abdullah, requested clarification of the meaning of "maximum degree of autonomy" and suggested holding state assembly elections in the fall of 1996. The APHC which has consistently called for tripartite talks between India, Pakistan and representatives of Jammu and Kashmir and made such talks conditional upon New Delhi's recognition of the "disputed nature" of Jammu and Kashmir appeared ambivalent. In early June, its chairman Moulvi Omar Farooq signalled the group's willingness to open talks with the Indian government and to involve Pakistan "at a later stage".

At the same time, Abdul Gani Bhatt dismissed the Indian government's proposal as it failed "to meet the basic demand of the people, which is the future dispensation of Jammu and Kashmir in accordance with the wishes of the people". The JKLF similarly argued that "we are fighting not for autonomy but for the reunification of the entire state and free expression of the unfettered will of its people about their future". On 7 August, the Election Commission announced that elections for the 87-seat state legislative assembly would take place on four separate days beginning on 7 September, with subsequent polling on 16, 21 and 30 September. The National Conference shortly afterwards announced its intention to participate in the polls along with several national parties including the Janata Dal and representatives of renegade groups. The APHC called for a boycott of the elections.

In the Pre-election Phase

In the months leading up to the Lok Sabha elections in Jammu and Kashmir, Amnesty International received reports of human rights abuses by government agencies, renegades and armed opposition groups, directed primarily against human rights defenders, journalists and prominent political leaders. Amnesty International has been told by some of the few remaining human rights defenders in Jammu and Kashmir that their position has become untenable as the use of force and the threat of use of force have made it impossible for them to collect information and consistently document human rights violations.

Only a high level of security arrangements made some electioneering possible. Candidates, many of whom were unknown locally, were given police cover and bulletproof cars. Many lived outside their constituencies and only visited them to file their nomination papers and to hold rallies under police cover. Despite government orders of 17 April, prohibiting candidates from carrying arms, many had hired their own armed escorts. As armed opposition groups had warned people not to attend election rallies, attendance was thin and apt to disperse at the hint of violence- renegades, visibly supported by various law enforcement agencies, enforced attendance of election rallies of their candidates, threatening people with "dire consequences" if they desisted. Candidates of the Indian National Congress threatened to withdraw from elections if armed opposition groups were not disarmed as their rallies were frequently disrupted and candidates and their followers were threatened. Only days after general elections were announced in Jammu and Kashmir on 19 March 1996, 23 members of the JKLF's Amanullah Khan faction were reportedly deliberately killed by state police.

Six days earlier, at least nine JKLF members and two officers of the Jammu and Kashmir Armed Police (JKAP) had died in an exchange of fire at Hazratbal Shrine in Srinagar after which the JKLF occupied it in protest against JKAP and Border Security Force (BSF) presence there. The JKLF group left the shrine on 26 March to return to their party office just outside the shrine's southern gate. Governor K.V. Krishna

Rao on 27 March said that "I was planning an operation in the night. If they had not come out, they would have all died. The force was ready. They were lucky." Among claims and counter-claims about the substance of the preceding negotiations, Shabbir Siddiqui on 29 March told journalists that the *status quo ante* had been restored but that the group had in fact been arrested; similarly Governor K.V. Krishna Rao asserted that the JKLF men had been "taken into custody". Before dawn of 30 March, the Special Operations Group of the police, with support from the BSF and the Central Reserve Police Force (CRPF), cordoned off the JKLF office and ordered those inside to surrender.

After three men, three women and four children came out, security forces opened automatic fire and fired mortar shells at the building, killing 23 members of the JKLF, including its president, Shabbir Siddiqui, and two boys aged between 10 and 12. Police claimed that the Siddiqui group had tried to retake the shrine and had opened fire, but the JKLF and the APHC have stated that the group was unarmed at the time of the killing. According to media reports, police suffered no loss in the incident; however, Additional Director General of Police, A.K. Suri said that in the gun battle which ensued between police and JKLF when the latter refused to surrender, six police officers were injured. To Amnesty International's knowledge, no inquiry into the incident has been undertaken. The APHC, which in peaceful demonstrations and house-to-house canvassing across Srinagar called on people to boycott elections and urged separatist groups not to resort to violence during elections, was itself the target of repeated attacks, apparently by renegades. On 2 May a fire broke out in the APHC headquarters, at a time when it had scheduled a meeting, later postponed, to discuss its anti-election campaign.

On 9 May, six senior APHC leaders were fired at by gunmen identified as renegades of the Ikhwan-ul Muslimoon, near Bombai village, Baramulla district where

Abdul Gani Lone, Shabir Ahmad Shah, Mohammad Yasin, Syed Ali Shah Gilani, Javid Ahmad Mir and Abdul Gani were canvassing house to house against elections. Police escorts of the APHC leaders intervened and overpowered the attackers. On 11 May, a landmine exploded on the highway on which Yasin Malik and Javid Ahmed Mir travelled, without injuring anyone. On 16 May, a rocket was fired at Syed Ali Shah Gilani's house in Hyderpora, Srinagar; it missed the main building but caused extensive damage to surrounding buildings; Gilani's house had earlier been attacked in October and December 1995, January, March and on 9 May 1996. Grenade and automatic weapons attacks on the house of Abdul Gani Lone were also reported in January, February and April 1996. Renegades reportedly interfered with electioneering of candidates from other parties.

For instance, Indian National Congress candidate Taj Mohiuddin from Anantnag claimed that renegades of the Ikhwan-ul Muslimoon had tried to prevent him from electioneering in mid-April; "... near a point where I had to address a rally in Anantnag town, I saw two gunmen approaching me. ... They said they will not allow me to address the rally and when I argued, they cocked their guns". Police claimed that the two men were Special Police Officers on duty in Anantnag and registered a case of assault against Mohiuddin who claimed in turn that the government was shielding the renegades. Human rights defenders and journalists have been particularly at risk when they exercised their right to freedom of expression over the last few months prior to elections, both from government forces and renegade attacks. On 27 March, the decomposed body of civil rights lawyer and chairman of the Kashmir Commission of Jurists, Jalil Andrabi, with his hands tied up and his face mutilated, was found in the Jhelum River.

The autopsy report later stated that Andrabi had probably been killed some 14 days earlier; he had apparently died of gun shot injuries to his head which also bore injuries inflicted by a blunt weapon. On 8 March, Andrabi had been taken from his car apparently by personnel of the 35 Rashtriya Rifles unit stationed at Badgam, headed by a Sikh major and accompanied by renegades who acted as "spotters" identifying the victim to army personnel. Andrabi's wife Rifat who had witnessed the incident, attempted to file a First Information Report (FIR) in the Sadar police station naming the army as responsible for the abduction, but was refused. The Inspector General of Police reportedly assured Rifat Andrabi on the phone later in the night that Andrabi was "with them" and would be released after completion of investigations. On the following morning, the Kashmir Bar Association, of which Andrabi was a member, filed a *habeas corpus* petition in the High Court, which directed all the law enforcement agencies in the state to declare whether they were holding Jalil Andrabi; the army in a sworn affidavit stated before the High Court on 11 March that "Rashtriya Rifles do not operate in the said area, neither was any member deputed/present at Parrayapora at 5.30 pm nor did any member of the Rashtriya Rifles apprehend or receive the alleged detenue on the date and time given ...".

Police reportedly urged the family to alter their FIR so as not to mention army involvement but to declare that Andrabi had been taken away by unknown persons; the family agreed to do so on the condition that they could meet Andrabi. On 13 March the FIR was finally registered but the family was not informed about Andrabi's whereabouts. On the following day, the High Court said it was not satisfied with affidavits denying the custody of Andrabi which junior officers of the army and the home ministry had filed and ordered the secretaries of the Defence and Home Departments to file their affidavits relating to the whereabouts of Jalil Andrabi. The court also directed that a special inquiry into Andrabi's whereabouts under the Deputy Inspector General of Police be set up. The Inspector General of Police was directed to carry out an investigation and report to the Court every day on the progress of investigations. The inquiry into the detention of Jalil Andrabi, then into the circumstances of his death, has not concluded yet; Amnesty International is not aware of any preliminary findings.

The composition and task of the investigation team have apparently been arbitrarily altered by the Inspector General of Police; while the original team had been directed to take instructions in the investigation only from the court and to report to it alone, the team appointed by the Inspector General of Police on 5 June is to report to him on a day to day basis. In response to these changes, the Andrabi families have filed a contempt of court petition. A hint left by Andrabi himself does not appear to have led to any breakthrough in the investigation. He had told journalists on 30 January 1996 that two unidentified armed men, possibly renegades, had tried to lure him from his house a day earlier and that he had covertly photographed them.

Jalil Andrabi had fought for improved prison conditions in Jammu and Kashmir and documented cases of custodial killings, arbitrary detention and "disappearances". A petition filed by Andrabi had led to a High Court order in October 1994 that district committees consisting of judicial, police and medical authorities should make regular visits to all jails, detention centres and police lockups in the state. As far as Amnesty International is aware, visits were restricted to only one district in the state during December 1994 and have not subsequently taken place. The visits found widespread evidence of illegal detention, torture and ill-treatment. In October 1995, following another petition filed by Andrabi, the state government gave assurances that no prisoner would be detained outside the state. Jalil Andrabi was to have represented the Kashmir Commission of Jurists before the United Nations Human Rights Commission in Geneva on 18 March 1996; in January 1996, Andrabi told newsmen that he knew that he was on the government hit list since attending the Commission in Geneva the year before. Shortly before his death, Andrabi attended a conference in New Delhi at which he condemned human rights violations committed by state authorities in Jammu and Kashmir.

His death is a further obstacle to the free documentation of human rights violations in the state and is seen by many as a deliberate attempt to end human rights monitoring in the state. Shortly after Jalil Andrabi's death, on 10 April 1996, the body of another human rights defender and editor, Ghulam Rasool Sheikh, was found in the Jhelum River near Pampore. Ghulam Rasool Sheikh had been abducted on 20 March, according to his relatives, by renegades accompanied by army personnel. State officials have denied the charge and stated that Ghulam Rasool Sheikh was abducted and killed by militants. Sheikh had recently publicly condemned the rise in killings and arson in his hometown Pampore. Kashmiri journalists pressed for an inquiry into the abduction and killing but to Amnesty International's knowledge, no such inquiry has been undertaken. About a month earlier, on 6 March, Ghulam Nabi Khayal, correspondent for Pakistan Television and veteran member of the local press community, was attacked in the compound of his home in the Rawalpora area of Srinagar by unidentified gunmen who tried to abduct him and threw hand grenades into his house.

While officials blamed separatist groups for the grenade attack, Khayal stated that Rawalpora was heavily patrolled by Indian security forces making it highly unlikely that members of an armed opposition group could have reached his house undetected. Prominent citizens have also been targeted by armed opposition groups and renegades in the pre-election period. Dr Yousuf Omar, chairman of the Kashmir Public Relief Trust, Trustee of the Rufaidah Blood Bank and president of the apolitical Islamic Study Circle, was shot at and critically injured in his office in Srinagar, on 16 April, allegedly by renegades who tried to abduct him. When he resisted, they shot him in the arm and the stomach.

Armed opposition groups threatened election officers and the public with "dire consequences" if they participated in elections. On 11 May, seven armed opposition groups issued a statement threatening to kill any official who carried out election duties in the state; the statement was signed by Hizbul Mujahideen, Tehrik-ul-Mujahideen, Al-Jihad, Al-Barq, Hezbollah, Al-Umer and Hizb-ul-Momineen. They also directed government officials to close their offices from 13 to 31 May. The Indian government simultaneously ordered state employees to report for duty during the election period. When some 10,500 central government employees were flown in to supplement local staff in elections duties, Hezbollah spokesman Kalim Siddiqui on 18 May declared that "by May 22, if the employees of other states fail to leave, our group will kill them and their families". Most, but not all schools and government offices remained closed during the period as people feared opposition groups more than the government. Earlier, in mid-April, the Jammu and Kashmir Islami Harkatul Mohmineen and the Khalistan Liberation Front had issued a 24-hour ultimatum to candidates contesting elections to withdraw from the contest; if they did not co-operate, it was threatened that the candidates or their families would be killed.

Armed opposition groups carried out their threats in a number of cases, abducting or killing government and army officials and candidates. On 9 April, Ghulam Hassan Pinglana, a former parliamentarian of the Indian National Congress in his seventies was shot dead in his village home in Pulwama district, allegedly by the Hizbul Mujahideen. A bomb planted in an election office in Anantnag on 12 April injured six occupants of the building; no group claimed responsibility. On 16 April, Al-Jehad group claimed responsibility for a landmine blast in Srinagar which killed at least two people, including the deputy commandant of the BSF, Subhash Sharma, and a child. Hospital sources stated that over 25 civilians, including a child, had been injured; witnesses said that many of the injured were victims of the BSF's arbitrary firing in retaliation after the attack. Al-Jehad warned that it would undertake more such attacks if elections went ahead.

The brother of Wali Mohammad Wani, who was

contesting elections on a Awami Tehriq Party ticket from Baramulla, was shot dead on 20 April when members of an armed opposition group could not find the candidate himself. The Awami Tehriq is a party formed by renegades; one of its activists had been shot dead by unidentified members of an armed opposition group in Srinagar two days earlier while distributing campaign literature. On 3 May, members of an unidentified armed opposition group reportedly killed three men in front of the assembled village of Bapsar, Udhampur district, allegedly to intimidate them and prevent them from participating in elections. On 4 May, in a hand grenade attack on Congress leader Mohammad Ayub Khan, his wife and two children were killed in Rajouri.

On the same day, three Hindus who were reportedly members of a local village defence committee were lined up outside their homes in Sudhmahadev village in Udhampur district and shot dead. Eleven other Hindu neighbours were abducted and their guns, given to them for self-defence purposes, taken away. About 20 houses were set on fire. Before leaving, the group reportedly pasted a poster on a wall threatening more killings if the villagers took part in elections. Increasingly, local residents are being trained and equipped as "village defence committees" to assist official counter-insurgency units.

The setting up of 100 additional committees in Doda and Udhampur districts, each consisting of some 10-15 mostly ex-service men, was sanctioned by state authorities in June 1996; 30 such committees had reportedly been set up in the district since the beginning of the year. The powers and structures of command and accountability of such committees are not known to Amnesty International at present. Often it was unclear which side was responsible for abductions and killings; for instance, on 5 May, eight Nepali workers were shot dead by members of an unidentified armed opposition group or a renegade group at Lasjan village, near Srinagar. Ten Nepalis had been abducted the night before from the stone quarry where they were working. Two captives managed to escape; no group claimed responsibility but authorities said the incident was intended to disrupt polls. APHC declared that renegades were responsible for the killings.

Journalists have been severely restricted in the exercise of their professional duties and right to freedom of expression by threats and attacks from both sides, the government and the renegades, as well as from armed opposition groups. From 19 April 1996, the Kashmir Press, a representative body of local newspapers suspended publication for an indefinite period after the Hizbul Mujahideen issued threats against any newspaper publishing any government statement or advertisement. Earlier, on 17 April, the union government had issued a circular directing newspaper not to carry any statement of any member of an armed opposition group or anything that might hamper the election, such as threats to candidates contesting the elections or to government officials. Any violation of this directive, the Union Home Ministry said, would invite penal action.

Human Rights Violations During Elections

During the first stage of elections, held on 7 May in Jammu and Ladakh, little violence and a high voter turnout of about 55 per cent approximately the same as in 1989 and 80 percent 6 per cent below the 1989 turnout respectively were reported. During the next stage of elections on 23 May in Baramulla and Anantnag, independent Indian and foreign correspondents and human rights monitors reported witnessing the Indian army, the paramilitary Rashtriya Rifles and renegades coercing people at gunpoint from their homes to participate in elections. Officials claimed a turnout of 35 per cent in Baramulla and of 43 per cent in Anantnag, compared with less than 5 per cent in parliamentary elections in 1989. A team of Indian human rights activists, including representatives of the Committee for the Protection of Democratic Rights, Lokshahi Hakk Sanghatana and Andhra Pradesh Civil Liberties Committee, reported that the Indian army went from house to house on May 23, forcibly evicting people from their houses at gunpoint, scuttling them like cattle towards the polling booths.

The army had threatened them that if they returned without a mark on their finger which is applied by election officers to mark those who have cast their vote, they would be considered sympathizers or militants." Renegades belonging to the Ikhwan-ul Muslimoon reportedly threatened people in Pampore that they would be beheaded if they could not show the ink mark on their finger. Demonstrators in Baramulla and Sopore towns and village Muchpora in Anantnag constituency, protesting against the army's coercive methods, as well as journalists covering the demonstrations, were subjected to heavy lathi-charges by the army, the human rights activists reported. *Agence France Press* photographer Tauseef Mustafa was beaten with gun butts and had his film taken away when troops noticed him taking pictures of women injured by troops. Journalists reported an army unit rounding up and detaining some 50 children in Baramulla till their relatives, who had attempted to boycott elections, had voted.

At least one election related death was reported from Ajar, Kupwara district, after 7-year old Shah Naza was hit on the head by army troops, probably with rifle butts on 23 May. The villagers had gathered in front of the mosque to protest against being coerced to vote when army forces resorted to indiscriminate beating. The girl was taken to an army hospital for treatment, and then transferred to the civil hospital in Handwara, later to the Institute of Medical Science in Srinagar where she died on 24 May of brain edema. Some armed opposition groups appear to have engaged in punitive killings after the elections in Anantnag and Baramulla. Two election agents of the Anantnag candidate of the Indian National Congress, Ghulam Qadir Ganai and Ghulam Mohamad Khan, were abducted from their homes in Beigam village in Kulgam, Anantnag district, on 26 May by armed men; their bodies were found two days later. The Congress candidate alleged that the Jammu Kashmir

Ikhwan (Liaqat group) had killed the men in retaliation for the high voter turnout; officials denied that the two men had been Congress election agents.

Srinagar, where the last stage of elections took place on 30 May, was relatively quiet during the elections in Anantnag and Baramulla due to prolonged strikes (20 to 23, 26 to 30 May) called by several opposition groups protesting against the elections. However, some incidents were reported. On 23 May, five renegades were shot dead by paramilitary troops in Kupwara after being mistaken for separatists moving in a suspicious manner. On 24 May, four unidentified members of an armed opposition group were shot dead by Indian troops during a shootout on the outskirts of Srinagar, according to official sources. Witnesses, however, were quoted as saying that the four men had been dragged out of their homes and shot dead at point blank range. Armed opposition groups repeatedly tried to disrupt election preparations and elections and especially targeted government officials.

Vehicles carrying officials on election duty were repeatedly attacked in different parts of Jammu and Kashmir, for instance on 18 May at Kanthpora in Kupwara district. Seven members of the Border Security Force (BSF) were slightly injured in the Lal Chowk area of Srinagar on 20 May when a grenade missed their jeep and exploded in front of it. On 25 May, a powerful bomb blast at a bus stand in Doda killed three people and injured 47 others; most of those injured and killed were government election officials travelling in a heavily guarded convoy from Doda to Bhanderwah. No group claimed responsibility for the bombing. On 28 May a rocket, fired at a hotel in Srinagar where over a hundred election officers and doctors, brought to the state for emergency medical service during the elections, were staying, narrowly missed its target, injuring no one. Armed opposition groups fired four rockets that exploded on 29 May in the outskirts of Srinagar without causing any damage.

Four soldiers on election duty were injured on 30 May when their vehicle struck a land mine in Brindaban in Udhampur. Grenade attacks on the same day injured two paramilitary men; five rockets fired at the city early in the morning produced no casualties. Armed opposition groups were reportedly responsible for some bomb attacks outside Jammu and Kashmir; these included a bomb blast on 21 May in a New Delhi market which killed 13 people and injured 56 others for which two Kashmiri groups (Jammu and Kashmir Islamic Front and Lashk-e-Sajad) and a Sikh group (the Khalistan Liberation Front) claimed responsibility. On 22 May a bus was blown up in Rajasthan killing 22 passengers; no group claimed responsibility but police suspected Kashmiri groups' responsibility. As in the pre-election phase, some abuses including targeted killings were committed by unknown persons or groups. On 15 May, Bashir Ahmed Mattoo, a senior physics professor and member of the Muslim Welfare Trust, was shot dead by unidentified gunmen when boarding a bus in Srinagar.

Several people were arbitrarily detained and ill-treated by security forces, apparently to intimidate whole neighbourhoods to participate in the elections or to put pressure on political leaders. On 13 May, Ghulam Hassan Mukhdoomi, the son-in-law of APHC leader Syed Ali Shah Gilani, was arbitrarily arrested by the paramilitary Rashtriya Rifles who acted in conjunction with a group of renegades in Tujjar Sharif, Sopore, and detained for three days in Bomai camp, Sopore. No charges were brought against Mukhdoomi, a medical assistant, who had no apparent political affiliation. His arrest was widely seen as intended to put pressure on the APHC leadership. On the day before the elections in Srinagar, most APHC leaders, including Chairman Umar Farooq, Yasin Malik, Syed Ali Shah Gilani, Shabir Ahmed Shah and Abdul Gani Bhat were placed under house arrest, apparently to prevent them from making public speeches against the elections. A police official was quoted as saying, "we are taking all measures to counter any trouble".

The house arrest was lifted after the election. JKLF leaders Javed Mir and Shakeel Bakhshi were arrested on 30 May while holding demonstrations against the elections, but were released later in the day. Two carpenters, Mohammed Ramzan and Abdul Rashid, who had no apparent political involvement, were arrested from their homes in Solina Balla in Srinagar on 29 May by the BSF, accompanied by members of the Special Task Force of Jammu and Kashmir police. A South Asia Human Rights Documentation Centre investigation team was told by eye witnesses that the men were beaten during arrest and in Shergadi police station where they were taken. Both men were later transferred to an undeclared detention centre in the Jawahar Nagar neighbourhood of Srinagar to which local residents had seen some 21 young men recently being taken.

Local people believed that the arbitrary arrest and detention of Mohammed Ramzan and Abdul Rashid was intended to intimidate their neighbourhood to caste their votes during the next day's elections in Srinagar. Like residents of Baramulla and Anantnag, people living in Srinagar's outlying areas reported that troops had threatened them on 29 May that their hands would be chopped off if their fingers did not bear the blue mark proving they had participated in elections; similar complaints were made in Udhampur. Some Srinagar residents told foreign correspondents that security personnel had threatened them with "dire consequences" if they did not go to vote. Officials later claimed a 37 per cent turnout in Srinagar and 55 per cent participation in Udhampur while independent observers touring the Srinagar area were quoted as estimating the turnout to be less than half this figure.

Invalid votes, according to official sources, were some 10 per cent of votes cast in Srinagar, compared to 7.5 per cent in Baramulla; this percentage was considered low by officials and an indicator that people were not coerced hence did not see the need to invalidate their ballot papers. Several journalists were beaten by troops in Srinagars Batamaloo area when they took photographs of police beating a women demonstrator. A photographer working for the *Press Trust of India* news agency reportedly fell to the ground bleeding after a BSF man hit him on the head with the butt of his rifle. A journalist said, "the photographers rushed when a BSF guard started roughing up a lady demonstrator. They then turned and charged us." Five other journalists, some from Delhi-based newspapers, were injured in other parts of the city covering the elections. Senior police official Gopal Sharma was reported as saying about the beating of journalists, "What has happened should not have happened.

We condemn the incident". BSF used teargas to break up protest demonstrations gathered outside the city's main mosque, injuring some 20 people. A witness said, "the troops just stormed in and began indiscriminate firing of shells at the crowd". A *Reuter* correspondent was prevented by troops from approaching the mosque area but witnessed many injured people being put in a van. Three people were killed in Srinagar on 30 May and dozens injured as hundreds of people demonstrated in the streets shouting anti-Indian slogans. The dead included Ghulam Nabi, who died when paramilitary forces opened indiscriminate fire at a protesting crowd in the city's Dalal Mohallah area, possibly in retaliation against an earlier attack on a BSF picket. Police, however, claimed that Nabi died in cross fire between armed opposition men and security forces. Another BSF guard died when he reportedly accidentally shot himself in a stampede outside a polling station following an anti-election demonstration. Another border guard died in a grenade attack by an armed opposition group during the last hours of polling.

Indian authorities have denied the truth of eye-witness accounts of coercion and the use and threat of force against people unwilling to participate in the elections. Jammu and Kashmir Chief Secretary Ashok Kumar, who acknowledged that he had not been to the relevant districts during the election process, stated in a press conference that what reporters had seen was troops offering protection to voters against reprisals by insurgent groups: "I am speaking the truth: there was no herding of people." A spokesperson of the federal government home ministry asserted on 24 May that complaints of coercion were a "defence mechanism" of people against possible reprisals by militants who had called for a boycott and that the heavy army presence was needed "to protect candidates, voters and government officials conducting the polls".

Lieutenant-General Jagjit Singh Dhillon declared that army officers may have asked people to vote, but that they had not been ordered to coerce anyone to do so. Similarly Director General of Police Manohar Nath Saberwal after the conclusion of elections in Srinagar dismissed reports of coercion as part of a "disinformation campaign". Governor K.V. Krishna Rao stated that "The people are fully aware that these elections have been absolutely free and fair. However, if there are any complaints these will be thoroughly investigated." The Election Commission termed elections in Jammu and Kashmir "relatively free and fair"; Chief Election Commissioner T.N. Seshan in response to allegations of coercion during a press conference said that no written complaint had been received by the commission. Despite these protestations, the overwhelming weight of evidence available to Amnesty International suggests that the electoral process was marred by intimidation and threats of human rights violations and abuses.

The Post Election Situation

Peace did not return to Jammu and Kashmir and human rights abuses have not stopped with the end of the Lok Sabha elections. On 2 June, at least five counting agents, reportedly belonging to the renegade groupings Muslim *Mujahideen* and

Jammu Kashmir Ikhwan, died and some 40 people were injured when paramilitary forces opened fire at them as they were allegedly disrupting the counting process in Anantnag district. Chief Secretary Ashok Kumar announced that a senior magistrate would investigate the "circumstances which led to the firing on militants". On 8 June, 10 Hindu civilians were deliberately and arbitrarily killed in Kalmari village in Doda district. According to reports, members of a separatist group broke into the house of Jagan Nath, a forest officer who had been on poll duty during elections despite threats; they first beheaded him, then his wife, father, son, a six-year old daughter and a female guest. When relatives in the neighbouring house raised the alarm, the armed men killed four members of that household and injured several others. No group has claimed responsibility for the killings.

A day earlier, in the night of 7 June, a powerful car bomb exploded outside the Rawalpora house of APHC leader Abdul Gani Lone, slightly injuring five people and extensively damaging his home and neighbouring houses. Lone, who escaped unhurt, held the authorities responsible for the assassination attempt. In the same night, unidentified gunmen opened fire and threw a grenade at the house of another APHC leader, Syed Ali Shah Gilani. Men in army uniform were reportedly seen at the scene of the attack and later to drive off in an army truck. Nobody was injured in the attack. Earlier, in the night of 1 June 1996, Gilani said some gunmen accompanied by army personnel, had attempted to kill him in his home. On 17 June, BSF personnel reportedly raided the office of APHC leader Shabir Ahmad Shah and beat five political workers found there.

Attacks by armed opposition groups on state officials have continued as well; on 12 June, a bomb exploded in the car of Superintendent of Police and telecommunications, Bupinder Singh at Nashri Nallah, on the Jammu-Srinagar highway, injuring two persons. The right to freedom of information was only slowly restored. On 17 June, Kashmir based newspaper editors announced the resumption of publications despite armed opposition groups' persistent threats against the press. With the announcement of the forthcoming state assembly elections which are to begin on 7 September, threats and incidents of violence have re-surfaced.

A newly formed organization of pro-Pakistan armed opposition groups – the United Jehad Council – which includes the Hizbul Mujahideen, Harkat-ul-Ansar, Al Jehad, Tehreek-ul-Mujahideen and Al Umer Mujahideen, called for 38-day strike from 24 August to boycott the elections and reportedly announced that "Anyone found violating the strike call will be regarded as a traitor and dealt with accordingly". On 19 August Mohammad Shafi Khan, a candidate for the Janata Dal party was shot dead, allegedly by members of an armed opposition group. The government has promised security to candidates and has reportedly drafted in an extra 70,000 troops.

Amnesty International's Recommendations

Amnesty International believes that there is urgent need for the Government to ensure that the right to life and safety of the civilian population of Jammu and Kashmir is fully respected. In particular, human rights defenders and journalists must be adequately protected to pursue their duties without fear in Jammu and Kashmir. The organization urges the Government of India to take all possible measures to ensure that the upcoming elections are not marred by further human rights violations.

Amnesty International urges the Government of India to:

- Promptly set up impartial and independent inquiries into every reported human rights violation in Jammu and Kashmir, including torture and threats of torture, extrajudicial executions and arbitrary arrest of political prisoners, and make their terms of reference and findings public;

- Ensure that all perpetrators of human rights violations are brought to justice and that the cycle of violations and impunity is broken;
- Disarm and disband the renegade groups reported to have committed human rights abuses;
- Provide protection to human rights defenders including journalists who report human rights abuses and to permit UN human rights mechanisms including the Special Rapporteur on torture, the Special Rapporteur on extrajudicial, summary and arbitrary executions and the Working Group on disappearances, as well as international human rights organizations including Amnesty International to visit Jammu and Kashmir. The continued refusal to grant access to such bodies creates the impression that the Indian Government fears international scrutiny of the human rights situation there.

The organization further urges all armed opposition groups to:

- Respect the basic standards of humanitarian law which require that all people taking no active part in hostilities should at all time is treated humanely.
- Desist from the practices of hostage-taking, torture and ill-treatment of those in captivity and the deliberate killing of civilians. In particular civilians should not be killed for expressing their views or because of political views attributed to them, or because of who their relatives are or because they belong to another religious community.

4

International Aid, Politics and Human Rights Violations

In Sri Lanka

Alarmed by allegations of human rights abuse, several donor countries have recently cut aid to Sri Lanka in an effort to force the government to address their concerns. The United Kingdom (UK) froze aid in May 2007, citing concern that government forces have been responsible for violence against civilians in government-controlled territory. UK officials expect that the decision will demonstrate symbolically that the Sri Lankan government cannot act with impunity. Britain says that resumption of aid will be considered after talks with the Sri Lankan government concerning its human rights record.

Germany cut aid several months earlier, in October 2006, worried that continuous conflict was preventing implementation of the projects the aid money was intended to support. Germany also urged other donor nations to refrain from making additional pledges to Sri Lanka. The United States (US) has partially followed suit, suspending some, though not all, development aid. Citing "a deterioration of human rights on the island", the US government stressed that the government must rein in paramilitary forces, which are fighting the Liberation Tigers of Tamil Eelam (LTTE) alongside government troops.

International aid to Sri Lanka

Though international aid to Sri Lanka as a percentage of GDP has declined over the course of the conflict (from 9% in 1983 to 2% in 1997), the nation still depends heavily on it. In 2006, for example, donors gave a total of $912 million in loans and $301 million in grants. Sri Lanka has seen a resurgence of international aid in the aftermath of the devastating 2004 tsunami; donor assistance rose from $275.7 million in 2000 to $1.2 billion in 2005. Furthermore, the Sri Lankan government says that it expects an additional $4.5 billion over the years 2007-2009, though donors have yet to make pledges.

Sri Lanka receives aid from a variety of sources, the most significant of which are the World Bank, the Asian Development Bank, and Japan. Japan alone reportedly accounts for more than 60% of Sri Lanka's international aid. In addition to Japan, India and China are key bilateral donors due to their regional power and trade ties, respectively. Other bilateral donors, including the US, UK, and EU, have substantially less influence. Generally speaking, Western donors have focused on issues of "human rights, democratisation, and liberalisation" to a greater extent than have Asian donors, who "have been more concerned with geostrategic interests and trade objectives"—though naturally, geo-strategic interests also underlie many Western donors' decisions. Nevertheless, explicit discussion of human rights issues on the part of countries like the US and UK has contributed to the belief that Western involvement in the peace process is compromising Sri Lanka's national sovereignty.

As a result, the Sri Lankan government has shown a marked preference for developing ties with non-Western donors. While much of the international aid supplied by these nations is closely tied to development projects—a safeguard against misuse—there is nevertheless concern that even apparently innocuous aid could indirectly finance the government's human rights abuses. Project aid was identified as potentially troubling in International Alert's 1987 report because it "frees resources that would otherwise be spent upon these development projects...enabing the government to run a larger defence budget than would otherwise be possible".

This realisation has been the catalyst for a re-examination of international aid policies among many of Sri Lanka's donors. In addition to development aid, Sri Lanka receives direct military aid from several nations. The US ambassador to Sri Lanka, Robert Blake, has said that the US is "a strong supporter in assisting Sri Lanka combat terror...by providing training and equipment to help the Sri Lankan military". Similarly, debates in the British Parliament indicate that "£7 million worth of [UK] arms were licensed for delivery to Sri Lanka in the last quarter for which figures are available" as of May 2007. Recently, Sri Lanka has sought further military aid from the Indian government, and has threatened to approach Pakistan if India is not willing to supply weapons.

In fact, India allegedly already supplies the Sri Lankan military with weapons, although the government claims that only training, not equipment, are provided to Sri Lankan forces. Given concerns over the government's alleged human rights abuses, the continued military funding of Sri Lankan forces by these nations has raised criticism, both from their own citizens and from supporters of the LTTE.

Sri Lankan Government and LTTE Opponents

The Sri Lankan government has expressed disappointment with these developments, portraying the aid freezes as a victory for terrorism. Foreign Secretary Palitha Kohona says that the aid suspension "achieves a political and propaganda objective that is essentially in favour of the LTTE". At the same time, the government has so far avoided expressions of serious concern in an effort to downplay the significance of the aid cut. Foreign Minister Rohitha Bogollagama, of the ruling Sri Lanka Freedom Party, dismissed the news of Britain's aid suspension, saying that the amount of money involved was "too insignificant to bother about".

The widespread sentiment, however, is that the aid freeze is an illegitimate attempt to infringe upon Sri Lanka's national sovereignty. Some see it as evidence of Western support for the LTTE; an opinion piece in Sri Lanka's *Daily News* interpreting the aid freeze as a "great victory" for the LTTE is fairly representative of this sentiment. The aid freeze is also seen as an instance of Western hypocrisy, since the same Western nations that have frozen aid to Sri Lanka denounce terrorism regularly and have labelled the LTTE a terrorist organisation.

Yet while many Sri Lankan opponents of the LTTE view the aid cuts as a victory for the group, LTTE supporters reject this view, pointing out that Western governments continue to supply the Sri Lankan government with military aid. TamilNet, for instance, claims that British arm sales to Sri Lanka now match Britain's contributions of tsunami relief aid. In addition, the US has provided approximately $500,000 annually to the Sri Lankan government under the International Military Education and Training Program (IMET), with additional, more variable financing ($1 million in 2006) under the Foreign Military Financing (FMF) programme. Faced with these statistics, many supporters of the Tamils questions American and British claims of cracking down on governmental human rights abuses. Tamil National Alliance (TNA) parliamentarian Gajendrakumar Ponnambalam asks, "How is one to interpret this other than as support for the Government's military approach?"

Sri Lankan NGOs

Sri Lankan human rights organisations, like many of the political and social institutions within the country, tend not to support the linkage of international aid to human rights standards—though for different reasons than the government. While convinced of the importance of upholding human rights standards, these organisations are concerned that tying international aid to such goals is not an effective method of defending citizens against abuses. The Consortium of Humanitarian Agencies, an association of over 70 Sri Lankan nonprofits, provides valuable insight into Sri Lankan NGOs' response to the aid freeze, arguing that donors need to "rethink their strategy" if they are to effectively help those in need. Instead of linking aid money to issues, like human rights, surrounding the government-LTTE conflict, the CHA recommends a focus on local concerns such as landlessness, unemployment, and poverty.

International Human Rights Organizations

In contrast to the local organisations represented by the CHA, international human rights organisations have lauded donors' decisions to link aid to human rights benchmarks. Human Rights Watch (HRW), in particular, has been very vocal in supporting international donors' decisions to freeze aid, and in encouraging other nations—namely Japan—to do the same. An HRW delegation visited Tokyo after the recent decisions by the US and UK to cut aid, hoping to convince Japan, Sri Lanka's top donor, to follow suit. Japan, however, said it had no intention to suspend or cut its aid to Sri Lanka.

The debate over Sri Lankan aid is not without precedent. In the last several years, aid freezes have been imposed upon countries as diverse as Uzbekistan, Zambia, and Colombia, among others, in response to poor human rights records. While it may be too soon to evaluate the long-term efficacy of these recent precedents, a study of Norway's 1998 decision to cut all development aid to Ethiopia during its two-year war with Eritrea suggests that aid freezes are not necessarily a useful method of pushing foreign governments to change.

The conclusion that "Norway introduced sanctions not primarily in order to influence the course of the war between Ethiopia and Eritrea, but rather for internal

Norwegian reasons" echoes a common criticism of sanctions—that decisions about aid are based on the interests of the donor country, not the recipient. Ultimately, the lessons of this case study of the Norway-Ethiopia aid freeze indicate that "sanctions must be internationally coordinated, with clear and limited objectives". Such lessons will be central for evaluating the efficacy of recent freezes in Western aid to Sri Lanka.

In India

The new coalition government led by the Congress party, which replaced the Hindu nationalist Bharatiya Janta Party (BJP) after elections in May 2004, has taken some important positive steps with regard to respect for human rights. These include repeal of the oft-abused Prevention of Terrorism Act (POTA) and a re-evaluation of federal government educational policies that have fostered communitarian resentments. Attacks on civilians by militant groups and Indian security forces continued unabated before and after the change in government. Notwithstanding the repeal of POTA, the government continues to use other legislation to shield security forces from accountability. Indian military, paramilitary, and police forces have engaged in serious human rights abuses not just in conflict-zones such as Kashmir, but also when dealing with criminal suspects and detainees.

The Gujarat government's failure to bring to justice those responsible for massive communitarian riots in the state, in which thousands of Muslims were killed and left homeless continues to be a source of tension throughout the entire country. However, the Supreme Court and the National Human Rights Commission have taken several positive steps to secure justice for the victims of the riots. The new government of Manmohan Singh also has to contend with the Indian government's systematic failure to protect the rights of Dalits, other marginalized castes and religious minorities.

The Congress Party itself has failed to provide any justice to the victims of serious abuses against the Sikh community in Delhi and Punjab twenty years ago. India faces a burgeoning HIV/AIDS problem, as people with HIV and their families face government and social discrimination.

Rights of Dalits and Indigenous Tribal Groups

Despite legislative measures to protect marginalized groups, discrimination based on caste, social, or religious grounds continues widely in practice. Local police often fail to implement the special laws set up to protect Dalits and members of tribal groups. Dalits, or so-called untouchables, continue to face violence and discrimination in nearly every sphere of their lives. Abuses against Dalits range from harassment and use of excessive force by security forces in routine matters, to mutilations and killings by members of other castes for attempting to cross caste barriers. *Dalit* women are targeted with sexual violence. Not only do authorities regularly tolerate such discrimination and violence, in some instances they actively encourage it. In one widely noted incident in July 2004, for example, police used excessive force against Dalits who tried to participate in a religious festival in Tamil Nadu.

Indigenous peoples, or *Adivasis*, have suffered from high rates of displacement. Scheduled Tribes that make up 8 percent of the total population constitute 55 percent of displaced people. This has had a serious effect on the overall development of these communities, particularly tribal children. The government continues to use the Land Acquisition Act of 1894 to displace the indigenous peoples from their lands without sufficient compensation, as is evident in the Narmada Valley Development Project. Tribal groups who have converted to Christianity have been targeted for attack by extremist Hindu organizations.

Impunity of Security Forces

Indian security forces, including the military, paramilitary forces, and the police, routinely abuse human rights with impunity. The Indian federal government rarely prosecutes army and paramilitary troops in a credible and transparent manner. The result has been an increase in serious violations by security forces throughout the country. The government's repeal of the controversial Prevention of Terrorism Act (POTA) was a major step forward for civil liberties in India. POTA empowered security forces to hold individuals for up to 180 days without filing charges, broadening the scope of the death penalty, dispensing with the presumption of innocence by placing the burden of proof on suspects, and admitting confessions into evidence despite the frequent use of torture.

The law was often used against marginalized communities such as Dalits, indigenous groups, Muslims, and the political opposition. But POTA's repeal has not ended the legal impunity that security agencies enjoy. Laws such as the National Security Act, the Disturbed Areas Act, the Armed Forces Special Powers Act or the Armed Forces (Jammu and Kashmir) Special Powers Act have spawned abuses in various parts of the country, including many deaths in custody and widespread allegations of torture. These laws give security agencies unchecked powers of detention that often foster torture during interrogation.

For instance in Kashmir and Manipur states, the sites of long-standing insurgencies, Indian military and paramilitary forces have held suspects in army camps and barracks and have routinely tortured them, in violation of domestic and international laws. In July 2004, Manipur state witnessed unprecedented civilian protests against the Armed Forces Special Powers Act after army troops sexually assaulted and killed a woman in custody. That Act provides security forces virtual immunity for crimes committed in the course of duty. The new government recently agreed to review the act.

Other laws such as the Public Safety Act and section 197 of the Criminal Code of Procedure also raise human rights concerns. Section 197 extends immunity to public servants by requiring government authorization to initiate the prosecution of public servants for crimes that result from the discharge of their official functions. In effect, it allows the government to shield security forces from any legal accountability. In Kashmir, military, paramilitary, and police forces continue their practice of torturing detainees and custodial killings. There has also been a nationwide rise in allegations of extrajudicial executions by security forces, who typically justify their actions by claiming to have killed suspects in an exchange of gunfire.

Since November 2003, a cease-fire along the Line of Control in Kashmir has provided tremendous relief to residents on both sides of the de facto border. During the intermittent shelling, however, neither Pakistan nor India took adequate precautions to protect civilians. The violence inside Indian-controlled Kashmir continued. Bomb and grenade attacks by militants in crowded market places constituted the intentional targeting of civilians. Attacks, apparently by separatist militants, on moderate Kashmiri leaders have hindered the peace process. Indian police and security services often use excessive force, and have been responsible for arbitrary detention, torture, and extrajudicial execution. Since 1989, when the insurgency began, thousands of people have disappeared at the hands of both militant and government forces.

Legacy of Communal Violence

Large-scale episodes of communal violence remain unpunished. This injustice continues to foster communal resentments throughout India. There has still been no accountability for the deaths of more than two thousand Muslims in the western state of Gujarat during communal violence that erupted following an attack on a train carrying Hindu pilgrims in 2002. In Discouraging Dissent, a report released in August 2004, Human Rights Watch documented the continued discrimination, intimidation of witnesses, faulty investigation, and apparent interference from members of the BJP state government in efforts to prosecute those responsible for the anti-Muslim violence.

The Indian Supreme Court has already ordered two Gujarat cases to be retried in another state. The criminal justice system in Gujarat, the Supreme Court concluded, had been "abused, misused and mutilated by subterfuge." Human rights activists and lawyers have petitioned for fresh investigations and trials in a number of cases where it was felt that the local courts, prosecutors and police were hostile to Muslim complainants. Despite these positive developments, rights activists in Gujarat continue to be harassed on the basis of what police claim are their "anti-national activities." Witnesses, however, remain vulnerable to threats.

2004 marked the twentieth anniversary of Operation Blue Star, a focal point in the conflict between Sikh nationalists and state security apparatus in the Punjab in the 1980s; and the anti-Sikh riots in New Delhi, which resulted in more than three thousand Sikh deaths. In July, the National Human Rights Commission called for claims in cases of summary execution in Punjab. The assignment of individual criminal responsibility for those and other crimes committed during the period, however, remains elusive. Also in July, the Nanavati Commission of inquiry served former Prime Minister P.V. Narasimha Rao, who was home minister in the Congress Party government in 1984, a notice for his failure to act to prevent the attacks on Sikhs. Two others who have similarly been served notices have recently been appointed ministers in the new Congress government.

Rights of Children

India has the largest number of working children in the world, millions of whom work in the worst forms of child labour, including bonded labour. The Indian government knows about these children and is required by its own laws to protect them. Instead, for reasons of apathy, caste bias, and corruption, many government officials deny that they exist at all. Both literacy and school enrollment rates overall have improved in the last decade, but according to UNESCO, approximately half of students completed grade five.

Proportionately fewer girls than boys attend school, and those that do, drop out at higher rates. Dalits also have higher illiteracy and drop-out rates and face significant discrimination in education.

Rights of those Living with HIV/AIDS

The government estimates that 5.1 million people in India are living with HIV/AIDS, though many experts suggest the number is much higher. People with AIDS, as well as those traditionally at highest risk – sex workers, injection drug users, and men who have sex with men – face widespread stigmatization and discrimination. People with AIDS are denied employment and access to education and healthcare. Those at high risk face police harassment and other state-sponsored abuse that undermines HIV prevention and AIDS care services for them. Married women are also at risk because they are frequently unable to demand condom use of their husbands, who may have extramarital sexual partners.

At least hundreds of thousands of children are living with HIV/AIDS. Many more are otherwise seriously affected by India's burgeoning epidemic – when they are forced to withdraw from school to care for sick parents, are forced to work to replace their parents' income, or are orphaned (losing one or both parents to AIDS). Children affected by HIV/AIDS are being discriminated against in education and health services, denied care by orphanages, and pushed onto the streets and into the worst forms of child labour. Gender discrimination makes girls more vulnerable to HIV transmission and makes it more difficult for them to get care. Many children, especially the most vulnerable as well as the professionals who care for them, are not getting the information about HIV they need to protect them or to combat discrimination.

Gender-based Discrimination and Violence

Women and girls confront discrimination and violence in practically every aspect of life. A strong preference for sons over daughters has led to sharply skewed gender ratios in several states. Sex-selective abortions, female feticide, and inadequate provision of food and health care to girls has led to ratios of less than eight hundred women for every one thousand men in some places. Despite several legal provisions for gender equality, women still struggle to realize equal rights to property, marriage, divorce, and protection under the law. Gender-based violence, including domestic violence, sexual harassment, sexual assault, and trafficking into forced labour and forced prostitution remain serious and pervasive problems in India. Domestic violence includes dowry-related abuses and "bride-burning."

Activists continue to campaign for reform of rape laws to protect women and children from all forms of sexual violence. The pervasive understanding of 'rape' is that it occurs only when a stranger uses force on a woman. A marital exemption protects men from being prosecuted for raping their wives. Marital rape is not recognized or penalized unless the wife is under the age of fifteen or if she lives separately from her husband. There is inadequate legal protection for abuse against girls, boys, and men, or for sexual violence between spouses.

In the absence of a more suitable law, section 377 of the Indian Penal Code, which penalizes consensual sexual activity deemed "unnatural," is also used to prosecute the sexual abuse of children and women. This provision has also been used to penalize men having sex with men, and has been used as justification for harassment of HIV/AIDS educators. The Delhi High Court dismissed a legal challenge to section 377, dealing a disappointing set back for activists working to improve the rights of gay and lesbian people in India.

Key International Actors

India receives 60 percent of its aid from multilateral donors such as the World Bank. India decided in 2003 to stop receiving bilateral assistance from all but six countries, including the United States, the United Kingdom, and Russia. The decision is widely perceived as an effort to bolster India's image as a world power. Increasingly, India has been providing significant amounts of financial and military aid to its smaller neighbors, but has not used its increasing influence to make public calls for better compliance with human rights standards.

The thawing of relations between India and Pakistan began in earnest in November 2003 with a ceasefire across the line-of-control. That was followed by a meeting between then-Prime Minister Vajpayee and President Pervez Musharraf of Pakistan in January 2004. The Congress government continued its predecessor's policy of dialogue with Pakistan to resolve outstanding issues of conflict. The two countries' leaders met in New York in September, where Singh and Musharraf reiterated a commitment to the bilateral dialogue to restore normalcy and a peaceful negotiated settlement in Kashmir.

The easing of tensions between India and Pakistan has allowed the United States to focus its dialogue with India on strengthening bilateral relations between New Delhi and Washington. U.S. Secretary of State Colin Powell visited India in March 2004. Human rights issues were not discussed. The increasingly warm relations between the two countries, despite the U.S. conferring the status of "major non-NATO ally" upon Pakistan, will likely continue under Congress Party leadership. Deputy Secretary of State Richard Armitage visited New Delhi in July, reaffirming to Indian leaders that the United States sees India as an important partner. India has also been strengthening its military-to-military ties, conducting joint exercises with United States and other NATO forces.

India is the largest provider of military assistance to Nepal, which is in the midst of a brutal civil war. India has not used its position of influence to push the Nepalese government to improve its human right records, and has resisted calls for a multilateral peace conference, presumably to avoid similar calls for resolving the Kashmir dispute.

India has been increasingly close to the brutal military government of Burma. A delegation of Burma's political opposition was not allowed to enter India to attend a conference on human rights. In September 2004, the Indian government welcomed a delegation from the Burmese military government, but did not raise any concerns about Burma's dismal human rights record. Thousands of Burmese continue to seek refuge in India, where they are not granted proper protections under international law.

National Human Rights Commission of India

The motto of the National Human Rights Commission is "Sarve Bhavantu Sukhinah". Happiness and health for all is sought to be achieved through a rights-based regime where respect for human beings and their dignity is cardinal. The Constitution of India provides the basic framework for this rights based regime. The constitutional framework is complemented by several legislations and institutional mechanisms that serve to respect, protect and promote human rights. In addition to this domestic framework, the international conventions to which India is a party also form the basis of human rights protection.

The National Human Rights Commission of India was set up in 1993 for "better protection of human rights and for matters connected therewith or incidental thereto". It is a statutory and autonomous body, which works independently. It has full financial and functional autonomy and has a wide mandate. Over the last 14 years, the Commission has endeavoured to give a positive meaning and content to the objectives set out in the Protection of Human Rights Act, 1993. During this period, the Commission has also worked vigorously and effectively to create awareness and to sensitize public authorities for promoting and protecting human rights in the country.

In the early years after inception, the Commission focused on civil and political rights like terrorism and insurgency, prisons, monitoring of custodial deaths, cases in detention, including mental homes and juvenile justice homes etc. However, in the succeeding years, the economic, social and cultural rights have also been given prominence. It is the belief of the Commission that all rights are inter-related and inter-dependent. Apart from working for the eradication of bonded labour and child labour and the rights of the children, women and other weaker or marginalized sections of the society, the Commission has also undertaken work in other fields, such as, right to health, food and education, right of displaced persons due to natural and man made calamities etc.

The Commission received only 496 complaints of violation of human rights in 1993-94, the first year of its establishment. The number steadily increased over the years and during the financial year 2007-2008, the Commission received 100,616 complaints. The Commission disposed off 101,272 complaints which included complaints carried forward from the previous years. The phenomenal increase in the number of complaints is indicative of growing awareness amongst the people in the country as well as increased faith in the Commission. In 188 cases, the Commission recommended immediate interim relief of Rs.5,64,26,500 during 2007-2008 and in Punjab Mass Cremation case the interim relief is to a tune of Rs.25, 75, 25,000/-.

Economic, Social and Cultural Rights

The following are some of the important activities undertaken by the Commission to monitor the economic, social and cultural rights:-

Human Rights Awareness Programme in 28 backward Districts

The Commission selected 28 backward districts in the country, one in each State, for direct interaction with their field level functionaries with a view to spread human rights awareness at cutting edge level in the administration and also to facilitate better assessment of enforcement of various measures related to human rights. In this effort, the special attention will be on (i) food security, (ii) right to education, (iii) right to health, hygiene and sanitation, (iv) custodial justice, (v) human rights issues of Scheduled Castes (SCs) and Scheduled Tribes (STs), (vi) right to culture and protection of Community Assets and (vii) right to life, living conditions and nature of responsibility of Government and *Panchayat* (unit of local self-government).

In pursuance of this programme, the Chairperson and officers of NHRC visited Chamba District in Himachal Pradesh from 1st to 5th July, 2008 and had detailed discussions with district level functionaries, elected representatives in local bodies and NGOs.

Right to Health

The Commission has been stressing that health and education are two basic human rights and are part of our fundamental rights. Keeping in view the rights approach, the Commission has been impressing upon the State functionaries that they are duty bound to do their best to realize these rights. With a view to discuss the availability of trained manpower in remote parts of the country, a meeting with the Medical Council of India, Indian Nursing Council and Ministry of Health & Family Welfare, Govt. of India was held on 30 August, 2007 in the Commission.

After extensive deliberations, the Commission recommended to the Government to make necessary changes in the Indian Medical Council Act to have one year compulsory rural attachment of the MBBS students before their registration. To increase intake of students for Psychiatry courses, the Commission has recommended to the Medical Council of India to relax its norms. With a view to improve the emergency medical service in the country, the Medical

Council of India approved a course in M.D. (emergency medicine) on the recommendation of the Commission.

The Indian Nursing Council, on the recommendation of the Commission, approved the syllabus of Nursing, Midwifery to ensure effective service to the population. The Commission has also taken up among others, the issues of unsafe drugs and medical devices, silicosis and availability of anti rabies vaccines. The representatives of the Commission have been visiting Mental Hospitals across the country to monitor the implementation of its recommendations on 'Quality Assurance in Mental Health'. To review and update the Manual on Quality Assurance in Mental Health, the Commission organized a conference of all Health Secretaries and State Mental Health Authorities at Bangalore in May, 2008 in collaboration with the National Institute of Mental Health and Neurosciences, Bangalore (NIMHANS).

HIV/AIDS and Human Rights

In order to spread human rights awareness among people, the Commission has taken the initiative of producing a series of short films on selected human rights issues. One such film and a video spot are on the rights of persons infected/affected by HIV/AIDS. This film and video spot were telecast by Doordarshan (National Channel) and other private channels. This is also shown in various awareness programmes.

Persons with Disabilities

The National Human Rights Commission of India played a major role in the drafting of the UN Convention on Rights of Persons with Disabilities and advocated for inserting Art.33 relating to national implementation and monitoring mechanisms. Therefore, it advocated for its early ratification with the Government of India, which has since been done in the year 2007. As a follow up action, the Commission appointed a Special Rapporteur on Women, Children and Disability related issues and constituted a Core Advisory

Group on Disability to advise the Commission on matters connected with and incidental to the promotion, protection and monitoring of rights mentioned in the Indian Constitution and laws for persons with disabilities and also envisaged in Art. 33 (2) of the UN Convention on the Rights of Persons with Disabilities.

In the light of its role as envisaged in Art.33 of CRPD, the NHRC, India is organizing regional workshops during the year in different parts of the country to assess the enforcement of rights of the persons with disabilities with particular reference to their education, employment, access and services. The Commission has evolved a format to collect detailed information with regard to right to education, employment, access and services being provided to persons with disabilities.

The Commission, deeply concerned about the education of deaf children, identified the lack of training in sign language as the major constraint. In order to standardize the sign language for deaf persons which can be introduced in teachers training, the Commission played a catalytic role to evolve a project entitled " Indian Sign Language for Deaf Persons" through the National Institute of Hearing Impaired, Mumbai.

Rights of the Internally Displaced Persons

To discuss the human rights implications of displacement following conflict, development projects, and natural and manmade disasters, the Commission organized the National Conference on "Relief and Rehabilitation of Displaced Persons" on March 24-25, 2008 at New Delhi. All key stakeholders, including Chairperson/Members of State Human Rights Commissions, government officials of both the Central and State governments, officials of the National Disaster Management Authority, UN agencies and NGOs participated in this conference. The participants deliberated on various human rights issues related to displacement and made several recommendations on land acquisition and relief and rehabilitation of displaced persons from human rights perspective. The Commission is currently finalizing the recommendations which will be sent to all concerned agencies.

Trafficking

The National Human Rights Commission of India is working relentlessly to help in prevention and combating of human trafficking. Special attention is being given to the plight of women and children being exposed to such a heinous crime. At the request of the UNHCHR as well as recommendation of the APF of NHRIs, the NHRC, India nominated one of its members as a focal point on Human Rights of women, including human trafficking. The Commission in collaboration with the National Commission for Women has assisted the Ministry of Women and Child Development in the Government of India in formulating a Plan of Action to Prevent and Combat Trafficking with special focus on women and children.

Food Security

The National Human Rights Commission has consistently maintained that the Right to Food is inherent to living a life with dignity. The Commission has expressed the view that the Right to Food includes nutrition at an appropriate level. It also implies that the quantum of relief to those in distress must meet those levels in order to ensure that the Right to Food is actually secured and does not remain a theoretical concept. The Commission is of the view that mortality alone should not be considered as the effect of starvation but destitution and the continuum of distress should be viewed as indicators demonstrating the prevalence of starvation. There is thus an accompanying need for a paradigm shift in public policies and relief codes in this respect.

The Commission has constituted a Core Group on Right to Food with experts in the field. In last meeting of the Core Group, it was observed that *Panchayats*, being burdened with so many other responsibilities may not be in a position to pay focused attention to this aspect in all the areas in their jurisdiction. Hence a need for the constitution of watch committees at various levels in States was felt. The purpose of these independent committees is to see implementation of the related schemes, availability of food grains and their proper distribution and report to the concerned authorities in the State or to the SHRC/NHRC directly in some select cases, as the case may be.

Civil & Political Rights

Besides evolving stringent reporting system and guidelines, the Commission continued to monitor custodial deaths, rapes, deaths in alleged fake encounters etc. Besides redressing individual complaints, the Commission also stressed the need for systemic reforms in the Police and Prisons. The Commission continued to monitor conditions in prisons. The Commission took up, among others, over crowding in prisons, medical treatment of prisoners, sensitization of prison staff. In October, 2007, the Chairperson, NHRC, India addressed a letter to Chief Ministers of all States and Union Territories highlighting the need for modernization of jails and also the Chief Justices of all High Courts requesting them to take steps for speedy trial and we are receiving the response for the same.

There are 15024 deaths in judicial custody and 2222 in police custody since 1.9.1993. These deaths are reported within 24 hours to NHRC and analysed by NHRC. Out of the above, 10658 deaths in judicial custody and 1485 deaths in police custody are due to natural causes but in 153 deaths in judicial custody and 158 deaths in police custody, the NHRC has recommended interim relief, prosecution and departmental action against defaulting personnel.

Violent Incidents in Nandigram Area

The Commission intervened in the matter of violence that occurred between the ruling party supporters and the

Bhoomi Ucched Pratirodh Committee (BUPC) – an organization to channelize the protest against the proposed land acquisition by the State Government and resultant police firing on 14 March, 2007 and the incidents of group clashes in November, 2007 in Nandigram area of East Midnapur District of West Bengal. The incident has its origin in the decision of the State Government of West Bengal to set up a Special Economic Zone (SEZ) and a chemical hub in an area of about 10,000 acres in Nandigram area of East Midnapur District of West Bengal. The police firing on 14 March, 2007 resulted in death of 14 persons and injuries to 300 people including 52 policemen. In the subsequent event of blockade and group clashes from 6th to 12th November, 2007, seven persons were killed and 32 persons, including 16 police personnel sustained injuries.

Several houses and other properties were damaged either fully or partially. The Commission, after considering the reports of the State Government and its own investigation team, made certain general observations regarding the role to be played by the ruling party, opposition, media etc. It also constituted a Committee under its Secretary General for suggesting quantum of compensation for damage that occurred and to ensure that monetary relief does not fall into wrong hands and reaches the genuine persons. The Committee visited the areas and has made recommendations which have been accepted by the Commission and conveyed to the State authorities for implementation.

Incidents of violence by Salwa Judum activists and Naxalites

The petitioners Ms. Nandini Sundar & others in their complaints before the Supreme Court of India prayed for directions to the State Government (i) to refrain from supporting the activities of the Salwa Judum, (ii) independent and impartial inquiry into the incident of killings, abductions, rapes and gross violation of human rights by the security forces and the Salwa Judum activists, in endeavouring to counter the Naxalites and to investigate the killings by the Naxalites, (iii) grant of compensation etc.

The Supreme Court of India on consideration of the matter on 15.4.2008, directed thus:- "After hearing both sides, we feel that in view of the serious allegations relating to violation of human rights by Naxalites and Salwa Judum and the living conditions in the refugee settlement colonies, it will be appropriate if the National Human Rights Commission examines/verifies these allegations. We leave it to the NHRC to appoint an appropriate fact finding Committee with such members as it deems fit and make available its report to this Court within eight weeks."

Pursuant to the directions of the Supreme Court of India, the Commission deputed a Fact Finding Team comprising its Deputy Inspector General of Police, two Senior Superintendents of Police and other officers in the Investigation Division to inquire into the allegations of large scale human rights violations by Salwa Judum activists, naxalites and security forces in the State of Chhattisgarh. The team of the Commission undertook strenuous visit to the remote tribal and forest areas for collecting facts. There were incidents of attack on police by some groups during the visit of the team. Threat to their lives did not deter the team from performing their assigned task and they completed the visit displaying enormous courage. The report of the team was being finalized for submission before the Apex Court for its consideration.

State Human Rights Commissions

Section 21 of the Protection of Human Rights Act, 1993 provides for constitution of State Human Rights Commission (SHRC). Seventeen states in India have constituted SHRCs. The National Human Rights Commission of India is keen that such State Human Rights Commissions are set up in every State so that the redressal mechanism is easily accessible to the citizens in all parts of the country and NHRC can concentrate more on the larger issue rather than individual complaints. The Commission has suggested to those States which have not yet constituted State Human Rights Commissions to favourably consider the same at the earliest. Further, the Commission has taken initiative to hold regular interactions with the State Human Rights Commissions to explore and further strengthen areas of cooperation and partnership.

A meeting of the NHRC and SHRCs was held on November 19, 2007 in New Delhi for better coordination and to develop joint strategies for emerging challenges. Under the capacity building of the State Human Rights Commission, the National Human Rights Commission of India has made a special provision in its own budget to strengthen the SHRCs by way of installing Complaint Information and Management Systems (CIMS) and impart training to those Commissions which want to incorporate it in their Commissions. Towards achieving this, on the recommendations of the Commission, the Planning Commission, Govt. of India has approved allocation of Rs.10 crores in the 11th Five Year Plan with an annual allocation of Rs.2 crores each year to NHRC to strengthen the SHRCs and to complete the installation of CMS package in the SHRCs expeditiously.

Human Rights Courts

Section 30 of the Protection of Human Rights Act, 1993 has provided for setting up of Human Rights Courts for the purpose of providing speedy trial of offences arising out of violation of human rights.

Commission's Interaction with NGOs

Encouraging the efforts of the Non Governmental Organizations (NGOs) working in the field of Human Rights is a statutory responsibility of the Commission under Section 12 (i) of the Protection of Human Rights Act, 1993. A Core Group of NGOs has been constituted to encourage the efforts of the NGOs. The Core Group provides the

Commission with crucial inputs regarding the hopes, aspirations and expectation of the civil society from the Commission. The Core Group of NGOs is expected to play a positive role in this regard.

Besides the Core Group of NGOs, the Commission has also set up Core Group of Experts on specified subjects related to Human Right issues to advise the Commission on complex technical issues. Some of the important Core Groups that have been set up by the Commission are:

- Core Group on Mental Health
- Core Group on Right to Food
- Core Group on Disability·
- Core Group on Health
- Core Group of Lawyers

The Commission constantly associates NGOs in its programmes related to human rights issues. For example, Jan Swasthya Abhiyan is associated in Right to Health survey. In the programme in 28 select districts local NGOs are being invited in the deliberations in regional workshops on disability the regional NGOs collaborate actively with NHRC.

Special Rapporteurs

The Commission has appointed 4 Special Rapporteurs on the subjects of (i) Bonded/Child Labour and conditions in Mental Hospitals (ii) Women, Child and Persons with Disability, (iii) Civil and Political Rights and (iv) Economic, Social and Cultural Rights. Besides, Special Rapporteurs have been appointed in five zones to visit the areas and give feed back to the Commission on human rights issues.

International Cooperation

The Commission participated in the Expanded Bureau Meeting of the International Coordinating Committee (ICC) held on 12-14 December, 2007 in Geneva and later in the 20th Session of the meeting of the ICC from 14 to 18 April,

2008 at Geneva. There was appreciation for the Commission's offer to host the web-site of all NHRIs. The Commission actively participated, among others, in sessions relating to UPR and role of NHRIs in poverty alleviation. On two points the Indian delegation laid special emphasis. The first related to fund raising by ICC. India expressed that the funds raising should be transparent and funds should be accepted only from the sources whose credibility is well established. The second related to the accreditation procedure.

Cooperation and Coordination

The NHRC, India has been participating in technical cooperation and assistance programmes with the NHRIs in the Asia Pacific Region for better protection and promotion of human rights. A four day Sub-Regional Workshop on National Inquiries was hosted by the National Human Rights Commission of India from October 29 to November 1, 2007.

The workshop was jointly organized by the Asia Pacific Forum of National Human Rights Institutions and Raoul Wallenberg Institute (RWI) of Human Rights and Humanitarian Law, University of Lund, Sweden. The workshop aimed to provide the representatives with a step by step understanding of the process of conducting National Inquiries. The deliberations included a number of issues like the Right to Food, Mental Illness, accessible public land transport for people with disabilities, torture, homeless children and Right to Health.

The Workshop on Strengthening the Advisory Council of Jurists was organized by the National Human Rights Commission in collaboration with the Asia Pacific Forum (APF) of National Human Rights Institutions of NHRIs in New Delhi on February 27-28, 2008. The purpose of the workshop was to bring together a representative group of Forum Councillors and Jurists to consider, among other things, the most effective ways to utilize the expertise of the ACJ; how to improve procedures for the selection and development of references and the implementation and monitoring of their recommendations; how to clarify and strengthen the relationship between the Forum Council and the ACJ and between NHRIs and their ACJ nominees.

Universal Periodic Review (UPR) Mechanism

The National Human Rights of India, in partnership with others, advocated for the effective participation of NHRIs in the Human Rights Council which resulted in the Human Rights Council Resolution 5/1 on "Institution-Building". In pursuance, the Commission has taken a very pro-active role at every stage relating to preparation of papers for UPR and in holding consultations with stakeholders.

In its independent paper for UPR, the Commission flagged important human rights challenges relating to education, right to food, right to health, rights of women, children and persons with disability. While reviewing international human rights commitments, the Commission stressed the need to ratify the 1951 UN Convention relating to the Status of Refugees and the Torture Convention. The Commission's statement has been placed on our own website as well as on the website of OHCHR.

The representative of the Commission attended the plenary session of the Human Rights Council to adopt the final outcome relating to India under UPR on 10th June, 2008 and presented a statement on behalf of the Commission. The representative stressed that the UPR process held great potential for the protection and promotion of human rights.

International Seminars and Workshops

The Commission participated in various seminars and workshops abroad which included (i) the workshop conducted by the UNHCR Centre, Tokyo on "Basics of International Humanitarian Response' from 2-9 October, 2007 (ii) placement programme with the National Human Rights Commission from 9-17 October, 2007 at Seoul, South

Korea (iii) Regional Workshop on the Establishment of National Human Rights Institutions in Asia from 15-17 October, 2007 (iv) training programme on human rights and migrant workers in Asia Pacific Region from 15-19 October, 2007 (v) Commonwealth Asia Colloquium on Gender Culture & Law from 30-31 October, 2007 (vi) 'Common-wealth National Human Rights Institution Forum meeting from 19-20 November, 2007 at Kampala, Uganda (vii) Regional Training Programme in Human Rights from 19-28 November, 2007 (viii) Sensitization Course on Trafficking and Migration of Children for Labour organized by the ILO in Italy from 21-25 January, 2008 and (ix) the UPR meeting organized by the Commonwealth Secretariat in London from 17-18 March, 2008.

The Commission exchanged views on protection and promotion of human rights with various foreign delegates who visited the Commission viz. (i) Lutyens Trust, UK, (ii) the Members of Royal College of Defence Studies, UK (iii) Mr. Brad Adams, Executive Director, Human Rights Watch (iv) a team from All China Women's Federation, China (v) Mr. Paul Hunt, UN Special Rapporteur on Right to Environment to the enjoyment of the highest attainable standard of Physical and Mental Health' (vi) a delegation of Mongolia on "Access to Justice and Human Rights" (vii) Prof. Michael Stein, Executive Director, Harvard Project on Disability, Harvard Law School, Cambridge (viii) Ms. Asma Jahangir, UN Special Rapporteur on "Freedom of Religion and Belief" (ix) Mr. Pierre Sane, Assistant Director General, Social and Human Sciences Sector, UNESCO, Paris (x) a delegation from Irish Parliament's Joint Committee on Constitution, (xi) a delegation from National Human Rights Commission of Rwanda (xii) Mr. Erik Kurweil, Political Consular, German Embassy, New Delhi and (xiii) two staff members of Indonesian Human Rights Commission.

A delegation of two staff members along with the vice president of the National Commission for Human Rights, Rwanda visited the Commission on a study trip from 29

March to 9 April, 2008. The delegates exchanged their experiences with our Commission. Another delegation consisting of two staff members of Indonesian Human Rights Commission also visited the Commission from 28 April to 12 May, 2008 on a study trip. The delegates were given first hand knowledge of the functioning of all divisions of the Commission. Based on the request of the OHCHR, the National Human Rights Commission of India sent two of its staff members to Rwandan Human Rights Commission to assist them in developing their Complaint Management System from 26 November-7th December, 2007. The Commission also sent two staff members to the Ugandan Human Rights Commission from 11 to 25 February, 2008 respectively.

A high level delegation led by Chairperson, NHRC, India visited the Irish Human Rights Commission at Dublin, Ireland on 11th April, 2008 and held discussions with Mr. Maurice Manning, President, and Irish Human Rights Commission. The two sides discussed about the various activities undertaken by both the Commissions for better protection of human rights and agreed to collaborate and cooperate closely with each other in future. The NHRC, India delegation later visited the Belfast and held discussions with Prof. Monica McWilliams, Chief Commissioner, Northern Ireland Human Rights Commission. The discussions covered activities taken up by both Commissions and scope for collaboration. Later, the NHRC, India delegation visited the United Kingdom and held discussions with the Secretary General, Commonwealth Secretariat and the Foreign and Commonwealth Office, U.K. on matters of mutual interest.

During the meeting of International Coordinating Committee (ICC) held at Geneva, Switzerland from 11 – 15 December, 2007, it was decided that the National Human Rights Commission of India will develop, host and maintain the Website for NHRIs. The Grant Agreement between the Office of the United Nations High Commissioner for Human Rights and the National Human Rights Commission of India was signed on 14 March 2008.

Human Rights Awareness Programmes

The Training Division, established in September, 1993, is imparting training to the officials of the Central and the State Governments, field functionaries and the representatives of NGOs, Universities etc. The main objective is to sensitize the participants of various levels/groups on Human Rights and equip them to work with more sensitivity in their respective fields with a Rights Based Approach. The methodology adopted in the seminars/workshops/trainings is lecture method, group discussions, syndicate report, action plan etc. The participants are exposed to international and national level Human Rights Conventions and Law and Culture.

Internship Training Programme

The Commission has been conducting the "Summer Internship Programmes" since 1998, and in 2000 the Winter Internship Programme was introduced with a view to spread awareness of human rights issues among university students. The Winter Internship programme 2007 organized by the Commission was commenced on December 17, 2007 and ended on January 16, 2008. This year the programme covered 102 sessions on various issues including interaction with Chairperson and Members of the Commission, State presentations, project work presentation, field visits to SOS Children's Village, Faridabad, Tihar Jail, Sulabh International, Social Service Organizations in Delhi, Government Hospital etc.

The project report covered issues like prisons, development and Human Rights, child rights and trafficking, religion and Human Rights, Human Rights Development Index, farmer suicides, migrant workers, fact finding, scrutiny of complaints, IT in Human Rights Promotion etc. In all 46 interns comprising 19 girls and 27 boys from various States of India completed their internship. The Publication Wing under the Information and Public Relations Division of the Commission plays an important role in creating awareness amongst the people regarding their human rights.

The Wing has a good number of publications relating to Human Rights. They include Monthly News Letters, National Old Age Pension Scheme: Issues of Policy and Governance, Journal of National Human Rights Commission, Human Rights Manual for District Magistrate (sent to all 605 districts), Human Rights Best Practices relating to Criminal Justice in a Nutshell, Handbook on Human Rights for Judicial Officers (available with 12,000 judicial officers), Theme Based Wall Calendar, Right to Health Booklet for Elderly Persons and the Hindi journal *Nai Dishayien*. The 'Know your rights' series brought out by the Commission has proved highly useful in spreading human rights awareness.

Democratic Process and Electoral Politics

India is a Union of States, according to its Constitution, with state power distributed between a (federal) government at the Centre and the governments of the constituent States. The importance of the States lies not merely in their vast territory or population, but in their distinct social structure, well-developed languages, culture and history. This tremendous diversity gives rise to different patterns of politics in different States. The government at the State level is responsible for most of the usual functions of a government, such as making laws on a wide variety of matters, their execution, maintenance of law and order, adjudication, commerce, industry, agriculture, education and health. During the last 50 years of its existence as a republic, States have come to occupy an increasingly important place in India's political system.

The political processes at the State level became significant after the breakdown of Congress dominance in the late 1960s. With the emergence of the State-based parties in the 1980s, there has been growing divergence in politics at the State and Central (federal) levels. Different party systems have taken shape in different States and the electoral outcomes have begun to differ from State to State in the last two decades, bringing a great deal of diversity among the States too. The emergence of coalition governments since 1989, in which the State parties became important partners, brought the State to centre stage. The onset of liberalisation policies from the early 1990s further increased its prominence.

National and international financial institutions and agencies, companies and industrial houses began to deal directly with the States, whose governments have assumed an active role in the development of infrastructure in the State, determining a host of policies in accordance with the priorities of the ruling party at State level. It is almost clichéd to describe India as a highly plural society characterised by tremendous socio-cultural and economic diversity, continuously undergoing radical changes.

The bewildering variety of political forms at the State level would lead observers of Indian politics to think of it as in a state of perpetual flux, or 'pattern less', or a chaos out of which one could make little sense. To some extent, Indian politics today may be better comprehended by looking at the national politics as a cluster or coalescence of diverse State politics. Of course, there is a two-way interaction between the State and Central politics: while the States operate within the national policy framework and political situation, the Centre functions within the limitations imposed by the dynamics of State politics.

At the time India became Independent, the country faced, to use the phrase of Rajni Kothari (1970), the challenge of simultaneous change. It took upon itself the daunting tasks of reforming social structure, promoting agricultural and industrial development, and fostering democratic political institutions, all at the same time. The Constitution was a social covenant in democratic socialism, as it assured to its people liberty, equality and social justice, and elections have become the main agency through which democracy has been strengthened in the country. Commentators of Indian politics have observed that such a situation gave rise to both political development as well as political decay. New sections of people have been mobilised into the political firmament, participation of people in politics has been made possible on an increasing scale and activists and leaders have been recruited and nurtured.

At the same, demands from the newly mobilised sections of people have increased on the state. There have been attempts to strike a balance between the claims of diverse segments of society for political power, social wealth and other opportunities, which were often conflicting. This has proved to be a difficult exercise in recent years. The era of liberalisation and economic reforms has affected thinking about the nature and role of state and government in the country. The new economic policies, emphasising deregulation, privatisation and de-statisation, have raised new questions about development and welfare. The tensions in the process of change are excessive. The new *Panchayati Raj* (traditional institution of local rural self-governance) system mandated by the Constitution has recently opened new avenues of political participation to include increasing numbers of representatives from different sections of society in the decision-making bodies at the local level.

The importance of the study of elections as a means to understand the political processes is well recognised all over the world. As Norman Palmer pointed out, the study of elections provides an opportunity to study the political system in action. If we take a longitudinal view of the political system, elections are situated at its interstices, but they bring out in sharp relief the interacting social forces that are at work in the polity, provide insights into various aspects of the system and its actual functioning. In India, where a democratic political framework was suddenly thrust upon a post-colonial society with age-old traditions and culture, elections became the agency for the democratisation of society and politics, as they brought politics within the sphere of the common man and common man into the political arena. They played a central role in mobilizing millions of people into the political process, crystallising public opinion on a host of issues, institutional functioning and styles of leadership, and in the emergence and recruitment of a new political elite.

Elections have influenced the ways in which the priorities of the political parties and the broad parameters of the incumbent government were laid down. We have seen how elections have effected changes in the existing policies of the government, where rejection or renewal of a regime means rejection or acceptance of a political leadership. Indeed, it was primarily because of the compulsions of the electoral politics that the parties adopted pro-people policies, with an eye either to consolidate their existing electoral base or secure support from newer sections. Even after the introduction of new economic policies, the governments at the Centre and in the States are compelled to carry out welfare programmes and the rival political parties have to compete with each other in projecting themselves as protectors of the interests of the poor and the disadvantaged. Electoral support can be mobilised on emotional grounds and the feelings raised by caste, faction, gender, religion and region, but such attempts have to be backed by some tangible welfare benefits to the members of these groups.

The very implementation of the economic reforms have to be justified by the political parties on the ground that they enable the government to spend more on people's welfare. Elections have assumed further significance as hundreds of millions of voters, living under conditions of illiteracy, poverty, backwardness, pre-modern social relations, religious distinctions, and inequalities based on caste built over hundreds of years, were repeatedly called upon to exercise their political right to choose their representatives at the Central, State and local levels. Fears that elections in India would either fail because of the awesome structural limitations and unpreparedness of the country to institutionalise parliamentary democracy or that they would have destabilising consequences which the political elites could not control, proved to be wrong.

There may be several limitations, deficiencies and failures in the functioning of India's democracy, which need to be overcome, but there are also commendable achievements. Few might be happy with what has been achieved or the way things happen in India, but there is the satisfaction that Indians, by and large, are able to work to solve their problems under a democratic framework. So far, India has seen 13 Parliamentary elections and an almost equal number of Legislative Assembly elections in each State. It is indeed a great experiment in consolidating and operating democracy in a large and ancient country like India, trying to stand on its own feet after nearly two centuries of colonial rule.

For a country with relatively little experience of struggle for parliamentary democracy and franchise, afflicted by congenital defects and constrained by social problems, it was no mean achievement of its people, as they still attempt to resolve their problems in a democratic and peaceful way, that elections could take place at regular intervals, parties in government could be changed without violence, power could be transferred peacefully to new sets of leaders, political parties could transform themselves from the era of mass politics of the freedom struggle to competitive politics, and a government based on law with an assurance of basic freedoms to the people was made possible. It could equally offer lessons to some of the Western countries on how polities could be governed in a more democratic way.

An account of the democratic process and electoral politics in Andhra Pradesh during the last 50 years is presented in the following pages. An attempt is made to analyse the ways in which the regional, factional, class and caste factors have operated in State politics and shaped the electoral outcomes. As such, the paper discusses how the policies and programmes of the State government and also the strategies of competing political parties have been influenced by the logic of electoral politics. It examines the process of the emergence of the Telugu Desam Party (TDP) and the factors for its consolidation. It also focuses on certain aspects of political decay and the challenges to the political leadership in the State and investigates the multiple and shifting strategies of the ruling TDP and the Congress in winning the elections in recent years.

Since the Livelihood Options Research in South Asia project focuses on the *Panchayati Raj* system in Andhra Pradesh, the results of the recent elections to the local bodies are discussed in detail in a separate section towards the end of this paper. In the process it analyses the dilemma faced by the ruling party in balancing the need for economic growth through the implementation of radical economic reforms and the compulsions of competitive electoral politics as they manifest in the continuation of the welfare programmes for the benefit of the poor and the disadvantaged. Some of the major aspects of Andhra Pradesh State politics and issues that require further study are discussed in the Conclusion.

Economy

Andhra Pradesh, like most States in India, has a multi-structured economy, ranging from shifting cultivation in Agency areas of Srikakulam district to high-tech industries in Hyderabad. As mentioned earlier, agriculture is still the mainstay of the Andhra Pradesh economy. The net area irrigated was 4.38 million hectares (41% of net sown area) in 1999–2000, constituting about 8% of the total irrigated land in the country, slightly above the national average (39%). But the area irrigated and sources of irrigation vary from region to region. During the early decades of the State existence, canal irrigation was given priority, but for some time now, progress in bringing more land under canal irrigation has been negligible. Food grains account for about half of the total cropped area: rice alone accounts for nearly half of the total area under food crops, and pulses, oil seeds, especially groundnut, cotton, chillies, sugarcane, tobacco, and turmeric are the principal commercial crops of the State.

Agricultural productivity per hectare has shown an increase since 1970–71 in the regions and crops that came under the influence of the agrarian revolution. Commercialisation of agriculture in the State became prominent from the early 1970s, but this has also had an adverse effect on the peasant economy. Agriculture has become capital intensive and losses due to natural disaster, pest or price fluctuations in the market, often depriving the peasantry of remunerative prices for their product, have meant the collapse of their economy. Several members of the peasant classes, who in search of prosperity opt for commercial crops and incur heavy investments mostly raised through loans, end up as paupers. Such 'pauperisation' from the status of an independent peasant results in loss of dignity for the peasantry as they cannot pay back their debts, marry off their daughters or support their children in their education, and the living standards of the family experience a sudden fall etc. This in turn drives the peasant to a state of despair and loss of interest in life. Suicide among farmers, especially those who grow commercial crops such as cotton, tobacco, chillies and groundnut, has become a recurrent phenomenon in the last two decades. Andhra Pradesh has the dubious distinction of recording the highest number of suicide deaths of farmers in the country in recent years.

The share of agriculture in the Net State Domestic Product fell to about 25% in 2000–01, from about 60% at the time of State formation. This decline in itself would not be cause for concern, provided it is accompanied by a corresponding decline in the proportion of the population dependent on agriculture. This, however, has not happened. The agrarian population in the State is thus sharing this sharply diminished share of the total income, which means an increasing relative deprivation for the rural classes. Data on the number and distribution of operational landholdings and the area operated under different landholding size-classes show that the number and percentage of marginal and small holdings and the area operated by them have been increasing, while the medium and large holdings have been declining over the last three decades.

While in the early 1970s the medium and large landholdings accounted for 15.6% of the total holdings and operated an area of 57% of land, in 1995–96 they accounted for only 6% of the holdings with 30% of the total land. There has been a sharp decline in the number of large holdings and the area operated by them. 'Deconcentration' of land has been taking place in the State due to a multiplicity of factors, such as agrarian struggles by the communist and peasant organisations in the early decades, land ceiling laws enacted by the government, and emigration of members of landowning families to urban areas. Old style landlordism has broken down in many parts of the State and land ceiling laws have lost their appeal.

In the pre-Independence period, land passed from the *zamindar* (a type of landlord, holder and rent receiver of an agricultural estate during the British rule) and non-agricultural families to the members of intermediate castes, but it seems that land is now being passed from peasant families, who have lost interest in agriculture or are unable to keep their land, to members of backward and scheduled castes who are engaged in agriculture. These changes in the agrarian structure have far reaching socio-political implications. Andhra Pradesh was a late entrant into the country's industrial scene. The share of the manufacturing sector in the Net State Domestic Product has increased from 7.2% in 1960–1 to 12.9% in 1999–2000 (at constant prices, 1993–94).

The share of the secondary sector as a whole stood at 19.4% in that year (GoAP, 2001). Growth of industries in the State was mainly propelled by public sector industry, especially in pharmaceuticals, electrical equipment, heavy engineering and machinery, iron and steel and fertilisers. Three-quarters of total employment in the organized sector was in the public sector in 1998 (1,513,000 out of a total of 2,065,900), although it may have come down due to the stoppage of further investment and also disinvestment in the public sector in recent years.

According to the data available for 1998, the most prominent industries, judging by employment figures, were the manufacture of food products (22.9% of factory employment), followed by non-metallic mineral products (16.4%). Other important industry groups included machinery equipment and metal parts (10.9%), cotton textiles (7.1%), chemicals and chemical products (5.1%), metals and alloy industries (5.1%), paper and printing industries (3.3%), beverages and tobacco products (3.1%). During the 1990s, the textiles, chemicals, paper, machinery and metal industries recorded faster growth. Much of the industrial growth took place in and around Hyderabad and Visakhapatnam cities. Computer software exports have also seen an impressive growth in recent years and the most prominent of household industries is handlooms.

The growth of industry in the State in recent decades has been identified as one of the offshoots of agricultural growth since the 1970s. Higher agricultural productivity and incomes have contributed to the pace of industrial development through the supply of entrepreneurs and investment resources, as well as a rising demand for manufacturers. It is said that the rapid accumulation of agricultural surpluses among the top segment of peasants and landlords during the agrarian revolution, limited opportunities for further investment in agriculture in these regions due to land ceiling legislation in the early 1970s. The rise of members of peasant families to political prominence and their ability to influence the industrial and credit policies contributed to the flow of agricultural surpluses into industry. The decade between 1975 and 1985 is considered a golden era for industrialisation in Andhra Pradesh State.

Poverty remains one of the major challenges to the government and society in Andhra Pradesh, as elsewhere in the country. The estimates of poverty by Minhas et al., Expert Group, Planning Commission and the World Bank using State-specific poverty lines, show that poverty in Andhra Pradesh has been declining since 1957–58, although the rate of decline varies from one estimate to another. The rate of decline has however been sharper since 1973–74, and it has been greater in Andhra Pradesh compared to several other States and India as a whole. The Planning Commission's estimates of rural and urban poverty in Andhra Pradesh show that poverty declined from 48.9% in 1973–74 to 22.2% in 1993–94. The figures for rural poverty were 48.5% and 15.9% and for urban poverty 50.6% and 38.3% for the respective years.

The latest government figures show that there has been a significant decline in recent years in the prevalence of both urban and rural poverty in Andhra Pradesh: rural poverty had fallen to 11.1% (5.8 million) in 1999–2000 and urban poverty to 26.6% (6.1 million), the combined poverty level being 15.8% (11.9 million) (Government of Andhra Pradesh, 2002). However, the National Sample Survey Organisation's (NSSO) 55th Round on Employment–Unemployment shows that the rate of poverty decline in Andhra Pradesh was not so high (Sundaram, 2001). Studies point out that rural poverty is inversely related to agricultural production: in years of higher production, poverty falls, and in years of low production or drought, it rises.

But it is surprising that the pace of reduction of poverty has slowed down since 1983, during a period in which the poverty alleviation programmes, including food subsidy (Rs2 per kilo rice), were implemented on a very large scale. Thus, it is difficult to establish any likely inverse relation between large-scale welfare schemes and poverty levels or a direct relation between economic reforms and poverty levels. Despite several welfare schemes, the incidence of poverty tends to be higher among the backward and scheduled castes and scheduled tribe population. While poverty causes hardship to those who have to live under it, it has its own political and electoral implications.

The promise of providing basic physical needs has dominated the election strategies of the political parties in recent decades because of the prevalence of poverty. It is often heard that votes are purchased with money and other allurements and the politicians seek to divide the poor people on caste and communal lines. The 'public servants' become arrogant and behave as if they are masters because of the preponderance of poor people, who tend to be fearful of the elites and hence submissive; the politicians tend to be corrupt and populist at the same time.

The majority of the tendencies and issues that have come to the fore since the formation of Andhra Pradesh could be seen in embryonic form during the period of State formation itself. The period between Independence in August 1947 and the formation of the State in November 1956 witnessed a series of militant struggles in the Andhra and Telengana regions, policy measures that brought about far-reaching changes in the agrarian structure, shifts in caste and class relations, the emergence of new leadership from peasant communities, factional strife within the Congress and also its consolidation, and political realignments among various political forces of the State.

At the time of Independence, the Congress Party in Andhra was rife with factional rivalries, which often made use of caste identities. There were two prominent factions in the APCC (Andhra Provincial Congress Committee). One was led by the legendary figure, Tanguturi Prakasam, known as *Andhra Kesari*, the 'Lion of Andhra' (Rudrayya Chowdary, 1971). The other group was led by Pattabhi Sitharamayya, another senior Brahman Congress leader, and later all-India Congress President in 1949–50 and the party's official historian (Prasanna Kumar, 1978). The elections to the offices of Madras Congress Legislature Party Leader and APCC President provided the occasions for a trial of strength between these rival groups. In a keen contest for the APCC presidency in April 1951, Sanjiva Reddy, sponsored by the Pattabhi group, defeated Ranga, whom Prakasam supported.

The struggle between Ranga and Sanjiva Reddy was seen as a turning point in the Kamma–Reddi rivalry that was emerging in Andhra Pradesh in the post–Independence period. The outcome of the election led to the exit of Prakasam and Ranga from Congress and their formation of a new party, called the Praja Party (PP). Subsequently, when the Kisan Mazdoor Praja Party (KMPP) was formed in June 1951, the Praja Party in Andhra merged with it. But Ranga later wanted to dissociate himself from Prakasam and formed, in August 1951, the Krishikar Lok Party (KLP), with himself as Chairman (Lingamurthy, 1994b). Thus the Andhra Congress presented a picture of disunity and appeared to be quickly fragmenting, unlike in other States.

While the Congress appeared to be weak in the State, perhaps weaker here than in the other major States of India, the Communist Party appeared to be gaining in strength. The growth of the Communist Party prior to the formation of Andhra Pradesh was extremely fast in Andhra and in Telengana. The communists grew as leaders of the peasant associations and led militant peasant struggles in some of the zamindari areas; their strength began to increase at a rapid pace during and after the Second World War. But after Independence, in response to the militant struggles waged by the communists in Andhra and Telengana regions, the party was banned in the Andhra area in January 1948. When the ban was lifted, the Communist Party and its mass fronts, especially the student's wing, participated actively in the campaign and agitation for the formation of Andhra State. In the first General Elections to the Madras Assembly in 1952, the popular support enjoyed by each of the different parties became apparent.

The Congress in the Andhra area suffered a serious setback: many of its Ministers and stalwarts were defeated.

The Communist Party emerged as the single largest party in Andhra region with 41 seats (out of 63 contested) and about 25% of the vote. Only Kerala (then Travancore-Cochin) came close to Andhra in terms of electoral support enjoyed by the communists in those days. Although the Congress secured about 30% of the vote, it won only 40 seats out of the 133 it had contested. The Communist Party was highly successful in the central coastal region. Apart from the support it enjoyed among peasant classes and agricultural workers, the agitational activity of the party for a separate statehood strengthened its position.

The poor performance of the Congress was generally attributed to the internal factional rivalries, the presence of the KMPP and the KLP as its rivals and the evasive attitude of the Central leadership of the party towards the demand for a separate linguistic State. After the General Elections, the Legislative Members of the KLP agreed to join the Congress Legislature Party (CLP) as 'Associated Members'. The KMPP merged with the Socialist Party to form the Praja Socialist Party (PSP). Thus, when the Andhra State was finally formed in October 1953, Congress strength in the Assembly was only 40 Members, but with the support of the KLP and independents, it formed the largest group with 60 Members.

As a result, only a coalition government was possible. In apolitically astute move, the Congress offered the post of Chief Minister to Prakasam, the President of the PSP, if he agreed to return to them. Prakasam could not resist the bait of the topmost executive office and the prestige of going down in Andhra history as the first Chief Minister of the State; the 'old man' (b.1872) found little difficulty leaving the PSP and returning to the Congress to this end. As a result, the KMPP group, which supported the Prakasam Ministry, left the PSP and formed the Praja Party. N. Sanjiva Reddy, who also lobbied for Chief Ministership, became the Deputy Chief Minister.

From the beginning, the coalition government was a precarious one. The KLP withdrew its support to the

Prakasam Ministry over the issue of the location of the capital. The location of the capital at Kurnool in Rayalaseema region was seen as a victory for the dominant Reddi caste, some of whose leadership was emerging as a cohesive political group within the Congress Party. However, the Prakasam Ministry failed to survive for more than a year. It fell in November 1954 after a motion of no confidence on the issue of prohibition, supported by the communists, the KLP and the PSP Members, was carried by a majority of one vote.

The mid-term elections in Andhra were held in February 1955. It turned out to be a 'critical election' in Andhra political history. On the eve of the election, the Communist Party was confident that it would form the next Ministry in the State. Sensing the danger and the strength of the Communist Party and given the experience of the 1952 elections when the communists stood to win a large number of seats due to the division of the Congress vote, the Congress leaders realised the need to consolidate all the forces opposed to communism. They forged an electoral alliance with the KLP and the Praja Party to form the United Congress Front. On the other hand, the communists, due to overestimation of their electoral prospects and doctrinaire attitudes, failed to forge an alliance with either the splinter groups of the Congress Party or the PSP. While the anti-communist forces formed a powerful array, the communists had ideologically outdistanced themselves from other political parties and groups.

This proved to be disastrous to the communists, but highly advantageous to the Congress Party. The Congress leaders also launched a virulent attack on the communists as presenting a danger to family, private property and democracy. The combination of the socialist orientation of Congress Party policies, the impact of some agrarian reforms and praise showered on the Congress by the socialist Soviet leadership served to seriously deflate the Communist Party. The grand strategy of the Congress Party paid very well, as it secured a decisive majority of 119seats on its own, with about 40% of the vote. Out of a total of 196 seats, the United

Congress Front won 146 seats with an aggregate vote of about 52%. The communists won a paltry 15 seats, although they secured about 31% of the vote. The election also took a heavy toll on the other parties: all the candidates fielded by the Bharatiya Jana Sangh (BJS), 18 of the 45 PSP candidates and more than two-thirds (111 of 162) of the independents lost their deposits.

Paradoxically, the Communist Party polled more votes than earlier, both in absolute terms and in terms of percentage, but lost a good number of seats. It lost heavily in its stronghold of coastal districts such as Godavaris, Krishna, Guntur and Nellore. The rout of the Communist Party and the defeat of the other parties enabled the Congress to emerge as the dominant party in the region. Thus the results of midterm elections indicated the onset of a new era of Congress dominance.

5

Political Economy of Civil War and Conflict Transformation

Quite a few jaded observers of writings on war economies tend to view similar analyses with scepticism, amusement or even consternation. Similarly, it is always interesting to read work that attempts categorisation of social phenomena into neat and pat theories, which are then rigorously analysed. Undoubtedly, there is great merit to this approach, look at the achievements that result from thinking and working in this manner. But can different, and sometimes unrelated, phenomena really be observed, compared, analysed, characterised, and solved using this approach?

As we all know, conflicts are dynamic in nature and difficult to capture through linear analysis. How effectively does theory relate to on-the-ground lived practice and move from the theoretical realm to practice? Or do we stop at theory's use being merely to theorise? How closely do our theories approximate reality? How useful are these theories to the real phenomena of conflicts and the need to mitigate them, especially as we are dealing with real flesh and blood people with needs and feelings? Do our theories and research serve real policy purposes? This, to me, seems to be the crux of the matter. Of course a rebuttal could be that theories only serve as the laboratory for practice, and that analysis is the process of achieving the intended outcome: to mitigate or ameliorate sufferings caused by conflict.

Most people who work in this field must at times agonise over the usefulness of their theories in the face of, nay, increase in violent conflicts in several parts of the world. So can it be that we are asking the wrong questions and doing the wrong analyses or that we fail to order our thoughts in such a manner as to address the real issues? For example, as much as the nascent study of the role of economics in conflict is valuable, it continues to baffle several people why it has suddenly gained preponderance and focus. This comment therefore asks if the political economy perspective – by focusing largely and narrowly on the economic activities of 'rebels' and, to some extent, 'governments' – truly offers an understanding of the dynamics of conflicts. It also asks if it can possibly point towards future useful policy directions, particularly in understanding the impact of war economies on peace building activities.

It seems to me that the crux of the matter is that causes, nature, dynamics, and impact of conflict are highly complex, and that the political economy perspective is 'reductionist' in its attempt at examining these. Conflicts, as we all know, generally are the result of the interplay of a multitude of intervening variables. In my opinion, to give the role of economics an exaggerated role as the main motivation for conflict is not only to ignore the realities of those involved in conflicts, but also to ignore past work done by sociologists, anthropologists, and political scientists. Gravest of all is to dismiss a complex interaction of physical, psycho-social, political, and economic issues, and to label those who are constantly faced with the dilemma of resorting to conflict as being motivated only or mostly by 'greed'. This is not to completely foreclose the issue of 'greed' as playing a role in conflict. The question is, whose greed, how, when, and where?

Therefore, this short article takes an alternative view on the causes, nature, and dynamics of conflicts and also an alternative view on the nature, characteristics, impact, and role of war economies. Most of these recommendations are, in my opinion, self-evident and logical consequences stemming from an understanding of the dynamics of West African conflicts. Most of the policy recommendations are also freely available in the existing literature, particularly in the work of some non-governmental organisations and several Africanists.

Typologies of West African Conflicts

Despite the difficulty of drawing up broad categorisations, perhaps what could be called common characteristics in places that are conflict-afflicted in West Africa are such factors as: violent suppression of dissent, bad governance, military intervention in politics, lack of political and economic accountability, inequitable distribution of resources, and uneven development between the regions and ethnic communities. These conflicts have tended to straddle borders and exhibit what are now known as sub-regional dynamics and implications. Encapsulating the variables of conflicts in West Africa and categorising them is a difficult task, made more difficult by the distinctiveness of particular conflicts and the possible ideological interpretations and perceptions that can influence such categorisation. However, one could discern objective conditions that create discontent which fuels wars in West Africa.

These objective conditions by the nature of their manifestations are the causes that define these conflicts. The new trend to increasingly focus on the means of financing these conflicts, coupled with the failure of the conflict perpetrators to coherently articulate and achieve their objectives and war aims, has progressively led to a discourse to find 'rational' arguments to dismiss the politics of such movements. This inclination has sometimes led to frightening interpretations including purely economic ones, instead of a hard look at an amalgamation of factors. These factors differ in their level of significance, and often underpin or counteract each other. A conflict can occur where a group with strong affiliation feels threatened. This affinity can take several forms, including ethnicity or religion. The question of identity/ ethnicity then becomes an issue.

The conflict could manifest itself in wars of internal self-determination, self-preservation and self-assertion, wars against exclusion and wars for self-autonomy (none of these categories are considered valid under a purely economic interpretation). Examples in West Africa can be found in Nigeria, Liberia, Côte d'Ivoire and Sierra Leone. It should be stressed that it is not being said that identity/ ethnicity is the sole cause of conflicts in these countries, but rather that several factors cause conflicts and this is one. Needless also to say that it is not inevitable that there would be conflict in a location with a strong identity or ethnic crisis. Numerous countries in Africa are faced with the onerous task of *nation building*. Little significance is given to this cause, except by Africanists. Nevertheless, it is crucial to understanding conflicts in several parts of Africa.

This has its origin in the colonial history, heritage of the colonial state constructs. The unfinished task of nation building that impinges on the state's political, social and economic existence leads usually to a crisis of governance, corruption, lack of livelihood opportunities, and then violent conflict. In the case of West Africa, this has not included crises over land with current descendants of 'settlers' as in Zimbabwe and, potentially, Kenya, Namibia and South Africa, since the nature of West African colonialism and the manifestation of its legacy differ. In all of these conflict configurations, the intention of the perpetrators is simple: to gain primacy, not only over their lives, but also over the politics and economy of their terrain, for the simple reason that control over the political and economic landscape fulfils their aspirations. Resources then become a tool, rather than the end in itself. In a somewhat perverse and atrocious manner, a combatant once told me that violence and conflict were the same as the process by which politicians in 'developed' countries acquired power by 'civilised' means and then dominated and controlled their economic and political landscape.

Finally, using econometric indicators to arrive at particular conclusions in an analysis of the causes of war is not an exact and precise science, and can be utilised to justify or disprove a desired position. An example is the situation in Liberia before 1979, where, in 1972, private American investment totaled over $500 million, the largest in sub-Saharan Africa. Liberia had a thriving iron ore export industry, about the third largest in the world. It also had other natural resources such as diamonds, timber, etc. The GDP per capita was $420, and Liberia was listed as middle-income country by the World Bank.

Looking at available economic data, Liberia seemed stable and well. However, Liberia had to withdraw some of the subsidies on rice, the staple food in the country, to meet, among other things, payments to the London and Paris Club, which Liberia owed money. The subsequent riot, which followed the withdrawal of the safety net of subsidies, could be said to have been the first event in a series that has led to the present conflict situation in West Africa, since Liberia has been called the epicenter of the conflicts in West Africa. It is easy to say that the conflicts in Liberia were caused by only the economic factor of the withdrawal of subsidies, but that would be disingenuous. The Liberian war was as a result of a complex interplay of political, social and economic factors, not only economic ones.

The Dynamics of War Economies

Still, the significant role that economics play in conflict can be vividly demonstrated, but in a different way from the 'greed and grievance' school of thought. This is more poignant in the 'new' wars, where states are defined as collapsed or failed and violent conflict ensues between warring factions to acquire and control state resources, appropriating state authority for personal use. In these new wars, economics do play a preponderant role. This role, though, has more to do with neo-classical paradigms of development. Perhaps a rigorously alternative perspective and focused study of this correlation could offer useful alternative policy directions.

As a report puts it: "Recent scholarly research has also begun to shed new light on the links between Structural Adjustment Programmes (SAPs) and the incidence of conflict and disorder, although the crisis in Somalia and the genocide in Rwanda were largely attributed by the international media to 'clanism' and 'ethnicity', Michel Chossudovsky puts part of the blame on the draconian economic policies of the IMF and the World Bank which removed all official economic safety nets and left the Rwandan economy in shambles after the collapse of the international coffee market in the late 1980s. With the price of coffee plummeting and the Rwandan franc repeatedly devalued, the general population was left destitute and impoverished. This, according to Chossudovsky, created conditions in which power hungry officials and leaders could sow the seeds of civil war and genocide. Hatred, which in a prospering economy could not and would not have surfaced, soon became apparent and was followed by the collapse of civil society.

It should be obvious by now that it is often the absence of justice that is the principal cause for the absence of peace. Any economic reform programme that denies human dignity is likely to be resisted by those who are being victimised. It is also likely to lead to further conflict and human misery." Observers in West Africa have also linked the conflict in Côte d'Ivoire to the fact that the economy of that country was intensely susceptible to the whims and caprices of international financial institutions, particularly the global commodity cartels. When the price of its main export, cocoa, declined, and economic safety nets disappeared, ethnic alignments became the only remaining 'safety net' for survival. In Nigeria, several ethnic conflicts boil up regularly, centering around economic issues – not in the sense of 'greed and grievance' but usually around the distribution of wealth.

Withdrawal of subsidies on the advice of international financial institutions, particularly on petroleum products, has consistently increased tensions, with potential for further escalation into full violent conflict. In fact, a number of under-reported low intensity conflicts are already going on in several parts of the country, whose causes centre on the distribution of resources, inefficient governance, and withdrawal of subsidies. As John Steinbruner and Jason Forrester say, the pattern of growth associated with the process of globalisation has so far been inequitable. Concentrations of wealth have increased throughout the world. Standard of living improvements have disproportionately benefited the top 20 percent income bracket.

In many areas of endemic economic austerity that have emerged in the uneven pattern of globalisation the ability to preserve social coherence and thereby to control violence is already very seriously at stake. So, yes, economics do matter, but the question is in what direction and what kind of economics? For whatever reason, analysis and discourses on war economies skirt around the importance and supporting role of the international dimension. The supply side of commodities, for example diamonds, is always studiously analysed, paying scant attention to the demand side. With the exception of NGOs like Global Witness, Oxfam, and some others, most academics tend to give little attention to this, too.

While, at the same time, in the case of small arms the demand side is scrupulously attended to but not the supply side. (No doubt there are political and economic considerations imposed on researchers dependent on and constrained by funds from players who are themselves influenced by these very suppliers?) Africanists have always wondered why arms exporting countries could not simply clamp down on illegal arms' sales, or control more vigorously their 'legal' arms export. Some have suggested in exasperation that if only the means were available 'Third World' NGOs would have embarked on 'programmes' in those countries to dissuade arms' exports. Very little arms production is carried out in Africa and, similarly, very little consumption of diamonds happens in Africa.

One can make the bold statement that war economies are truly globalised economies. The connections and contacts between war elites in Africa and the internationals, who aid, abet and sustain war economies in one form or the other need to be given more attention in work on war economies. Perhaps studying this variable could offer policy recommendations for countries of both supply and demand. Even if 'greed and grievance' theories miss the role of internationals and the role of neo-classical development paradigms in wars, the valid and legitimate question of the possible connection of criminality and war still remains. Are wars being fought to acquire resources criminally, therefore transforming struggling economies into war economies, as is asserted?

Boldly stated, what Karen Ballentine and Heiko Nitzschke describe as "distinctive features of War Economies" constitute the nature of the economies of quite a number of developing countries, such as informality, cross border trade relying on ethnic contacts, and control of resources and assets by an elite group. Perhaps this is exactly what is wrong with the economies of Africa! "Combat economy", "shadow economy" and "coping economy" are terms which, if we must use them, describe in one breath a 'normal' undeveloped economy that becomes transformed into a 'survival and free for all' economy in the atmosphere of increased anarchy in a situation of escalating conflict. These conditions, however, do not universally justify the label of war economies, as even in peace times similar economic relationships and situations exist. Of course, in any extreme situation – such as a war – the negative consequences of these arrangements become accentuated.

Similarly, "lootable" and "unlootable" resources have always been available in several conflict zones, e.g. Liberia and Sierra Leone. The question to be asked is why it is that now, at this moment in time, they have become resources to be fought for and controlled by warring factions? Perhaps the answer lies in the simple fact that a generation of combatants who did not live under direct colonialism and the dynamics it unleashed –including the succession to political power by certain favoured groups after flag independence who continued the marginalisation of the people – has now grown up and wants a better quality of life in all ramifications. The chickens have simply come home to roost. The tension after evolving through several phases, including the awakening of the (false) consciousness of the masses, now results in violent conflicts.

Further, care has to be taken in accepting automated policy implications of a classification into 'lootable' and 'unlootable' resources. The example of Sierra Leone in relation to Botswana cannot be used to arrive at a general principle without taking into consideration the different political history and demography of the two countries, which have largely shaped their situations. Also, if the logic of 'lootable' and 'unlootable' is utilised, oil in Nigeria requires heavy drilling and is thus unlootable, yet Nigeria is rife with conflicts.

Finally, could the problem of conflict, particularly its economic dimension, be attributed to situations, as Karen Ballentine and Heiko Nitzschke say, "where corrupt, exclusionary, and unaccountable governments fail to adequately share the resources generated or provide adequate public goods and services, [so that] a sense of economic deprivation may fuel other local resentments and feed separatist violence..."? Resulting in the combatants believing that they can share and provide these resources, goods and services themselves – and not being merely criminally motivated?

Areas of Exploration for Policy Formulation

More studies and research are needed. Such studies require a better understanding of the context and dynamics of war situations and they must realign themselves with good and appropriate work done in the past. An illustration of the need for better socio-economic contextual understanding can be found in recent DDR programmes in certain parts of West Africa. Ex-combatants in two contiguous parts of West Africa were to be paid disproportional amounts in a DDR programme run by the UN. The decision for this was made based on (economic) statistics provided by international development agencies, showing that the standard of living in one country was higher than in the other. Obviously, ex-combatants in the poorer country would rather go to the better-off country to disarm. It would be obvious to the discerning interlocutor with good contextual understanding that, with this kind of arrangement, the DDR programmes in both countries are booby trapped from the start. Therefore, policies must be grounded in real understanding of the context. If the search is only for ground-breaking theories, they will not be very useful to those affected by conflicts.

Further studies of the following issues could guide more holistic and comprehensive policy prescription on the economic dimensions of war, and particularly on mitigating violent conflicts and their impacts:

- The economic dimensions of wars should be analysed not only from the reductionist perspective of lootable and unlootable resources. There should be more concentrated and in depth research on the linkages between Structural Adjustment Programmes, neo-liberal economic measures and conflict or peace building.

- The economic dimensions of wars should include critical analyses of the roles of suppliers of arms and consumers of resources, such as 'conflict' diamonds. The role of multinational corporations and internationals in business and conflict needs to be revisited.
- The effects of anonymous banking in the international banking system and the recovery of money stashed abroad by warlords and corrupt leaders need to be sorted out. There is a need to make clear categorically to conflict entrepreneurs that war or corruption do not pay, and that even if the loot is stashed in the 'developed' world, it would be recovered and returned.
- An analysis of the impact of natural resources on conflict dynamics is required, rather than the other way round. We should not apply the linkages *ex post facto*, as ethnic linkages and political dimensions could also be part of the configuration (whether the presence or absence of resources fuels the war is another matter).
- It is necessary to develop better contextual knowledge of the dynamics of the war situation, including socio-economic factors.
- The issues of youth unemployment and availability of livelihood opportunities to all need to be given greater consideration in an analysis of the economic dimensions, beyond merely the DDR stages. At the opening of the African Union Extraordinary Summit of Heads of Governments on employment and poverty alleviation in Africa, on 8 September 2004 in Ouagadougou, Burkina Faso, the Director General of the International Labour Organisation described unemployment, underemployment, the working poor, and unaccounted workers in the informal economy as the world's biggest security risk.
- The incorporation of explicit economic agreements into peace agreements could assist in quickly ending wars and in peace building. The ECOWAS sponsored

Comprehensive Peace Agreement for Liberia in Accra, August 2003 could serve as an example. There, such issues were addressed, including the establishment of a Contracts and Monopolies Commission to oversee the award of contracts, sound macro-economic policies, etc.

- We need to look at the role of the dichotomy of urban vs. rural areas dichotomy. The vanguard of conflicts is usually an urban-based elite – and those who suffer most as civilians or combatants are the rural poor.
- The developmental question needs to be taken into the equation. The issues of 'development', infrastructure, and the provision of goods and services need greater attention.
- An integration of programmes offering livelihood opportunities into *all* conflict transformation activities needs to be put into practice.

Georgia's Rose Revolution

Georgian people's Rose Revolution of November 2003 strove to achieve a democratic society, improve human rights and living conditions, reduce corruption, and enhance the national economy. Accordingly, the Revolution and its heroes, led by Mikhail Saakashvili, received the support of the Bush administration, the EU, and its member states. Three years later, the euphoria that followed the Revolution, both within and outside the country, has gradually been replaced by more realistic assessments of the results of the post-revolution policies to date. The sobering up from being drunk on revolution occurred somewhat sooner within Georgia than abroad, which is quite understandable: Georgian citizens have been experiencing the revolution firsthand, whereas Georgia's international friends often mistake what they would like to see happening for what is really happening. The unconditional support for all endeavors of the post-revolutionary government on the part of the Western nations and, most of all, of the U.S. government, is fostering the development of anti-Western and anti-American tendencies among Georgians.

Nevertheless, even those analysts who have been a priori supportive of the revolutionary leaders cannot ignore some recent antidemocratic developments in Georgia, such as executive authority dominating the judiciary and troubling incidents that are provoking discussions about the country's key values. But to date none of the analysis devoted to the revolution deals in any substantive way with economic problems. This article aims to explore the economic transformations in post-revolution Georgia and outline basic directions of Georgia's economic development.

The Pre-Revolution Economy

Georgia's economic development from 1991 until the revolution, which was characterized by some successes but also several significant mistakes, can be thought of in three phases: the years of disregarding economics (1991–94), then consistent reforms (1994–98), followed by the rise of corruption (1999–2003).

Disregarding Economics

The period from 1991 through the first half of 1994 saw almost a triple decline in production coupled with hyperinflation—in 1993–94, the inflation rate reached 50–70 percent a month. An interim Georgian currency, the coupon, introduced in spring 1993, devalued so fast that ultimately the only product it could buy was a loaf of bread. However, even that would have been impossible to do had the bread not been baked mostly by government-owned bakeries and had the government not artificially kept the bread price at a low level. The result was that the Russian Rubble was the only effective currency in circulation.

In 1993–94, the country had no parliament-approved national budget. Public expenditures were approved by the parliament on a quarterly basis. The only source of national revenues was loans from the central bank, the National Bank of Georgia (NBG). Commercial banks were extending limitless credit. Liberalizing prices (except for bread) in 1992 was the only important step taken toward a market economy. However, due to the lack of a national budget and uncontrolled issuance of money, it had adverse results, such as falling production, dramatically rising inflation, and the unprecedented devaluation of the national currency.

Reform

In the second half of 1994, the government finally began to pay attention to economics and institute reforms, a process that continued through the end of 1998. The first steps were to raise the price of bread; curb the NBG's uncontrolled lending to the government, which was underwritten by printing excessive amounts of money; and ban overdraft credit extensions for the commercial banks. Hyperinflation was brought under control, as was declining production. In 1995 Georgia's parliament approved a national budget, as it has every year since. This permitted implementation of a successful currency reform in fall 1995. A new national currency, the *Lari*, forced out of circulation both the coupon and the Russian Ruble.

In summer 1996, after gradual increases in the bread price and a simultaneous privatization of public bakeries, the bread price was entirely liberalized. All these reforms were carried out in close cooperation with the International Monetary Fund (IMF) and the World Bank. As a result, after 1995, Georgia turned to economic growth and finished its exit from the hyperinflation spiral. Fall 1998 posed a test for the strength of the reforms. Because of the August 1998 default in Russia, the Georgian currency started devaluing rapidly. The government lacked control of the South Ossetian and Abkhazian sections of the Georgian-Russian border, so there was smuggling of cheap (because of the default) Russian goods. Also, the Russian military bases in Georgia were used as a vehicle for flooding the Georgian market with devalued

Russian *Rubles*. All of this contributed to U.S. dollars streaming out of Georgia into Russia and the *Lari*'s is being devalued by 70 percent. However, the government took timely steps and the NBG ensured that not a single commercial bank went bankrupt during this very difficult period for the Georgian economy.

Corruption

Unfortunately, in 1999 President Eduard Shevardnadze began disregarding common sense and expert advice, especially in his government appointments. This period was characterized by the escalation of a budget crisis, the first symptoms of which became noticeable as early as 1998, when actual national budget revenues started lagging behind projections. The next year represents the most palpable example of the national budget failure: in 1999, the government collected only around 70 percent of the projected national budget. This state of affairs continued through 2003. One remarkable characteristic of the budget crisis was a many-year "budget war" between the central government and that of the Adjarian Autonomous Republic. In essence, the government of the autonomous republic refused to transfer to the central budget legally established quotas of tax revenues collected in Adjara.

To achieve the projected budget revenues on paper, the government resorted to deceptive accounting techniques such as "forwarding" budget funds from one budget line to another and making fictitious tax offsets. From 1999 onwards, the country was unable to obtain loans and grants from international financial institutions and donor countries, since it could not meet IMF requirements; in 2002, the IMF suspended its own funding. Other international financial institutions and donor countries followed suit, and Georgia's problem of external debt, which at that time had reached 50 percent of GDP, became critical. With the IMF suspension, the Paris Club door was locked for Georgia, and without restructuring, the country would never be able to repay its debts.

In 2000, the Georgian government invited the prominent Polish economist Leszek Balcerowicz to become an adviser to the president. But massive government ineptitude made futile his two-year effort to help the country's leadership overcome economic crisis. (In a move similar to his predecessor's, President Saakashvili recently invited the former prime minister of Estonia, Mart Laar, to become a presidential aide on economic affairs.) In June 2003, President Shevardnadze approved an Economic Development and Poverty Reduction Program for 2003–15. The program had been developed by the government agencies in cooperation with NGOs and Georgian economists, along with experts from the international organizations and donor countries in the final phase. However, owing to the lack of political will, the government failed even to begin implementing the program, thereby exacerbating tension between Georgia and the IMF and other international donors.

While GDP growth rate had begun to fall during this period, in 2003 Georgia succeeded in achieving a high economic growth rate, primarily due to investments in the construction of the Baku-Tbilisi-Ceyhan oil pipeline. But as a consequence of the government's failures in all aspects of the budgetary process, in 2003 the state budget deficit reached $90 million, or 15 percent of projected revenue. At the end of 2003, the total internal debt in unpaid salaries and public-sector pensions, which had been accumulating for the entire duration of the budget crisis, reached $120 million, even though monthly pensions amounted to less than $7. Half the population was living under the poverty level. This drastic deterioration of social conditions created sufficient dissatisfaction with the Shevardnadze administration that the ground was prepared for revolution.

Post-Revolution Economic Achievements

The concentration of power in the president's hands is the most notable characteristic of Georgia's development since the revolution. In February 2004, the parliament approved the president's initiative to amend the national constitution, giving the president the power to disband either the parliament or the cabinet in case of a conflict between the two. The constitutional amendments significantly weakened the parliament: a permanent threat of disbanding keeps parliamentarians loyal to the government. The strengthening of presidential powers and the weakening of those of the parliament has had both positive and negative consequences for the country.

Among the positive results, the broader executive powers allowed the government to drastically reduce redundancies and improved its ability to maintain financial order. For example, the unlawful accounting practices for state budget revenues have disappeared. Also, the May 2004 revolution in the Autonomous Republic of Adjara permitted a normal budgeting process to resume between the central government and this region, and Georgia's tax revenues significantly increased in 2004 for the first time since it gained independence in 1991. The new government succeeded in overcoming the budget crisis and in covering old liabilities, including paying pensions and salaries. Also, decisive steps were taken to intensify a war on crime in order to improve the business climate.

As part of its efforts to combat corruption, the government abolished the traffic police that had existed since Soviet times and created a Western-style police patrol. As a consequence, the practice of bribery across the country's roads and highways was ended, opening up new opportunities for the country's development as an important international transport corridor. No less impressive were the results of the reformed system of exams for admission to the country's universities, which had been infamous for their corruption since Soviet times. By taking the exams out of the control of university administrators and holding them on a national level, the government overcame the deep-rooted corruption in the admissions system.

State budget revenues were tripled as a result of such anticorruption measures as arresting and then releasing—for a "price of liberty"—former government officials and their relatives, especially friends and family of President Shevardnadze. Ostensibly this money was used to pay back to the state money and properties that had been stolen from it, but in many cases the "price of liberty" no doubt was different from the amount taken. The new government announced that during its first year some $200 million had been returned to the national budget, but the new "fighters against corruption" have certainly recovered much more than this.

Almost immediately after coming to power, the Saakashvili government started implementing an ambitious plan of large-scale privatization. The country's new image, improved by the Rose Revolution, enabled it to attract from the outset high-value privatization deals that exceeded by tens and sometimes hundreds of times the amounts raised for the whole period before the revolution. In addition to its other achievements, the new government reduced some tax rates and the adopted a new Tax Code in late 2004. In the new tax code, VAT decreased from 20 percent to 18 percent, the payroll tax decreased from 32 percent to 20 percent, and a flat income tax of 12 percent replaced the old progressive income tax.

At the same time, the number of taxes also went down: the more than twenty taxes under the old tax code and other laws were reduced to only seven through abolishment or combination. By summer 2004, the government had earned renewal of the IMF program, enabling it to begin negotiations on restructuring the country's foreign debt. Since then, donor countries have extended Georgia credit and grants amounting to $1 billion. In addition, In September 2005, Washington committed to extend the country $295.3 million in assistance under the Millennium Challenge Account.

Post-Revolution Economic Mistakes

One of the negative consequences of the strengthened presidential and weakened parliamentary powers is an intensified feeling of impunity among government officials, which has been manifested in their disregard for the rule of law. The judiciary has been degraded and denounced, and judges have turned into tacit executors of the prosecutors' wishes. The government's control over the media has become overwhelming. In this context, the process of democratization and improving human rights has encountered many barriers.

In almost all governmental ministries and departments, most of the experienced employees were swept away by the revolutionary wave, usually in violation of the law. Government employees with a comprehensive university education are now almost nonexistent. New employees were selected on a competitive basis, with preference given to young people who had received some Western education. In hiring young staffs, the government lost a great deal of institutional memory.

The flipside of the changes made in the country's budget system is that they have deprived local budgets of practically all tax revenue: if before the revolution some 99 percent of profit taxes were left for the local budgets, after the revolution 100 percent of such revenue has been collected by the central government and apportioned to local budgets through distributions. Such steps aimed at strengthening the central government fit perfectly with the government's failure to honour its electoral promises to introduce direct elections of city mayors.

The government established extra budgetary "law-enforcement development accounts" where those suspected of corrupt practices were compelled to transfer payments to buy their liberty. Thus, a new form of corruption had developed in the form of these extra budgetary accounts.

Since such revenues could not be raised on an ongoing basis, the government started replenishing these accounts by means of "voluntary contributions" from businesses. Just as in the mid-1990s, when the earlier government's extra budgetary accounts were closed under IMF pressure, in late 2005 the IMF demanded that the new ones be closed, to which demand the government reluctantly acceded only after several months of hesitation.

Another matter of particular concern is the process of "deprivatization" of privatized state property, which may drag the country back to its status at the initial stage of its transition to market economy. Furthermore, the government's new wave of privatization will probably make necessary sometime in the future another round of deprivatization. These initiatives only create the appearance of providing for "social justice." Their real purpose is redistributing property for the benefit of the new elite.

Russian-Georgian Relationships

As the West's support for Georgia has increased since 2003, so has irritation in Moscow, to which the Georgian leaders respond in kind. Themutual reproaches between Tbilisi and Moscow have become increasingly loud. What policy does Russia actually plan to pursue with respect to Georgia and the other post-Soviet states? Russia's policy toward these states today—the author of which is Anatoliy Chubais, the president of RAO EES (Unified Energy Systems), a huge nationwide utility—is an updated version of the "liberal empire" concept.

One of the key goals of liberal empire is to significantly weaken (if not destroy) Western influence over the post-Soviet states. According to Chubais, because Russia has never been invited to and actually could not be squeezed into either NATO or the EU, it needs to create an alternative to those organizations. One variant of such an alternative could be a liberal empire, which would be built not by means of coercion or even military occupation of the former Soviet republics, but rather by means of acquiring and developing assets located in their territories. Russia started fulfilling its master plan of incorporating the Caucasus in the liberal empire with Armenia, its strategic partner in the region.

In late 2002, just before the March 2003 presidential elections in Armenia, the countries agreed to a "debt-for-equity" swap. Russia gained multiple national Armenian enterprises, the aggregate value of which turned out to be enough for Armenia to pay off its $93 million debt to Russia. Georgia is a geographical obstacle on the way to Russia's creation of a united economic space between itself and Armenia. Should Russia succeed in implementing its liberal empire plan in Georgia, it will be an easy endeavour to get Azerbaijan involved in this imperial project, too, as all key Azeri transport and communications routes, including basic pipelines, cross Georgia's territory. In summer 2003, RAO EES acquired the Georgian holdings of AES Silk Road (a subsidiary of the U.S.-based power company AES Corp.), which held 75 percent of the equity in the Tbilisi electricity network and some other important components of the Georgian electric energy system.

In fact, most Georgian assets in the post-revolution years have been bought by Russian companies or their subsidiaries, registered in third countries. Russia has thus been able to pursue its strategy in Georgia because of insufficiently transparent privatization procedures. The Russian holding group Industrial Investors plans to invest up to $200 million in the Georgian economy over the next three years. Through a subsidiary, Stanton Equities Corp., it has already embarked on this by purchasing, for $35 million, Madneuli, a gold-mining enterprise (it paid an additional $16 million to pay Madneuli's state budget liabilities), and 50 percent of the shares in Kazreti, a gold alloy manufacturer.

Russian gas giant Gazprom is also moving aggressively in Georgia. Gazprom is willing to purchase dozens of major gas interests in Georgia and, most importantly, the main North-South natural gas pipeline through which gas flows from Russia to Georgia and, by transit, to Armenia. In addition to the numerous privatization schemes, there is the precedent of renationalization implemented by the Russian side and unfortunately welcomed by the Georgian government. In early 2005, Russia's state-owned Vneshtorgbank purchased the controlling shares in the United Georgian Bank, the third-largest bank in Georgia. Just one year earlier, Vneshtorgbank had acquired the controlling package of shares in the Armenian Armsberbank.

According to Vneshtorgbank management, the bank is planning to embark on an ambitious investment program in Georgia which may reach $1 billion in aggregate. The Russians started this program by spending $40 million to purchase the gas turbines for an electricity generator in Gardabani, south of Tbilisi. A major role in making Georgia part of the developing liberal empire has been assigned to RAO EES Russia. Russia's interest in acquiring parts of the electric power grid in Georgia in order to gain access to the huge Turkish market has been known since Soviet times. When Tbilisi indicated its interest in privatizing the Inguri Power Plant and renewing construction of the Khudoni Power Plant, RAO EES's leadership indicated its strong interest in both projects.

While most countries welcome FDI, it should be a matter of concern for Georgia that investments are coming from a not-quite friendly nation that has openly announced its intention of luring neighbouring countries into its liberal empire. Russian capital is always either directly owned or otherwise controlled by the state. Russia manifested its desire to destabilize Georgia in the "economic war" it opened in January 2006, when a gas pipeline to Georgia was blown up on the Russian side of the two countries' border. As a result, gas deliveries to Georgia and Armenia were disrupted for days during a particularly cold winter. In Spring 2006, Russia put a ban on the importation of Moldovan and Georgian wines, as well as plants and vegetables, claiming high levels of heavy metals and pesticides. (In 2005, wine accounted for 9.4 percent of Georgian exports, second only to scrap metal. More than 70 percent of these exports were to Russia.) Other Georgian goods, such as mineral water, also face expulsion from the Russian market. As a result, Georgia is considering quitting the Commonwealth of Independent States, but it is still welcoming Russian state investments. Georgia faces a historic choice: either to continue moving towards Europe, or to let it be drawn back into Russia's orbit. The West cannot ignore these developments in the Caucasus.

6

Human Rights' Impact on International Finance

Servitude or Entitlement

The title of this study implies the juxtaposition of two human dimensions: the affectional and the functional. Human rights relate to such concepts as care, respect, dignity and understanding among human beings, hence the affectional. International finance connotes transfer of capital across frontiers for gain and therefore the functional. Combining the human dimension with finance (in general and not necessarily international at this stage) we can conceive of different outcomes. At one extreme we are presented with financing for profit with little human consideration. But along the line we will find occasions when the affectional may, or may seem to, condition finance's functional nature.

Take, for instance, the financing of a friend or one's own child without interest—in a way giving ones money away. The motivation for the act, however, is more important than the altruistic appearance. The child may even be charged interest or be required to reimburse the capital; not because of a desire for direct material gain by the parents, but in order to make the child socially responsible. In this case despite the functional appearance of the transaction, the motivation is affectional. Inversely, a friend or a protégé may be advanced funds without interest, "out of the goodness of ones heart," yet the motivation may be a functional investment in the future and expectation of the return of the favour based on an evaluation of the recipient's potentials for success. The operation is functional.

Transferring these interpersonal instances of the affectional and the functional to the socio-political arena, we may find that the functional extreme of financial gain may reduce the human factor to a mere tool; producing the phenomenon of slavery. In such a situation, the relationship of the human factor to the capital is that of servitude. On the other hand, the human consideration may reduce capital to a tool whose use is not to produce profit but to serve social welfare irrespective of financial cost effectiveness. In the extreme case of the claim of social welfare on the capital the relationship of the human factor to finance will be that of entitlement. This situation may be approached in a social democracy with strong egalitarian labour unions or in a totalitarian state capitalism with centralized democracy.

While the interpersonal affectional/functional and the sociopolitical servitude/entitlement tendencies can be traced in time and space to different cultures, when they are transferred to the international domain, they acquire a patently Western characteristic. It is that international finance is associated with capitalism and the human dimensions translated into human rights and identified with democracy: both developments of modern Western culture. To some extent, this Western association of the proposition is a distorting factor; because it projects the interaction of capitalism and human rights into societies and cultures whose historical evolution has been different from the West. In order to better grasp the proposition it may be useful to briefly scrutinize the development of capitalism and human rights within the Western culture and see whether the two were interrelated and, if so, what the nature of this interrelation was and to what extent it can be transferred to modern international relations.

The developments we are concerned about here are those of post-reformation Europe. The Calvinist and puritan concept of the "elect" did not, as such, contain a direct human rights component. God had chosen the "elect" to become rich probably because they were pious, hardworking and frugal and did not indulge in the joys of the tavern. By the very fact of the godly distinction between the "elect" and the others, the elect did not have to feel guilty for the lot of the downtrodden. Of course, as they amassed wealth and their reputation as conscientious craftsmen and businessmen grew, the elect could expand their activities and provide employment for the poor.

In the course of the centuries, however, riches became the measuring rod dissociated from the pious characteristics which were to bring it about. Indeed, as Protestant ethics metamorphosed into social Darwinism in the nineteenth century, social institutions, notably the churches, tried to attenuate its impact by emphasizing Christian charity and creating charitable foundations. Human rights, however, were not originally developed in reaction to this state of affairs but as another concern of the emerging bourgeoisie and as a complement to capitalism. Locke's life, liberty and property were safeguards that the bourgeois capitalism wished to wrestle out of the monarchs. These ideas inspired the English Bill of Rights and the American and the French Revolutions. The human rights they proclaimed were civic and political, leaving free rein to liberal economy.

This free rein, combined with social Darwinism and the industrial revolution, caused economic and social disruptions in the nineteenth century. Christian charity was not enough to counter balance the encroachments of free enterprise capitalism. Trade unionist and socialist ideas and institutions emerged to counteract and interact with the free enterprise and the government to secure social and economic justice. Conflict, compromise and cooperation between the four dimensions (government, capital, labour, and, to some extent, the church) provided economic, social and political settings oscillating somewhere within the spectrum going from servitude to entitlement.

In the process, the intrinsic characteristics of most of these dimensions within the national boundaries of Western countries were compromised: governments assumed more and more social, economic and regulatory responsibilities beyond their political, military and judicial authority. Labour movements, originally inspired by Marxism, eventually sat down to negotiate with capital and government instead of wiping them out by revolution. And capital moved from sweatshops to unemployment and health insurance for the workers. These evolutions did not take place because they were intrinsic to the characteristics of each of these social dimensions but because of the presence and potentials of the other dimensions within the national boundaries and their input within the legal system.

International

In the course of the colonial and imperial expansions of the West, each of these dimensions produced different impacts on the penetrated territories. In general, and naturally, they reverted, circumstances permitting, to their intrinsic characteristics. The interactions in the new non-Western environments produced different complexes. The Western Governments, for example, while essentially political and military powers, were creating frameworks for the international economic penetration of their national capital. We thus could encounter home countries with well-developed human rights conditions whose international financial arms extending into other parts of the world needed not occupy themselves with human rights considerations.

Capital moved to non-Western regions of the globe in search of profit: its intrinsic characteristic. One of the incentives for the capital to move was the absence of the restraints encountered in the home country—notably in the domain of economic and social human rights. Of course, in some cases some residual developments of the interactions within the home country did move on with the capital. For instance, during the nineteenth century industrial revolution, capital had come to realize that the Malthusian misery of the workers was not cost-effective and that providing some standards of hygiene and housing were more efficient both for better production and better control of the workers.

Of course, the introduction of such standards in traditional societies could, at times, disrupt local ways of life and cultural patterns. Thus, in addition to possible lack of Western style civic, political, economic and social human rights in the countries penetrated by international finance and other dimensions of Western culture, such penetrations had the potential of disrupting the local traditional cultures. In the aftermath of World War II, human rights became one of the major concerns of the United Nations. With the moral implications of decolonization the United Nations' efforts to improve human dimensions through international finance were inspired by affectional factors defined earlier.

Governments were to contribute, with little or no interest, to such programs as the Special United Nations Fund for Economic Development or in later years finance arrangements made by the World Bank and IMF to help developing countries. Contributions to these international programs and institutions and aids and grants provided through bilateral arrangements between governments did not have profit or interest or capital as their direct functional goal. Their goals were economic and political and each government had its own ideological rationale to contribute to it. The indirect functional goals of such programs have become more apparent in the recent role played by the IMF in bailing out developing countries with huge debts which are unable to meet deadlines on their payments.

In 1948 the UN General Assembly adopted the Universal Declaration of Human Rights which served as basis for the "International Covenant on Civil and Political

Rights" and the "International Covenant on Economic, Social, and Cultural Rights," adopted by the General Assembly in 1966. The two covenants came into force in 1976. As the title of these covenants indicates, they are aimed at securing the two different kinds of human rights discussed earlier. But the forms and the circum-stances in which they have been formulated are far different from the evolution of these rights within the Western culture. At the UN, it is the governments of different countries who proclaim principles with little or no enforcement instruments at the international level. They can, of course, enforce the principles they proclaim within their national boundaries; although this is not always the case.

For international finance an international covenant or any other principle of behaviour is only effective to the extent that it is enforced by the governments of the countries within which they operate. This applies to the home as well as the host countries. International finance seeking gain on the international market place is not in charge of enforcing human rights. If the government of the United States forbids, under penalty, the U.S. firms to deal with the Soviet Union because the Soviet Union is helping the Polish government to suppress human rights in Poland, the U.S. firms will find it difficult to disregard such law—unless they can find some international trade practice or legal loophole permitting them to go around the prohibition. Similarly, where a host country has laws on minimum wage, workers insurance or taxes for welfare and education, international finance will find itself obligated to abide by those laws—unless it can negotiate concessions from the government. The side comments in the last two sentences above are, for some, the crux of the problem.

The Church

So far, we have touched upon the international projection of the attitudes of the governments and the capital towards human rights. A look at the international projection of the other dimensions, namely, the church and labour, which we discussed in the context of the development of human rights within the Western countries, will throw light on other human rights restraints on international finance. The church has, of course, an involved relationship with international finance; too extensive to delve into within the limits of this study. Suffice to say that over the centuries, while saving the souls of non-Western people, the church in general created favorable grounds for the international movement of capital and at times served, more or less, as the conscience of international finance in cases of flagrant abuses.

Churches have played important roles in influencing international capital in the field of human rights in the last two decades. They have, in fact, taken the lead in the popular pressure on multinational corporations to respect human rights. As distinct from other popular protesters, such as civic and student groups which act on the outside and around international capital by such tactics as demonstrations, lobbies, boycotts and using the mass media, the churches have had leverage within multinational corporations and financial institutions as shareholders and investors. Together with such other institutional investors as universities, they have been able to influence corporations and financial institutions by threatening to withdraw their investments and accounts. Above all, as shareholders, churches have brought human rights issues in the corporate policy making process through proxy resolutions.

In the domain of human rights the impact of churches on international finance can be significant due to the parallelism of church structures with those of international finance, extending from within the home and host countries into an international network. Some, such as the Catholic Church, have been inherently international. When the Pope tours Central America and tells the campesinos of their human worth, international finance and the government with which it works will have to cope with the new political awareness. When the Central Committee of the World Council of Churches adopts a resolution, as it did in 1977, considering multi-cultural corporations as oppressors and exploiters, it is addressed to its nearly 300 member churches and over a billion adherents around the world.

Trade Unionism and Socialism

The internationalization of institutions, which emerged as a consequence of trade unionist and socialist ideas, has had a checkered history. In the course of its evolution the trade unionist dimension did not lend itself to an integrated international growth. It enmeshed with the government and capital within the national frontier to gain job security, social benefits and favorable wages. This, of course, happened in those Western countries where negotiation—not always without conflict—among labour, capital and government was possible. In these contexts, labour movements recognized capital as a legitimate component of the social and economic process and distinguished between their claims on capital as syndicalist action for improvement of labour conditions and their political action for influencing the government through social democratic parties.

As the symbiosis between labour and capital developed, more often than not, it pitted the national labour against foreign labour. Where cultural, economic and political conditions were not favorable for symbiotic evolution, such as Southern and Eastern Europe, and later other parts of the world, the socialist dimension inspired by Marxism turned into militant political action. These evolutions can be traced through the history of the international labour and socialist movements. The International Secretariat of National Trade Union Centers created in 1901 fell apart in 1913, precisely because of the conflict between the pragmatic social democratic unionism and revolutionary socialism. When World War I started, workers of Western industrial nations picked up arms to defend their "bread baskets" against each other.

But the end of that War was marked by the implantation of Revolutionary Communism in Russia where international and national capital was nationalized. The conditions surrounding the Russian revolution, however, did not lend themselves to putting capital at the service of entitlement programs. Eventually a state capitalism was instituted which, under Stalin, brought human rights conditions closer to the servitude end of the spectrum. The 1917 Bolshevik Revolution further crystallized the differing characteristics of trade unionism and militant socialism. The post WW1 Western inspired international trade unions, whether the International Federation of Trade Unions (IFTU) founded in 1919, or the International Trade Secretariats of various crafts and industries, remained conglomerations of national trade unions.

Among the international labour organizations, the International Confederation of Christian Trade Unions created in 1921 by Catholic workers unions was probably, in aspiration, more universal because of its religious orientation. The Comintern as an international political arm of Soviet communism was to mobilize the proletariat under the slogan of "Workingmen of the world unite." In that spirit it created in 1920 the Red International of Labour Unions (RILU) to counteract Western inspired trade unions. It is interesting to note that RILU was dismantled in 1935 to permit its national units to act more freely within their respective countries. The brief cooperation of the Soviet Union and Western democracies during WW2 saw the end of the Comintern in 1944 and IFTU in 1945. By the end of WW2, however, the Marxist socialist ideology had consolidated its home and widened its sway.

The countries of Eastern Europe that had embraced it, despite the fact that they were not practicing it, had become the official standard bearers for the emancipation of the proletariat and in that role condemned international finance as the new form of Western imperialism. Soon after the end of WW2 the trade unionist and ideological dimensions of labour reorganized in modified forms reflecting the new realities at the international level; but with little change in their intrinsic characteristics. International Confederation of Free Trade Unions (ICFTU) created in 1949 can be reasonably considered a successor to IFTU while World Confederation of Labour (WCL) was the post-WW2 de-confessionalized merger of ICCTU and some Protestant unions.

The World Federation of Trade Unions (WFTU) provides an interesting case. Despite its trade union appellation, it contained within it the two trade unionist and ideological characteristics with striking emphases. Created in 1945 under the influence of the Soviet Union, WFTU is mostly composed of workers' organizations within the Eastern European countries. The national trade unions within these countries are enmeshed with the state capitalism of their government beyond recognition. An Italian trade union delegation to Moscow—having in mind Fiat automobile corporation which has factories in the Soviet Union—inquired from the Soviet unionists whether they would take solidarity action, if asked, against a multinational corporation within which workers in a Western country were on strike.

The answer of the Soviet workers was that "... this is a political question and trade unions in the USSR are not involved in politics." Inversely, the relatively small portion of the member organizations of WFTU which are outside Eastern Europe have been the more militant unions in the West and the developing countries such as CGT in France, CGIL in Italy CUTch in Chile, or CNT in Uruguay—the latter two suppressed by military regimes.

Underdevelopment and Nationalism

The main international thrust for the ideological promotion of human rights, however, has not been the use of trade unions—precisely because of their intrinsic characteristics of symbiosis with the national government and the capital. The international setting has not lent itself to the Marxian scenarios of proletarian consciousness and revolution in the highly industrialized societies. Instead, the consciousness has been that of underdevelopment and nationalism, and in some extreme cases, that of religious fanaticism. The methods have been those of militancy, creation of national liberation fronts, guerrilla warfare, coup d'états and terrorism. And the target has been imperialism and its manifestation in the form of international finance.

If there needed to be any proof for the justification of this scenario, Allende's attempt at gaining control through democratic process in Chile and the circumstances of his overthrow provided it. The threat of national liberation fronts and other forms of disruption have become a check on international finance for consideration of human rights; but usually they are perceived too late, basically because of capital's primary intrinsic characteristic of profit making and also because where the international finance does promote human rights in the host country, it generally does it according to Western standards which often disrupt the cultural pattern of the host country and accelerate the process of social change.

Unfortunately, when the political and social unrest become serious, consideration of human rights by international finance further precipitates the process. By trying to improve the economic and social conditions, it admits pate shortcomings and points the way. And by supporting the ruling class, yet nudging it to ease the situation by granting some civic and political human rights, it creates contradictions within the established order, thus weakening its position against the militant elements. The past history of these events, from the Soviet Revolution to Nicaragua has shown that once the process begins, the compromise between international finance and militant factors is unlikely.

Past history has also shown that once the revolutionary elements have succeeded, the regime they install is not that of entitlement. They invariably call international finance back in. By suppressing and controlling civil and political rights and by standardizing economic and social human rights they create favorable and predictable conditions for international finance to follow its natural goal to seek profit which, at the same time, helps develop the economy of the authoritarian "socialist" or "state capitalist" host country. This transition process has not yet fully taken shape. In the early seventies a number of Eastern European countries and more recently China passed laws to facilitate the influx of international finance. Some efforts were made in that direction. But the economic and political upheavals since the seventies have brought that movement to a practical halt. For other more recent regimes issue of revolutions, wounds are still too fresh for accommodation.

We thus return to the realities of symbiosis between international finance and the government, and by doing so to their intrinsic characteristics. Governments are, in the last analysis, political, military and legal entities. International finance is a balance sheet. Balance sheets don't have a soul. Whether it is Romania, Honduras, South Africa or Haiti, for the international finance to move across frontiers, its forecast printouts should show that the balance sheet will be in the black. The human dimensions of international finance lie outside of it, affecting and being affected by it.

Human Rights' Impact

The shareholders invest capital in a corporation for return and banks make loans for interest. If the shareholders do not know or do not care what happens in South Africa or Haiti, the corporation calculates the price of labour—in combination with raw material, capital layout, management, energy costs, etc.—and comes to the conclusion that it is profitable to invest in those countries. If, however, the shareholders do know and do care about human rights conditions in these countries and make a point of it as shareholders, then the corporation may have to take human dimension of the operations into consideration.

As mentioned earlier, interestingly enough, the church is the dimension which provides national and international structures parallel with the international finance and is actually intertwined with it, therefore having a leverage on it for the observance of human rights. The church has the intrinsic characteristic of saving human souls. It is true that it has been known to promise only post-mortem salvation and thus appease the downtrodden without chastising the profiteers. But in the present international conjunctures the church seems to have also taken the direction of promoting earthly human rights among private as well as state (e.g. Poland) capitalists. The structure and intrinsic characteristics of the church thus single it out as one of the more likely national and international dimensions to sensitize international finance to human factors.

It must, however, be noted that the churches themselves were largely sensitized to human rights issues by "radical" movements of the sixties and the seventies which, from within the universities and student movements, were trying to mobilize the public opinion. Although the "radical" movements subsided or became more institutionalized—such as the Greens in the German Federal Republic—they helped develop the intellectual components of the public opinion concerned with international human issues. The intelligentsia/public opinion dimension runs through the social fabric beyond the structured institutions so far covered.

International trade unions, despite the national orientation of their member organizations have taken some critical stands against international finance. It is, of course, in the interest of trade unions in the developed countries to promote social and economic human rights in the less developed countries. The more the labour force in the developing countries moves towards entitlement claims the more expensive the price tag for that labour will become and the less interested international finance will become to move away from its home country labour market.

Governments do have components within their intrinsic characteristics, notably the political and the legal, which do reflect human dimensions. Elected officials and even authoritarian leaders are sensitive to the intelligentsia/ public opinion dimension mentioned above. Thus, the home country may try to become the soul of international finance by, for example, prohibiting it from moving to another country because according to its criteria the target country does not respect human rights or forbidding certain practices such as bribing officials of other countries. In terms of international realities, these policies are subjective and peculiar to the home country's policy. To the extent that they are not universal practices, they may handicap the movement of international finance. Host countries, as we have already discussed, can also establish standards for human rights. This latter phenomenon, however, can be better observed from the other perspective.

International Finance's Impact

We pointed out that the international finance is a balance sheet. On the face of it, unskilled labour at $0.10 per hour in another country compared to $3.35 in the home country is attractive. Of course, it has to be fed into a complex of other factors to determine the feasibility of its use. The labour may be in the Andean Altiplano or Central Australia and when combined with such factors as transfer of capital goods, transportation, access to market, etc., may be found not to be cost effective.

In addition to these obviously functional factors, international finance will need to look into the political and legal structure of the potential host country in terms of foreign exchange convertibility, repatriation of capital and interest and other pertinent laws. These considerations should per force lead into other questions. It is appropriate for the international finance to find out why labour is at $0.10 per hour. The variables here will be enormous. For example, we may find that labour is cheap due to an archaic feudal social pattern where a small oligarchy of families exploits the masses. It would be quite disruptive and absurd if the international finance getting into the host country took upon itself to improve the lot of the people by offering the workers the minimum wage of its home country.

It may equally be the case that in order to have access to the labour, the market or the raw material in the host country, or simply to make its capital available there, the international firm may have to make some donations to the official oligarchs and power holders of the country. Indeed, the word "bachshish" usually used to imply bribe means donation. It is true that acceptance of favors by the prince consort of the Netherlands or the prime minister of Japan to influence a deal in the context of what we know as a modern culture can be considered reprehensible. But in our own culture, for many centuries, when the King bestowed titles to his officials, they were to collect tributes for their services and even pass on some to the King. The process is feudal and still in practice in some developing countries. It is not for the international finance or its home country to impose their value system on other countries.

It is, however, a fact of social dynamics that the introduction of a foreign agent into a body will influence it. Whether it is by "donation" to the ruling class or competing with local job givers for labour, international finance will contribute to the process of change; and as a factor, will acquire a certain image. The image, in the long run, is that of superiority and aggressiveness. The nineteenth century mandarins who looked down on the Western mercenary commerce soon came to realize its potency.

The influx of international finance does not only awaken a general sense of alienation but contributes to new radii of identification. The labour in developing countries working for foreign industries, when receiving special treatment, becomes, so to speak, a separate class. It may be considered lower by traditional societies which have pride in their own identity as was the case in China earlier, or it may be considered superior in cultures which do not have respect for their own identity.

Usually there is a combination of both because some segments of the society may remain traditional while others may aspire to modernism. At the same time, those who work for foreign firms, despite the fact that they may be better treated than the rest of the indigenous population, may become more conscious about the discrepancy between themselves and the foreign personnel and resent the discrepancy. Inversely, some, recognizing the discrepancy, become loyal to their foreign employers in that context and try to imitate the culture of the latter.

These phenomena, and others, such as the collusion between the ruling class and international finance, can trigger social upheavals which will use the concepts of human rights to justify their cause and in doing so will find international finance and its home country the appropriate villains. As past events have demonstrated, this process spirals into confrontation between the discontented elements and the international finance. The government of home country—especially when it is the USA—gets involved, and the market mechanisms by which international finance was attracted into the host country get distorted.

For example, the home country will provide military and economic aid to the government of the host country to suppress the social unrest and secure the continuation of the privilege of the international finance. The beleaguered host government will suspend whatever human rights which may have existed in the country and the international finance and its home country by association become implicated in the process.

At some point the situation loses its cost effectiveness in the overall picture of the home country. Whatever its international finance may be gaining in the host country may be offset by the expense to the taxpayers of the home country to maintain the government of the host country. Unfortunately, at this point the situation is no longer evaluated in terms of sound financial considerations but gets marred by ideological and political exigencies. Where social upheavals end up in successful revolutions, international finance takes a loss during the revolution and its usual aftermath of nationalization. Further, the antagonism and resentments between the new regime and international finance handicap the resumption of the activities of the international finance in the host country for a time.

The Islamic Regime in Iran

Democracy as a system of government is proclaimed to be superior to dictatorship. Since the collapse of the system in the Soviet Union and Eastern European countries, people in all countries are converging on the ideal of democracy to improve economic performance of their country as well as to ameliorate the human and civil rights of the people. For more than a century, the people of Iran have struggled to establish a democratic system of government. The Constitutional Revolution of 1907 in Iran tried to replace absolute monarchial regime with constitutional monarchy and parliamentary democracy, but it had limited success and a dictatorial monarchy was imposed. In the early 1950s a conflict emerged between nationalists, led by Prime Minister Mossaddegh, and monarchists, led by the Shah himself.

The conflict concerned the extent of power and control exercised by the Shah and the royal family in the state's affairs and the nationalization of oil. In 1953 Mossaddegh was removed from power and arrested in an American CIA-engineered coup. Mossaddegh's overthrow occurred in part because he had nationalized British property. Iran's long border with the Soviet Union, which had an active Communist party was considered to be in great danger of falling to communism. With harsh repressive measures, the Shah was reinstalled. Soon, the Shah, through repression, established an absolute monarchy and controlled all the affairs of the country. The popular uprising against the Shah's dictatorship in the late 1970s led to the Revolution of 1979. Although there were many political organizations and groups with different ideologies and political orientations during the revolutionary process, the Islamic clerics gained hegemony and hijacked the ideals of revolution: liberty, justice and democracy; and turned the rebellion into an Islamic Revolution.

The clerics eliminated other ideologies and tendencies in the system during the early years of the revolution and imposed a more repressive Islamic government on the people and the country. The Islamic regime has resulted in great economic and human loss and suffering since the Revolution of 1979. This paper identifies and defines the political system in Iran without going through the historical analysis of how the regime established itself. From a political economy point of view, the Supreme Leader uses the scarce economic resources to repress the opposition, buy political loyalty, and maintain political power. This paper uses a political power production function model to establish the conditions under which the Islamic regime in Iran obtains power and behaviour. The paper also shows the process by which the regime can be deprived of its power and move toward establishing a democratic system of government in Iran, using property rights theory and human rights theory approaches. These theories are used to compare different political systems in terms of their capacity to allocate power as well as to promote economic growth and efficiency.

In democratic societies, power is formally delegated to governments through free elections. Governments, in turn, use this power to affect the economy by regulating industries and providing public goods. Modem property rights theory allocates capital resources in the economy and human rights theory allocates political power. Property rights theory indicates that two conditions are necessary for private bargaining to allocate resources efficiently:

appoints the heads of TV and Radio organizations, appoints joint chiefs of staff, appoints the Commander of The Revolutionary Guard, appoints the Commander of the Army and Police, and he may remove the president from office. Moreover, in the Islamic Republic, the state owns and monopolizes power over heavy industries, foreign trade, all minerals, banking, insurance, electric power, radio and TV, postal services, and railroads in the country. The private sector in Iran is crowded out and plays an insignificant role in the economy.

Friedrich and Brzezinski define totalitarianism (in effect dictatorial) as a political system with these characteristics: a coercive ideology, a country led by a single person, a terrorist police force, the monopoly of mass communications, the monopoly of armaments, and state control of the economy. The Islamic regime in Iran possesses all of the characteristics of the dictatorial regime, which has tried to dominate every sphere of life of individuals in the country. In the following sections, an attempt is made to analyze the process of producing and maintaining political power by the regime, and how the democratic opposition may use this analysis to disarm the Islamic regime of its political power and move toward establishing a democratic government in the country.

Political Power Production Function Model

As previously mentioned, the political system of governance in Iran is authoritarian and dictatorial. The regime uses loyalty and repressive instruments in its political power production function to build and maintain political power. To repress and eliminate political opposition, the regime allocates economic resources to produce and implement repressive laws, monitor the activities of individuals, and punish the offenders. Also, in order to create an environment of fear and terror, the regime's agents at times kidnap, torture, kill, assassinate and hang the suspected opposition. Furthermore, the regime buys support from individuals by creating and distributing political rents. The rent seekers subsequently become loyal supporters of the regime. The resources that are used by the regime to repress the population and create loyal supporters are wasteful expenditures that represent deadweight loss to the society.

Application of the Model

The autocratic Supreme Religious Leader as the representative of the Allah's sovereignty on the earth uses repression and loyalty instruments to maximize political power over the population. For producing and maintaining the political power over the population, the regime represses the opposition and buys political loyalty from supporters. From a political economy view point, the central and basic question is not the maximum political power obtained by the Supreme Leader, but the importance of the nature of the constraints and limiting factors in political power production. From the Supreme Leader's point of view, the most important factor is the loyalty of the population. What constrain the Supreme Leader in the maximization of power is the economic resources under his control. The regime, in order to produce and maintain political power, represses the opposition and buys political loyalty by using up economic resources. In Iran, oil and gas, other minerals, and large industries are state owned. More than 80 percent of the economy is under state control. There are also huge economic foundations that are separate and independent from the government, with monopoly power under direct control of the Supreme Leader.

Theoretically, there is a conflict between maximizing the political power of the regime with total political repression and ignoring the loyalty factor. This will become apparent as the relationship between repression and loyalty is discussed below. As mentioned, autocratic rulers use two instruments to produce and maintain political power over the population of the country. These are:

1. *Repression*: To eliminate political opposition, the Islamic regime designates the opposition's political activity as

illegal and represses it. The repression of the opposition requires allocation of economic resources in order to pass repressive laws; establish revolutionary courts, which have been in operation for the last twenty six years since the inception of the regime; build more prisons and secret detention centers; employ special police and security forces; and hire vigilante groups and thugs to attack and kill people. According to a June 2004 report of the Human Rights Watch, the center of the human rights violations is the Islamic regime judiciary, a small group of judges accountable to the Supreme Leader; this judiciary has shut down public dissent through torture, indefinite solitary confinement, and denial of basic due process rights to all political prisoners. This report indicates that "The authorities have largely succeeded in their campaign to send a message to the broader public that the costs of voicing peaceful political criticism are unbearably high". The regime's judiciary system is part of the repression apparatus rather than a part of protecting the rights of citizens. The Islamic Republic is the only regime in the world that eliminated the opposition by calling them "the corrupt on the earth and the enemy of the God" and by telling them that their elimination is a God given order. The Islamic regime is one of the most repressive in the world today as documented by human rights organizations. According to July 2004 report of the International Federation for Human Rights, the Islamic Republic of Iran is ranked 160"1 out of 166 countries in term of freedom of expression.

2. *Loyalty*: The autocratic Supreme leader, by distributing political rent and creating rent opportunity among a portion of the population, buys their loyalty and support. The regime's top officials and bureaucrats consistently focus on their political survival by always ensuring adequate political support from social groups. The dominant strategy they use is material advancement in return for support and political loyalty. Politicians

and bureaucrats have turned the institutional arrangement of the country into instruments for their own political purposes. This also explains why they oppose changes while maintaining the status quo. Consequently, this has led to widespread corruption and economic mismanagement which has resulted in high annual inflation, high unemployment, a brain drain and the decline in economic growth and per capita national income.

Political rent donors themselves are rent seekers at a higher decision-making level. According to an Economist Intelligence report in early 2002, a corruption case was exposed and Shahram Jazayeri, a 29 year old business man, confessed he had given money to as many as 60 reformist deputies. This included more than $500,000 to the brother of the Supreme leader who is a reformist deputy, and to many government officials and clerics including the Supreme leader's office and $700,000 to President Khatami. In fact, all the 500 or so mullahs with political positions in the Islamic government are stockholders in the same corporations or serve on the board of the foundations established by the regime.

The government, by owning oil, natural gas, other minerals and the major industries, as well as by controlling about 80 percent of the economy, is the biggest contractor, buyer and employer. There are several Foundations which are involved in all lines of business and trade that are not accountable to any one but the Supreme Leader. The Foundation for the Dispossessed, for example, controls assets worth $80 billion and is Iran's second biggest corporation after the National Iranian oil Company. The foundation owns factories, banks, hotels and properties in Iran and foreign countries. It has purchased interest in 80 foreign companies. About 25 percent of banking business in Dubai is owned by this foundation. The foundation never publishes its accounts and reports only to the Supreme Leader. The second largest foundation is Imam Reza Foundation. By some estimates, the foundations under the control of the Supreme Leader control about 70 percent of the national economy outside agriculture and state-owned industries. These foundations emerged after the revolution when the Islamic regime seized the assets of the Shah's family, the rich people and individuals closely associated with the monarchy.

In the early 1990s, the government launched a privatization program of some of the state-owned enterprises. Often this has meant the transfer of ownership to these foundations, to politicians and mullahs and their family members and associates who actively campaign for the regime. Senior clergies and close associates, including Supreme Leader and former president Rafsanjani, are the major stockholders of more than 100 companies. The foreign trade is a monopoly of the government, and the regime is granting trade licenses to influential people in government and their associates as political rent. Trade with much of Asia, specially Japan and China, and many of the foreign investment deals in Iranian oil and gas are under Rafsanjani's control. In September 2003, it was revealed by Dagens Naeringsliv, Norway's daily newspaper, that Stat oil, Norway's state-owned oil Company, had given 15.5 million-dollar to Rafsanjani's son for obtaining an oil contract in Iran.

The regime not only uses financial resources of the country to buy loyalty domestically, it also gives special discounts in oil exports to foreign politicians and friends to buy their support in international diplomacy. The regime, by granting economic concessions to Russia, China and European countries, is obtaining international support and legitimacy to advance its political agenda.

The Islamic regime has developed a network of loyalty in the country that is estimated to be about 2 million people. These supporters are offered low interest loans to buy houses and set up businesses, priority in obtaining business licenses, admission to the universities, and pilgrimage to Mecca and other shrines. There are about 20,000 theology students in seminaries that receive stipends from the regime. The regime very often pays the loyalists' cost of hospitalization, weddings and vacations at state-owned resorts. Moreover, the regime is buying loyalty through a network of mosques and 400 Friday prayer leaders throughout the country." Now that the price of oil in the international market has risen to about $60 per barrel, the regime has more financial resources to buy more loyalty by providing more subsidies which give way to the loyal supporters mentioned above. Consequently, we may observe a new wave of repression in the country.

Iran has emerged from the era of Western imperialism as a renter state and the Islamic regime uses the state structure, including the parliament, to adapt and implement policies that are decided by a small group of mullahs and their advisors in secrecy, without being held accountable to the people. This in turn has affected the character of social classes and their political participation. The dichotomy results in elitist Islamists above a dependent citizenry. According to the 2002, Iran Statistical Yearbook, about 56 percent of working people in 1998/1997 were employed by the government, excluding the number of people working for the Ministry of Information, Defense Ministry, Armed Forces, Police and security forces and people working in companies affiliated with these government agencies. Considering the size of these parallel security and police forces and these government agencies in the country, the private sector in Iran's economy is insignificant. The majority of the working people depends on government for their livelihood and is scared of criticizing government policies. According to the United Nations report of January 2004, "the climate of fear induced by the systematic repression of people expressing critical views against the authorized political and religious doctrine and the functioning of the institutions coupled with the severe and disproportionate sentences imposed, lead to self-censorship on the part of many journalists, intellectuals, politicians, students and the population at large, thus in effect impeding freedom of expression".

The Islamic Republic, in addition to Information Ministry agents and spies, mandate that every public or parastatal economic organization has to have a clergy on its board; thus, every ministry, government agency, or university has an Islamic committee. All trade unions are run by the Islamic workers' council in order to control the employees. These employees are silenced by the fear of losing their jobs if they criticize the ruling clergy or express any opposition toward their policy. These support and loyalty-buying activities by the regime are consuming another major part of the country's economic resources. Therefore, the regime continues its reign of power by exploiting and controlling these two determining factors and the amount of the economic resources allocated between them.

The relationship and interaction between these two factors, namely repression and loyalty as the two determining factors in political power, are complicated and interdependent. The level and extent of the repression of the opposition are influencing the loyalty level of the regime's supporters. For example, as the regime becomes more repressive, repressions become less effective, and at the same time supporters of the regime require and demand more financial rewards for their loyalty. Analyzing the nature and mechanism of the authoritarian Islamic regime from a political economy view point helps us to understand the allocation of the economic resources between the above two factors and their interrelationship in political power production. This understanding is likely to help the democratic and secular oppositions in their struggle against the regime, especially in unraveling the regime from its political power base.

The level of the political repression is affecting the political loyalty to the regime. As the regime increases the political repression of the opposition, in order to produce and maintain its political power, the additional repression will diminish its initial effectiveness. In other words and in economic terms, the marginal product of the repression will decline. Nevertheless, if there is a decline in fear from repression, the expected big repression reoccurs as the regime reestablishes its credentials. That is why, after a period of harsh repression and control, it is observed that the regime lowers its level of repression in order to make the next repressive action more effective. Nonetheless, with the increased level of repression, the level of political loyalty among the regime's supporters diminishes. This is because the regime realizes that, with increased repression, people hate the regime more, and the regime's supporters are exposed to more risk for their political affiliation and loyalty.

The level of political loyalty and repression to the Supreme Leader depends on two other variables. The first is the price of the loyalty. Political parties and groups which are loyal supporters of the regime want and demand in return participation in the political power and share in economic benefits. The supply of loyalty has a direct and positive relationship with these economic benefits or rents, which are called the price of loyalty. Increasing this price increases the supply of the loyalty. The second factor is the regime's economic performance. If Iran's economy experiences more economic growth and improved performance, the regime claims the credit which improves its legitimacy. Moreover, the improved economy means that the regime has more financial resources available to repress the opposition, which increases the regime's political power. The added repression resulting from improved economic performance increases the risk of being associated with and loyal to the regime. The supporters of the regime then, for continuation of their loyalty, want to be rewarded for this additional risk; thus they are likely to demand more financial reward from the autocratic Supreme religious leader. This helps us to understand the factional politics within the Islamic regime between the so-called reformist faction and the conservatives.

In the 1996-1997 presidential election, Khatami ran for the position. It should be noted that election in Iran is not free. There is a Guardian Council, for which its members are selected directly and indirectly by the Supreme leader. This Guardian Council decides who is qualified to run for presidency and the Parliament. Only those who have shown their dedication to the regime and belief in Supreme Leader, in Islamic terms known as Velayate faghih, and the Constitution of the Islamic Republic, may run for these positions. In the 1996/1997 election, voters supported Khatami because he was aware of the public discontent and promised reform. The Supreme Leader favored the other candidate. Nevertheless, the people supported Khatami to express their opposition to the Velayate faghih and hope for reform. Khatami's presidency created an environment of hope and optimism for reform in Islamic regime. As president, he made promises and asked people to stay with him patiently. He wanted to make people, especially the young, believe that he would change things. He never followed his promises, but the regime could draw out and identify the opposition. With this strategy and 22 million votes for Khatami and his "dialog of cultures" campaign, the regime was able to gain legitimacy, particularly with Western countries. With this gain, and the now identified opposition, a new wave of repression started.

The autocratic Supreme Leader, without this strategy, lacked the power to impose his will on the Iranian people, with huge political risk for the regime associated with both "civil" and "uncivil" warfare. After Khatami was elected, torturing and murdering political activists, students, writers and journalists continuously increased. Mr. Daryush Forouhar, the general secretary of the Iran's Mellat Party, and his wife were murdered by the Ministry of Intelligence agents in his house in Tehran. In July 2003, Zahra Kazemi the Iranian-Canadian photo journalist was murdered by the Public Prosecutor of Tehran and his associates while in detention. The regime has been also very active in extending its reign of terror beyond Iran's borders by murdering Iranian political leaders and activists in the Diaspora. By murdering Dr. Shapour Bakhtiar, the last Prime Minister of the Shah's regime, in Paris; Dr. Ghassemlou, the secretary general of the Kurdish Democratic Party of Iran and his associates, in Germany; and about fifty other political activists outside Iran, the regime has tried to create an environment of fear and terror outside the country, too.

Khatami's first term (1997-2001) coincided with the conservative faction domination of the parliament. He claimed that his inability to make changes was due to this domination and people should vote for reformist deputies. In his second term, with reformist deputies in majority, and then, executive and legislative branches in the hand of reformists, the parliament passed legislation to redistribute and shift political power within the system and increase power of the president. This act was vetoed by the Guardian Council. From a political economy viewpoint interaction between the two factions of the regime during Khatami's presidency 1997 to 2005 needs special attention. During this time period, the so-called reformist faction created and capitalized on an image of change and reform. People, hungry for real reform, supported them politically. Then, this faction used this loyalty to bargain with the conservative wing, the Supreme leader.

The discredited conservative wing needed legitimacy for the regime domestically and internationally, and the other wing now could deliver this in return for more economic and political resources. For the Parliamentary election of February 20th, 2004, the majority of the reformists who had even served as deputies were disqualified. They staged a sit-in protest, and President Khatami, with the speaker of the Parliament, engaged in a negotiation with the Supreme Leader in order to remove this disqualification, but failed. The election was conducted and conservative deputies, as it was planned, were chosen. The reformist's deputies, while protesting, never appealed to the people for support in order to resist the complete domination by the Supreme leader.

People did not support them because deputies had lost their credibility with most of the people and the deputies never requested and appealed to them.

Deputies feared that the regime might lose control of the situation with violent conflict, and consequently, both factions might lose political power. Secondly, their rent-seeking activities and kickbacks while in office had made them a target of corruption investigation by the conservative wing in control of the judiciary, if they did not remain silent. According to a Human Rights Watch 2004 report, the Islamic Republic judiciary launched a politically motivated campaign against corruption in December 2001 that netted about fifty people in parliament deputies and government. Furthermore, because the president and deputies under the current Constitution are first selected by the Guardian Council of the Supreme leader to run for their position, they have a weaker bargaining position than if they are elected independently by the electorate.

The Supreme leader dismissed the so-called reformists. He knew that reformists had lost their credibility with the people and were unable to exert effective political pressure through resistance. Thus, they could no longer deliver loyalty for the regime as before. Therefore, from the political economy view point they were excluded from participating in sharing the political power. It should be noted that Khatami and reformist deputies were not able, nor wanted, to reform the system because they had pledged their allegiance to the Islamic Republic Constitution and Supreme leader. The latter are the required credentials to get and have any position in the government. The regime, with all the hanging and flogging in Iran's city squares and stoning and amputation in public places, has tried to create an environment of fear that increases the cost of political activism, such that the disgruntled do not get involved in political activities and remains silent. The regime wants to make sure that if they can not absorb the disgruntled as loyal supporters, they should become inactive and not engage in politics.

The regime knows that these people have the potential and may sympathize with and join the activist groups. The conservative faction and so-called reformist's faction are two sides of the same coin, or two faces of the Islamic government. The reformists' disagreement with the conservatives is over the harsh repressive acts in public, which they believe are damaging the Islamic Republic's international image. They also bargain for greater portions of economic resources, which are under the control of the conservative faction. Other than that, they believe in Islamic governance, the Supreme Leader, and the Constitution of the Islamic Republic, which guarantees the supremacy of the religious leader and his absolute power. The reform of the existing system and gradual transition to democracy are impossible with the current Constitution, which guarantees the Supreme religious leader absolute authority and veto power. The reform, gradual reassignment of policy-making power, and emergence of democracy are a possibility with a bipolar system of government in which power is gradually transferred from autocratic leader to a broadly freely elected representative government.

This is similar to the transition in many European countries from the king dominated system to the parliamentary system of governance. It should be noted that in the current crisis in Iraq, the Islamic regime is trying to create and take advantage of turmoil in the country to engage in a diplomatic dialog and exchange with the European countries and the United States. The goal is to warm up its relations and increase the regime's legitimacy. If the regime were able to achieve this goal, another wave of repression is anticipated for the reestablishment of the autocratic Supreme Leader credential. Moreover, it is important that Western countries and the US, in their foreign policy formulations toward Islamic regime should not compromise on human rights violations; they should ask for observation and respect for human rights issues.

Today in Iran, majority of the people do not believe in Islamic ideology and Supreme Leader with divine right, but rather, struggling for ideals of popular sovereignty and universal suffrage. Iranian people are the only people in the region with strong conviction for separation of religion and state with a democratically elected government. Western countries should help this movement with their political and moral support. A democratic system of government in Iran will greatly impact democratic movements in the region.

Western Countries' toward the Islamic Regime

The Islamic Republic of Iran was the first government established with the Islamic ideology in the region in 1979, and since then Islamic extremism and terrorism have increased. These are threats to the security and well being of the people and the country's economy. As it is observed in Iran and Afghanistan under Taliban, the Islamic Government is the most repressive regime, and it has tried to expand its influence in other Moslem countries, especially supporting the Islamic extremist groups in regional conflicts. The Islamic regime in Iran is using these extremist groups to gain and improve its negotiating power and legitimacy among western countries. Therefore, policies of the democratic governments, the United Nations, and international human rights organizations toward the Islamic regime are very important. The Iranian opposition groups and parties with democratic platforms should try to obtain the moral and political support of western democracies and international organizations to unravel the Islamic regime's hold on power.

With regard to democratic governments, especially western countries, it is assumed that the promotion and development of freedom, liberty, human rights, and democracy are their foreign policy objectives, rather than their economic interests which should be less significant and secondary. It is known that this assumption may not hold in some of the major western countries in which economic interests dominate their foreign policy objectives. Nevertheless, their values and major goals are the support and defense of liberty and human rights. Thus, the role of the Iranians in the Diaspora should be to lobby western governments and politicians to pressure the Islamic regime to respect human rights and liberty of individuals in the country.

Nonetheless, the fundamental questions for the democratic Western governments are should the democratic countries expand their economic ties with the Islamic and dictatorial regime in Iran? Or are they going to impose economic restrictions to limit the regime's ambitions? Should not the democratic countries of Europe, Canada, and the United States in their diplomatic and economic relations demand from the Islamic regime the respect and observation of human rights? Answers to the above questions should help in finding out which policies curb terrorism and repression and improve human rights conditions in Iran. The improvement of human rights conditions in Iran, supplemented with the moral and political support of the democratic opposition of the Western democratic governments, can unravel the Islamic regime's hold on power. An empirical study of 150 countries showed that ensuring human rights, civil liberties and freedom of press significantly reduces the chance of a dictatorial regime's survival.

In regard to the democratic countries' trade policy toward the Islamic regime, the following factors should be considered: First, the expansion of the economic relations of the democratic countries with the Islamic regime will improve Iran's economic growth and performance. With the improved economic performance, the regime will claim more credibility and legitimacy, and consequently, will increase the level of loyalty to the regime. The improved loyalty may result in more repression of the opposition and democratic forces, and more political power for the regime. Therefore, any expansion of trade relations with Iran, such as the case of the United States lifting trade sanctions, must obligate the Islamic regime to honor and observe the human rights conditions. This is the least that can be expected of the democratic countries. If they can not ignore their economic interests, they can use diplomatic pressures to force the regime to respect human rights of the Iranian people.

Second, some people may argue that expansion of western countries' economic ties with the Islamic government will improve economic conditions in the country. Once segments of the population accumulate wealth, they are likely to demand more freedom, thereby diminishing their loyalty to the regime. With regard to this point in Iran, with more than eighty percent of the economy owned by the government and Foundations under the control of the Supreme Leader, and most of the private sector owned by the clergy and their relatives and associates, those who benefit would likely want to preserve and maintain the regime which has endowed and provided them with the opportunity to accumulate such wealth. These wealthy individuals have their wealth both inside and outside of the country; thus, the argument in favour of the trade expansion with Iran does not hold. Third, expansion of foreign trade will increase the regime's revenue from tariffs. Also, trade may increase Iran's national income and tax revenue.

With the increased national income, the regime can claim credit for this improvement and loyalty to the regime is expected to increase. As a result, the Supreme Leader, being the guardian of the regime, has more economic resources in his disposal to maintain his hold on power by spending on repression and loyalty. The result is always increased political power and extension of the regime's political life. For example, in recent years, with the increase in oil prices, the regime has become more repressive. Therefore, the link between economic growth and political liberties and democratization in authoritarian states is weak. Economic growth, rather than being a force for democratic change in authoritarian states, can be used to strengthen tyrannical regimes.

The political implications of the above three factors are undoubtedly related to the increase or decrease of loyalty to the regime. Therefore, if the foreign trade tends to increase the level of loyalty among the regime's supporters, which in turn increases the level of repression against the group of the people called outsiders, such as students, writers, journalists and political activists, the trade contracts should be made contingent upon respect for human rights to prevent repression. Trade with the dictatorial Islamic regime can be expected to produce beneficial effects if it is accompanied by human rights constraints. The World Bank and International Monetary Fund should also consider these factors in dealing with the repressive regimes such as the Islamic Republic. It should be emphasized that all dictatorial regimes that have collapsed have done so due to the decline in economic resources and revenues available to them. For example, the Soviet Union collapsed partly because of its engagement in the arms race and its decline in economic performance. In China, with 9.4 percent average annual GDP growth, the highest growth rate in the world in the last 25 years, the level of repression has not declined.

The diplomatic crisis in the relationship between the United States and the Islamic Republic after the revolution was created by Khomeini who was facing the growing opposition to the Clerical Rule. By invading the United States Embassy and taking Americans hostage for 444 days, the regime diverted attention. He subsequently increased political executions, imprisonment, torture, and widespread repression in order to strengthen the regime's hold on power. This international crisis was followed by the Iran-Iraq war, which was continued for eight years. During this war, Khomeini said that the war had been a God given gift for the regime! The regime used the war to eliminate any opposition, improve its hold on power, and augment the regime's political power. When the regime ended the war in 1988, up to 30,000 political prisoners had been massacred in a period of three months during the summer of that year. During the earlier years, the regime used the international crisis to repress and eliminate the opposition, because it had legitimacy domestically due to revolutionary fervor.

These days the regime tries to improve its international relations and legitimacy, especially with the Western European countries and the United States. This is because the regime has lost its credibility and legitimacy with the people. If the regime succeeds in improving its international legitimacy, it is likely to see another wave of massive repression. If the aim of Western governments is to promote freedom and democracy and fight the international terrorism, it is critical that these governments stay on the side of the Iranian people in their aspiration for liberty and democracy, as well as to support their rights in determining their future political system. The public in non-Arab Iran has a better impression of the United States than in all other countries in the Middle East and is more ready for democratic change. It is important to note that a democratic and secular system of government in Iran has great political implications and repercussions for the Middle East and the rest of the world, especially Western democracies, given inter-national terrorism, which the Islamic regime in Iran sponsors.

The key to unraveling the autocratic religious leader's hold to power is to attack the instruments that are used to maintain that hold on the population, namely repression and loyalty support. With the political pressure of Western democracies on the Islamic regime and their support of the Iranian people in their pursuit of liberty, people become less fearful of the regime and can organize themselves through mass civil disobedience to remove this regime from power and establish a secular and democratic system of government.

7

Political and Social Economy Approach The Standard Concept of Human Rights

Human rights as they are usually and loosely conceived are the rights that one has because one is human. Before accepting this simple definition a series of questions must be asked. For example, what does it mean to have a right? How are being human and having rights related? Are there alternatives to the simple and usually minimalist definitions of human rights as the rights that one has because one is human? How are women's rights related to human rights? The social capabilities approach to women's right which we develop here emphasizes the positive freedom to achieve aspects of the right bearer and in this sense provides a social foundation for women's rights. However, first we discuss the universal human rights model which can also be justified from the social capabilities point of view.

The Universal Declaration Model

In recognition of the central role of the 'Universal Declaration of Human Rights' in establishing the contemporary consensus on internationally recognized human rights one can justify calling it the universal human rights model (UHRM for short). However, it is not thereby implied that the model is complete. In fact, extensions to women's rights are an example of a good use of the universalizing tendencies in the UHRM. As is well known, the Universal Declaration of Human Rights was adopted by the United Nations General Assembly on December 10, 1948, by a vote of 48-0 (with eight abstentions). Since then it has been endorsed, regularly and repeatedly, by virtually all states. This phenomenon accounts for the wide acceptance of the idea that "for the purposes of international action, "human rights" means roughly "what is in the Universal Declaration of Human Rights."

The purpose of presenting the list below from UHRM here really is to examine the implications for women's rights of the Universal Human Rights Model. This will be done not just for the sake of understanding the connection between UHRM and women's status though this is one of the goals of this paper. More important, however, is the goal of learning something about the specific policies of the state apparatus in light of its human rights obligations and commitments. It may be recalled that the approach to human rights in this book is based on the social capabilities theory which follows immediately after this section. Therefore the Universal Human Rights Model presented below is to be interpreted in that light.

The utilitarian tradition in economics, as Sen correctly reminds us is based on three distinct components. One of these is consequentialism. All choices of actions, rules, institutions etc. must be judged by the consequences of the particular choice made. In this sense, consequentialism is merely results oriented. It does, however, rule out purely or exclusively rights- based or deontological decision rules. A second constituting element of utilitarianism is what Sen has termed 'welfarism'. According to Sen welfarism 'restricts the judgments of state of affairs to the utilities in the respective states' Combining welfarism with consequentialism, one can derive the proposition that '...every choice must be judged by the respective utilities it generates.'

Finally, the third element, namely, sum-ranking of utilities imposes an aggregation scheme whereby utilities of different people can simply be summed together without bothering about their distribution over the entire population. This neatly sidesteps who gets what; but it is clearly the greatest good under the three conditions when utility is the only good to consider. Notice that Robbins attacked the classical utilitarian idea of interpersonal comparability and by implication sum-ranking of utilities in the 1930s. But the alternative, radically subjective view of personal utility also sidesteps the issue of distribution. No two Pareto optimal states are, strictly speaking, comparable. In general equilibrium theory the second theorem of welfare economics merely states that under a suitable redistribution of initial endow-ments, every Pareto optimal state can be achieved as a competitive equilibrium. However, there is no bias towards— or, for that matter, against— an egalitarian distribution.

What Sen's more radical critique of utilitarianism and his replacement of utility with capabilities have done is to change the paradigmatic terms of discourse. It is no longer necessary to debate the various meanings of utility and what the distribution of utilities should be. The talk about utilities has been replaced by talk about positive, concrete freedoms, as the Sen-Nussbaum list of capabilities above demonstrates. With this radical shift of the terrain of discourse, however, there is also a set of new questions that arises. What are the social, political and economic conditions under which capabilities are best promoted for all the people in an equalizing direction? Both the levels and distribution of capabilities are important. Perhaps responding in an indirect way to earlier criticisms Sen has outlined the 'perspective of freedom' more definitely. Freedom is important both for *evaluative* and for *effectiveness* reasons.

Evaluation of societies by the actual amount of substantive freedoms enjoyed by people is radically different from using utility, procedural liberty, real income etc.

Effectiveness reason rests on Sen's claim that freedom enhances the 'agency' of the individual leading to greater individual initiative and social effective social participation. Thus freedom can be viewed as both the primary end and the principal means for development. Sen also gives a five fold classification of instrumental freedoms as consisting of political freedoms, economic facilities, social opportunities, transparency guarantees and protective security. In the rest of this section we argue that a perspective of global 'deep democracy' consistent with Sen's characterization of freedom leads us to a consistent critique of the existing political and socioeconomic arrangements globally.

Following the enlightenment project as formulated by Kant, and the critique of Kantian understanding by Hegel, and finally, the 'this-sided' worldly critique of Hegel by Feuerbach and the dialectical critique of Feuerbach's one sided materialism by Marx takes us to a questioning of the existing institutions when these fail to promote and equalize social capabilities. The theory of 'deep democracy' captures many of these concerns. Building on both the contributions of classical thinkers from at least Rousseau onwards, but also on modern theories of participatory and strong democracy advanced by scholars such as Barber deep democracy advances the thesis of equalization of capabilities as a central concern of global economic justice. Most important from this perspective is the work by scholars such as Alan Gilbert on radical democracy that is internationalist and welcomes mass activism.

Extending the important earlier work of Gilbert, Khan in a number of essays and books establishes the claim of equalizing social capabilities along with global justice as central elements of a sufficiently rich conception of democracy which respects the rights of citizens underlying the core concept of democracy. Conceiving rights following Sen as 'goal rights' is one way to defend the centrality of capabilities. Another way is to view these rights— most importantly, the right to self-determination— as self-sustaining if and only if movement towards equalization of capabilities can be sustained globally.

Extending Gilbert's cluster conditions for democracy10 Khan (1992, 1998) establishes that three clusters are of particular significance. The political cluster begins with formal democratic principles of universal suffrage and elections, but does not stop there. Although this 'formal democracy' must be defended vigorously, it is seen as one aspect of a deeper form of democracy that various polities are moving towards. In order to gain insight into this deeper form, we need to ask what conditions can gain freedom which is the core idea underlying democracy. The answer is that as soon as freedom is conceived positively and not just as mere absence of coercions, capabilities come to the fore.

However, probing deeply into the project of enhancing and equalizing the capabilities of citizens even in rough, practical sense economic and cultural conditions come to be seen as crucial. For example, education, including critical ethical and political education is recognized as of utmost importance. In so far as democratic movements for a just society have been schools for political education— say, starting with at least the political movements from 17th century onwards including major movements in the 20th century and the new social movements of this century— these are not just disruptive moments, but are complex struggles where much political learning about freedom takes place. Thus deep democracy will necessarily involve a continuous engagement with the past, present and future of the democratic movements in a pluralistic context. Periodic individual and mass non-violent civil disobedience movements will of necessity be part of a deep democratic agenda.

Economically, the provision of leisure time for both personal private interest and the exercise of citizenship responsibilities will be necessary. Work place democracy is also a salient condition, since production is socially necessary and will occupy a certain amount of time for all able bodied and mentally competent adults. The capabilities literature has not always been clear on this point. However, it is logical to think that a person's capabilities will suffer deprivation if working conditions do not allow discussion, participation and 'ownership' of work conditions. The literature on flat organizations in knowledge economy generally makes a case for the newer 'intellectual' labour to be treated in this way; but the social capabilities approach leads to the conclusion that all work in organizations large and small should be treated this way so that work place alienation can be overcome without necessarily using labour saving capital-intensive technologies. Overcoming alienation also requires a vibrant culture where artistic and other forms of individual and collective expressive activities are as open as possible.

Capabilities in this dimension are vital for the protection of democratic values and practices, since these also involve internalization of mutual respect, integrity, tolerance and creativity. It can also be seen that using the advances in cognitive, social psychology and some schools of psychoanalysis capabilities can be further advanced through a therapeutic approach to social problems. A 'post-modern' insight is also the need to recognize the limits to certain types of economic growth. As Daly and others have pointed out the scale of production counts in a globalised, interdependent planet in a significant way. Ecological issues will often require a just global democratic procedure for deliberation and policymaking. In short all of the cluster conditions—political, economic and cultural— require a theory of global justice as an underpinning and justification. Khan (1998) has proposed such a theory in the context of a post-modern world by building on elements of Rawls and Sen.

In brief outline the structural forces in the global economy push towards integrating markets and regions. However, many markets are embedded in national economies; there are also non-market aspects of social and cultural lives of people that are threatened. As a result we find the contradictory phenomena of McWorld and Jihad. The creation of a genuine global society, which many see as the ultimate outcome of globalization then necessitates meeting the requirements of global justice.

Khan (1998) mentions at least 5 areas, where the norms of global justice must evolve (among others):

1. *International trade and monetary regimes*: The current asymmetric system of payments which penalizes the deficit countries by forcing only them to bear the costs of adjustment needs to be made a global burden sharing institution. The World Trade Organization, similarly, needs to acknowledge the historical imbalances in the world trading system. For example, specialization according to static comparative advantage may lock the developing countries in a relatively backward situation in the emerging global division of labour.
2. *International capital flows*: From the perspective of many people in the developed economies capital flight to LDC's (with or without free trade agreements) may constitute a barrier to well-being, at least in the shortrun. At the same time foreign direct investment in LDCs may create only low wage, marginal jobs. A just approach to FDI must consider the effects on both the north and south in terms of self-determination. A controlled capital flow accompanied by improvements of wages and working conditions in the south may be the most desirable solution.
3. *International ecological consideration:* Global interdependence has been increasingly recognized in this area. However, it is not clear what justice demands in terms of the relationship between the north and south. Other things being equal, the enforcement of strict environmental standards would seem to be just. However, such standards may destroy the livelihood of some people in the south, it is sometimes argued. A

global tax and transfer scheme would seem to be the precondition for applying a global set of environmental standards. The transfer of ecologically sound technology systems from rich to the poor countries is a precondition for justice in this sp here.

4. *Asset redistribution and human development*: Much of the foregoing discussion pinpoints the need for giving people the economic wherewithal in order for them to develop their social capabilities. Most studies have discovered that non-redistribution of assets to the poor hampers poverty alleviation strategies. Redistributing assets and developing their human capital so that the poor can have access to markets becomes a major necessity in our normative framework. In most parts of the world this will require structural reforms rather than marginal policy interventions.
5. *Gender justice*: The impact of globalization on women will have to be assessed carefully. The well-documented facts regarding gender inequalities that so far have affected women's capabilities negatively demand unequivocally that policymakers pay careful attention to enhancing (or at least not decreasing) women's capabilities. Will the globalization help women to overcome social limitations ranging from lack of nutrition to limits on participation in social, economic and political life? Unfortunately, the answer is unclear. In so far as many developing country women do not possess skills for the global market place, globalization is already hurting them.

These five examples are meant to be illustrative only. By no means do they exhaust all the pertinent issues in moving towards a just economy globally. (For example, we could add or highlight the growing rural/urban disparities with globalization and its implications for justice). But they do illustrate both the problems and prospects for justice in the age of globalization. One of the major political problems we have not discussed so far is the weakening of national sovereignty that the call for global economic justice entails.

Agreeing to a global mode of production and distribution constrained by the principles of justice does mean surrendering considerable authority to international agreements, conventions, and ultimately, perhaps to new international organizations. It should be observed, however, that even without the constraining role of justice the globalization process weakens national sovereignty, even for advanced industrialized countries. Thus, the call for a just economy must confront this (as well as other issues such as weakening of traditional cultural modes of living) head on in the light of reasonable principles.

The fundamental message is that among these principles that of freedom as rational autonomy of the individual must be the principal one. This is one rational (perhaps the only one) approach if we are to avoid both the Scylla of Jihad and the Charybdis of McWorld. The McWorld aspect of globalization is a result of a fractured but real economic, financial and technological integration. Following the collapse of the Bretton Woods Agreement in the early 1970s, the financial market (including interest rates and exchange rates) was deregulated, thereby enhancing the flow of capital between nations. Until then the world financial system was governed by the Bretton Woods agreement of 1945 which provided for fixed exchange rate where currency values were expressed in terms of dollars and gold. When the system was abolished in 1971 by the Nixon administration and replaced by a floating exchange rate, the grounds for a global market were laid.

This was reinforced by the resurgence of a neo-liberal free-market ideology of liberalization, privatization and deregulation that became the "only game in town" following the ascendance of political conservatives — Reagan in the U.S., and Thatcher in Great Britain. It was further reinforced by the collapse of the former socialist countries and the emergence of the neo-liberal thinking as a dominant and unchallenged school of thought. All these factors created a conducive environment for the free movement of goods including capital goods, and services as well as finance, thereby seemingly creating an integrated global economy. However, an alternative set of policies that can address the problems of slow growth and external payments while promoting the equalization and enhancement of social capabilities is also possible.

However, the links between "social" capabilities and process aspects of women's right. Sen points out correctly that while his version of capabilities approach is superior to others —e.g., the Rawlsian primary goods framework— in terms of opportunities and positive freedom aspects; it is weak at the same time with regards to the procedural aspects of freedom and justice. Indeed, Rawls's 'first principle' of justice centers on the priority of liberty. The first part of his 'second principle' involves procedural fairness. In particular, it demands that 'positions and offices be open to all'.

If we take Rawls seriously, the process aspect of liberty must be emphasized properly in any foundational theory of human rights that claims to have some degree of comprehensiveness. Here the attraction of the "Social" and political interpretation of capabilities is that to some extent the social rules that respect this emphasis on process can be included. A full articulation of this position is beyond the scope of this paper. The intuition behind this claim, however, is that a Hegelian approach that explicitly recognizes the importance of social and political institutions in defining freedom and social individuality can go some distance in incorporating the process aspect within the ethical community.

The Political Economy of India

Economic processes are everywhere political in that in order to operate they require political conditions, both at local level and from the state. These processes are also political in that their in egalitarian and exploitative character leads to political struggles over the ways that the economic processes work and over their distributive outcomes. Similarly, the political conditions require, and are influenced by, economic conditions. For example, economic processes influence the extent to which the state can be involved in re-distributive e projects and the conditions under which the lower classes can struggle for better living standards.

Issues in India's Political Economy

The edited collection by Sathyamurthy analyses the agricultural, industrial and technological policies of the Indian state. The overall outcome of these policies has been a development process which is skewed in favour of certain regions and classes at the expense of other regions and classes. In the process, contradictions of a vertical nature (for example, between dominant and dominated classes, upper-middle castes and lower castes) have come to coexist with horizontal (for example, intra-ruling class) contradictions. In sum, the Indian political process has been characterized by two significant trends. These are a growing regionalization of the polity and the emergence of new social groups as significant actors on the political scene. One of these actors is the 'classes of farmers. Their political action and their relation to the state are the thrust of Varshney's work.

He argues that a democratic system introduced before an industrial revolution has led to a rise in farmers' political power. All political parties, including the left parties, support their demands for higher farm prices and subsidies. Farmers have therefore succeeded in preventing the worst-case scenario from taking place, this being the fall in producer prices that normally accompanies an accumulating grain surplus. But the best-case scenario, that is, continual increases in farm returns irrespective of the rhythms of technical change, remains unrealised. That is because rural power is subject to serious constraints. On the one hand, the farmers' organisation, which aimed at putting pressure on the state for more resources, is impeded by crosscutting cleavages within the farming community (for example, caste, ethnicity and religion). On the other hand, millions of poor Indians cannot afford costly food.

Besides, there is also a limit to the extent to which the state can subsidise the rural sector, which is very large compared to that in more developed countries. State subsidy is especially a problem because farmers are only one group among many competing for the state's resources. Dre'ze and Sen points to a different type of state failure in India, namely, its failure to remove poverty, illiteracy, disease and inequality of opportunity. Nevertheless, they argue that the state, or more generally public action, can contribute to a people-centred economic development aimed at the expansion of human capabilities. They suggest that economic development requires the mutually supportive interaction of public action, including state policies, and market stimulation. The pro-market (or neo-liberal) reform policy of the Indian state is the theme of Kurien's book.

Since the introduction of these reforms in 1991, the Indian economy has been increasingly connected to global capitalism. Kurien discusses the nature and the implication of that connection. Reforms have been sponsored by a tiny minority to promote its specific interests, although neo-liberalism has been promoted politically as being in the national interest. India's balance of payment situation has improved, but its debt situation has worsened. Industrial exports have not significantly increased. This is partly because of quota restrictions imposed by western countries, and because exports have remained concentrated in traditional areas such as textiles. Finally, the way that neo-liberal reforms have impacted on the poor is the theme of the Rao and Linnemann collection. It draws our attention to the significant rise in absolute poverty in villages in the immediate post-reform period, reversing the earlier trend of a decline in poverty. The claim is that the reduction in public investment and social expenditures as part of neo-liberal policy has contributed to poverty.

Class Character of the Indian Society

The class character of either Indian society as a whole or only the countryside is considered in almost all the works.

But their approach to the issue varies. For Varshney, India is a predominantly peasant land. He uses the terms 'peasantry' and 'farmers' interchangeably because both peasants and farmers produce for the market. First, work suffers from an under-conceptualization of class relations. His discussion of rural India and, in particular, his characterization of India as a peasant land, which is consistent with the view of the Rudolphs, completely ignores the celebrated mode of production debate that looked at the class character of India's agriculture. Indeed, he rarely refers to the vast literature on the radical political economy of agrarian India that deals with the capitalist nature of Indian agriculture.

This neglect is partly a reflection of his overall theory of India's social change as industrial–technological change, rather than a change in class relations effected by the socially and spatially uneven development of capitalism. Second, to the extent that he does discuss class, his discussion has three flaws which will itemise briefly. Partly, it is that his view of class is sectoral. He talks about class relations as if industrial classes do not exist. In the other works under review, there is a good discussion of India's class map in several chapters of the Sathyamurthy collection and also in Kurien. During the last four decades, says Sathyamurthy, the Indian capitalist class has vastly expanded. In addition to the national industrial large bourgeoisie, the capitalist class also includes the agricultural bourgeoisie, the provincial industrial bourgeoisie and the non-resident Indians.

The non-capitalist class includes the poor peasantry, the landless, agricultural workers, the urban petty bourgeoisie and the industrial working class, including its semi-skilled and unskilled segments and the casual and contractual labourers. However, the regionally important feudal, semi-feudal and the feudally exploited people (for example, bonded labourers) are not discussed. Given that feudal elements tend to impede the exercise of bourgeois state power, this is an important omission. Several writers stress the significance of the political actions of classes. Thus classes are seen as both classes in and for themselves. This is to the good. The political action of farmers, in particular, has received considerable attention.

According to Basu in the Rao and Linnemann collection, is one of the most expensive in the world. This is not because wages are high but because of high indirect costs of labour (for example, strikes). Clearly, Basu wants a quiescent labour, waiting to receive adequate wages by virtue of the sweet will of employers. This is, of course, somewhat different from Dre'ze and Sen's general acceptance of the role of public action, which, significantly, includes working class organi-sation, in economic development, although they do say that too much adversarial public action can hurt economic growth, as in Kerala. Turning now to farmers' political action, for Varshney the claim that the new farmer agitations are class-driven is weak. Rather than having a narrow class base in the surplus-producing rich peasantry, the new farmers' movement has the support of all sections of the landed peasantry.

For example, there is widespread support by small farmers for higher prices for cash crops as well as for food crops and lower input prices. Marginal farmers (that is, the food de. cit farmers) can also be expected to support higher prices for cash crops and lower input prices, but they do not unless strong political reasons (for example, organization as a check on the bureaucratic abuse of input delivery) and visible employment effects are simultaneously present. Labourers tend not to support these agitations, but, where they do, it could be mainly due to their dependence upon the rich farmers for wages and loans. Capitalist farmers are trying to build a hegemonic project which includes some concessions to non-hegemonic fractions of the landed (for example, poor peasantry) and perhaps even labourers (the view that 'higher prices will increase wages', which he himself refers to).

A movement does not have to be exclusively about the interests of the capitalist farmers to be (called) a capitalist farmers' movement. Indeed, and in contrast to Varshney's stance, Patnaik and Hasan in Sathyamurthy say that the farmers' movements represent the interests of the new rural capitalist producers clearly and consistently. They explicitly argue that those poor peasants and labourers who are substantial net purchasers of food grains are the classes who stand to lose from farmers' agitations and are therefore entirely outside their support base. Varshney, however, asserts that marginal farmers can support the price agitations on non-economic grounds. But he never problematises the so-called non-economic benefits of new agrarianism, such as making the bureaucracy more accountable. Its bureaucratic character is an inherent aspect of the capitalist state, partly, at least, aimed at keeping the masses away from state institutions. It is true that the state is an arena of struggle, which means that it can be made more democratic, within limits, through political action. But lack of recognition of the obstacles to making this possible can lead to politicism, that is, the explanation of things solely in terms of political variables and especially in abstraction from economic processes.

On the other hand, Patnaik and Hasan never even entertain such a possibility and thus smack of mild economism (the opposite of politicism). For his part, Varshney suggests that, while the normative order of patron-client relationships has been gradually disintegrating, class conflict has not always replaced it. Labourers are increasingly conscious about their rights, induced by continuing social deprivations and indignities. But this increasing political awareness has not generally been translated into organised collective action. This is because, unlike the landlords or rich farmers, those who mobilise labourers are unable to provide credit, insurance or employment. Further, over time, even the organisers, including the communist parties, have been trying to mobilise on multi-class lines, not concentrating exclusively on labourers' interests.

On the other hand, there is relatively little in the Marxist works, for example, the Sathyamurthy collection and

Kurien, on the topic. To generalise, while Varshney tries to combine structural and agency-oriented analyses (although his view of structure and agency is far removed from class approaches to these matters), the Marxist works are more structuralist and unfortunately pay only lip service to agency. However, Varshney's analysis of class politics, like his analysis of class relations as discussed above, has several problems. First, he says that both mainstream parties/movements, as well as the communist parties, organise on a multiclass basis. But he does not ask why the leadership of these multiclass organisations is usually in the hands of capitalist farmers or rich peasants. Can there not be a multiclass mobilisation led by labourers and poor peasants, who constitute 70 per cent of the rural population?

To the extent that the communist organisations are based on the support of multiple classes, including both exploiting and exploited classes, what is the contribution of state repression to this form of organisation? Second, Varshney says that there are obstacles to labourers' organisation and that farmers' power is also self-limiting. But, if both farmers and labourers are constrained in their political organisation, why then do the state policies benefit farmers, the rich farmers especially, while there is little attempt at (for example) implementing minimum wage legislation? More specifically, if farmers have a surplus commodity, the state ensures its sale at a profitable price, but, if labourers have a surplus of the only commodity they have (that is, labour power), why does not the state guarantee its sale and at an adequate price? What does this differential treatment of farmers and labourers say about the nature of the Indian state? Varshney (and others) seem to suggest that what farmers and labourers get depends on their political organisation, but they neglect the prior issue of the structural source of the power of these classes: their class power and relation to the state.

The Nature of the Indian State and its Interventions

Several types of state interventions have been discussed in the works under review. These include policies aimed at processes of socioeconomic change such as land reforms, poverty alleviation, the Green Revolution, industrial development and economic liberalisation. The discussion of the policies aimed at these changes is important in its own right, but it also sheds light on the ways the authors look at the nature of the Indian state and will focus on this aspect. In particular, I want to discuss the class character of the state and the determinants of the state's actions and their effectiveness.

Class Character of the State

The class character of the state points to the classes that are the primary beneficiaries of state actions (or in-actions). Chaudhuri says in the Sathyamurthy collection that 'Indian planning was meant to benefit the industrial capitalists and the rich farmers'. This is a premise that is indicative of the class character of the state and which is supported by Byres, among others. Exercise of power over the state is facilitated by, although it does not necessarily require, the instrumental control by the dominant classes over the state apparatus. Instrumental control occurs both in terms of these classes actually occupying positions within the state apparatus and also in terms of their capacity to influence ideologically the actions of state actors. There is considerable discussion of instrumental control in the works under review.

In India, the state apparatus, says Bandyopadhyay in Sathyamurthy, is controlled by the propertied classes. For example, as Varshney rightly observes, the local level state apparatuses (e.g. the local police and village-level bureaucracy) are dominated by upper caste landowners and share their biases. This fact, he says, was responsible for the failure of the attempt to nationalise the grain trade and also to promote land reforms. However, Varshney's discussion of the nature of the state is inadequate on several grounds. In the main, his sectoral view of the class character of society, referred to earlier, leads to his sectoral view of the class character of the state. He suggests that only some parts of the state, such as local level apparatus and the CACP, the agency that recommends farm prices, are influenced by the landed class or their politicians, but these institutions are less powerful than institutions such as the finance and defence ministries.

The state in Delhi therefore might not have been a preserve of landlord power, but Varshney does not say which dominant class has the primary influence over the finance, defence and other ministries. He is also often quite uncritical of state actors and institutions. This is evident in his treatment of (for example) Nehru and the Planning Commission. But readers get quite a different view from Sathyamurthy's contribution to his own collection. One learns, for example, that 'Nehru entrusted all the economics portfolios to non-Congress "experts" who would have won the enthusiastic approval and unqualified trust of a latter-day World Bank or International Monetary Fund! From 1957 onwards, the Prime Minister appointed [Congress] "experts" to these ministries.... These largely consisted of men who were themselves industrialists or traders, or who enjoyed the confidence of the Indian national bourgeoisie.'

The post-Nehru period was no different. 'In all the central ministries that have been in power since 1977, economic portfolios have been held by ministers openly committed to free market, capitalist, pro-liberalization , and denationalization policies.' The Planning Commission has the same story. 'With the partial exception of Mahalanobis and Gadgil none of the executive heads of the Planning Commission ... had a vision of India's economic development that could be deemed to be a genuine alternative to that projected by the successive ministers of the central government in charge of economic portfolios.' Not surprisingly, the policies of the Indian state have been basically in favour of the propertied classes, especially the capitalist class, as seen in its current neo-liberal policy. Baru in Sathyamurthy says that the post-independence industrial policy sought to create the basis for an independent capitalist economy in India (even though, in practice, it was forced to yield considerable space to foreign capital).

The state has also promoted capitalism in rural areas in several ways. Consider land reforms. The thrust of these reforms was the attempt to push and cajole frontiers to turn themselves into capitalists. Land reform measures simply created a suitable institutional framework for the growth of capitalist production, which in the last resort required the stimulus of profitability. This was provided in several ways. First, with the state-promoted Green Revolution, richer landowners could reap a profit of 50 per cent or more, which was more attractive than merely renting out land and usury business.

Second, the implementation of a strategy of planned investment and other expenditures by the Indian state on a large scale from the mid 1950s onwards created an expanding domestic market for necessities, particularly food grains. This, in turn, substantially raised the profitability of food grain production. The ratio of prices of food grains relative to manufactured goods rose (an issue Varshney also documents well). The problem with Varshney is that his exchange view of class and his sectoral view of the state ignore the land reforms' (limited) success in creating conditions for the emergence of a class which would pressure the state for (the continuation of) a favourable price policy, the issue on which he focuses.

Determinants of State Actions and their Performance

A general question is: why does the Indian state do what it does? The works under review give different answers to this. Dre'ze and Sen, for example, say that what the government does can be influenced by public pressures. But much depends on what issues are politicized and what is, or is not, politicised depends on the visions and pre-occupations of opposition parties. This is, in my view, very politicist for (non-communist) opposition parties do not oppose ruling parties on crucial issues such as payment of compensation to landlords in the land reform laws. In other words, on class-related issues that do matter to the lower classes, opposition parties do not matter. This happens, in part at least, because both ruling and opposition parties work within the framework of a state that supports the fundamental interests of the propertied classes and share an anti-lower class ideology which, in turn, contributes to the de-politicisation of the crucial issues. Dre'ze and Sen ignore the fact that the ideology of the propertied classes and the coercive character of the state, among other things, influence what enters into political debates and what does not. Varshney's explanation of Indian state interventions is marred by statism, another form of politicism.

He assigns the state more causal power than it can possibly possess. The state, he says, introduced a price- and technology-oriented strategy (the Green Revolution) in the 1960s when the countryside was actually less powerful in the polity than it has been in the period since then. He notes that this 'change in agricultural policy in the mid-1960s had been primarily a state initiative', which indicates that Varshney has an under-conceptualised view of the class character of the Indian state. His approach is sectoral in that he ignores the national class context of the state. He does not consider the fact that there is an imperative on the state to reproduce class relations in the country (not just countryside). The capitalist state has generally to create conditions for capitalist accumulation and for the reproduction of capitalist property relations. Here cheap food is crucial. One major reason for the pro-farmer policy is to help richer farmers produce food cheaply, since this is important for industriali-sation, private capitalist profits and industrial peace. Indeed, the surplus production from the developed regions of north India has been used by government in purchasing urban peace.

If cheap food is not provided, urban discontent and unrest on a mass scale may be confidently anticipated as Patnaik and Hasan point out happened in the early 1970s. Thus what is, for Varshney, an autonomous state action to a large extent emanates from the overall capitalist context of the state. No matter how autonomous it appears to be, 'the state power does not hover in mid-air', as Marx correctly recognised. The state, in short, must be seen in its class context. There is much discussion too of causes of failure in the implementation of state policies. Varshney, for example, provides two explanations of the failure of the land reforms policy: factional struggle at the top levels of the Congress party and the absence of political mobilisation of the intended beneficiaries. Local governments (*panchayats*) were supposed to help in the political mobilisation of the poor. Instead, the local 'notables' captured them. How this happened is explained by the imperatives of 'party building in a new nation'. The lower wings of the Congress party—the district and *taluka* (sub-district) levels—came under the control of landlords and substantial landowners. These groups saw the advantages of entering the party in power. For me, this is again statism.

More specifically, Varshney tries to explain the failure of state actions entirely in terms of the failure of state structure (local level of apparatus; political parties). Varshney's modernization theory of Indian politics fails to ask: is party building a class-neutral project? Is not party building in a class society such as India's largely about creating the political institutional framework within which the masses can be controlled so that in egalitarian property relations can be safely reproduced? Varshney' politicist /statist discourse is a part of a more 'general statist paradigm' in (India's) political economy literature to which Bagchi (again in Sathyamurthy) draws attention.

This paradigm is the widespread assumption that the Indian state is an autonomous active agent which impinges on a passive society, galvanizing it into appropriate responses as desired by the planners and policy makers. In sum, Varshney, like Dre'ze and Sen (and most authors in the Rao collection as well), does not look at the necessary class character of the state, especially the fact that large landowners are a part of the class base of the state. They all ignore the fact that the state seeks to ensure that property relations are not attacked. In contrast to Varshney's approach, there is a class approach to the failure of state policies. Bagchi argues that the failure of such policies as land reform and cheap loans for poor farmers is generally seen by planners and others as merely a defect of implementation.

It is not seen as the integral, constitutional birthmark of a society in which landlords, usurious moneylenders, privileged bureaucrats and policemen thriving on criminality remain in control of change. Varshney, as well as Dre'ze and Sen, all share this premise which Bagchi criticizes. Commentaries on land reforms by these authors fail to observe that 'policies towards land reform were never part of any Plan strategy, in spite of the pages devoted to it'. Indeed, as the constitution stood, land reform was not a sphere of activity for the central government, although, according to Chaudhuri, it is dif. cult to believe that a government that took the matter seriously could not have made a better show of progress.

Indeed, he complains, the Five Year Plans never provided for an alternative set of policies that would be contingent upon a failure to implement land reforms. Consider too in the same light the state's unsuccessful attempt to promote balanced industrial development. This also shows the importance of the class context of state actions. The state has intervened more effectively in favour of industrialization where the regional capitalist class has been strong (as in the north-west, western and southern parts of the country) and where it has traditionally played a more important political role along with the rich peasantry. Aversely, support given to industrialization has been less in areas (such as the eastern states) with a weak indigenous capitalist class.

Democratic State-form in India

Dre'ze and Sen, Stuijvenberg (in Rao and Linnemann) and Varshney, among others, all characterise the state and the political system as democratic. Varshney discusses the ways in which India's democracy facilitates what he calls 'democratic peasant mobilization' against state policies. He argues that, if the state can repress farmers without any electoral or political sanctions, rural mobilization can be easily stilled at its birth. However, a democratic system places serious constraints on the state's repressive capacity *vis-a'-vis* farmers, particularly as they themselves are well represented in the upper tiers of the polity. Additionally, opposition parties have a vested interest in embarrassing the government and a free press puts further constraints on the government. Very similar points were made by Dre'ze and Sen. Readers will also know that Sen is a long time admirer of India's democracy.

A government that has to face criticism from opposition parties and free newspapers, and that has to seek re-election, cannot afford to neglect such problems as famines, Dre'ze and Sen note. Similarly, Stuijvenberg asserts that mature democratic institutions and the freedom of press (along with numerous eminent economists) are safeguards against too reckless an implementation of neo-liberal economic reform. It is only in the Sathyamurthy collection that one (occasionally) hears about 'the authoritarian practices of a quasi-democratic state apparatus' and their implications, such as the fact that women are among the worse victims of predatory capital and the repressive state apparatus. In short, in the conventional literature the democratic character of the state-form is not problematised and, in particular, the class character of its particular democratic form is not treated critically. Varshney says that, in a democratic system, it is unlikely that 'drastic measures', such as repression, could be taken against protesting farmers.

But how did the state repress the famous Telengana peasant resistance? How does the state repress the day-to-day struggles of the masses for better living conditions? He ignores the fact that the power of farmers is mainly due to their control over property. Their power does not stem from democracy, although they may have received some concessions from the state through mobilisations that are facilitated by democracy. In my view, democracy in India has been mainly reduced to the resolution of conflicts, through elections and otherwise, between dominant classes/class-factions and their electoral representatives.

Indian society and the Indian state are more undemocratic than democratic from the standpoint of the under-privileged majority. Go to urban neighbourhood s and rural areas and you will see that lawlessness is ubiquitous; laws are up for sale and/or in musclemen's pockets nearly every-where. If democracy could empower people irrespective of their class background, one must wonder why the majority of Indians are below or very close to the line of absolute poverty.

Poverty and Development

Dre'ze and Sen argue that poverty lies not merely in the impoverished state in which the person actually lives, but also in the lack of real opportunity to choose other types of living. Poverty is thus, ultimately, a matter of 'capability deprivation'. The 'expansion of human capability such as ability to read, live a long life and so on can be, broadly, seen as the central feature of the process of development' can also seen as a gendered concept. Economic progress on its own does not necessarily reduce the gender gap significantly. Indeed, India has an exceptionally low female–male ratio. Adult men have disproportionately benefitted from improvements in living conditions and medical care. The fact that professional attendance at birth remains so rare in several Indian states, while modern medical treatment is very often used to cure diseases that are not specific to women, is a good illustration of this point.

As Dre'ze and Sen again rightly argue, the emancipation of women is an integral part of social progress, not just a 'women's issue'. Nor is, in their view, the growth rate of GNP to be regarded as the ultimate test of developmental success, although at the same time one must not reject the importance of economic growth itself. There has to be growth for it to be participatory or redistributive. In sum, Dreze and Sen offer a people-centred concept of development which may be appropriate for India and other less developed countries, given their multiple aspects of deprivations, including income deprivation.

While poverty and economic development have been appropriately conceptualized in Dre'ze and Sen, the causes of poverty and the causes of slow economic growth in India have been discussed in the other books as well. Varshney notes that agriculture may not have contributed a significant amount of savings to the industrial sector, which may partly explain India's slow industrial growth rate until the late 1970s. More important, though, it seems, have been the actions/inactions of the state. As Dre'ze and Sen argue, the state has neglected primary education. This is important because inequality in basic education translates into inefficiency, as well as further inequality, in the use of new economic opportunities.

This distributive failure supplements the effect of educational backwardness in restricting the overall scale of expansion of skill-related modern production. The Indian state has also presided over a decline in public investment. There are many reasons for this. First, the allocation of resources by the state has led to a proliferation of subsidies and grants to placate different competing groups. This reduces the surplus available for public capital formation, an issue Bardhan has also pointed to. Second, the state has been unable to raise adequate resources from the affluent. The decline of investment for all these reasons, in turn, has led to disincentives for private investment, given the existence of a direct relationship between public investment and private corporate investment. However, for Dre'ze and Sen, the cage that most effectively keeps the Indian economy tamed is that of bureaucracy and governmental over activity.

Bureaucratic control, says Basu, emanates from the particular nature of India's democracy. This is based on a system of overlapping rights: every one has the right to decide on every matter in contrast to a system of partitioned rights where everyone has a domain over which he or she has the full right to decide. Indian-type democracy thus allows many to exercise veto power and presents individuals from effective decision making because they need clearance from others at every stage. This system impairs flexibility and stifles economic development. In my view, this latter argument is but a softer version of the neo-liberal explanation of state failure to promote development, which is 'based on … the assumption that an all-powerful state has been the root of all economic evil and the progenitor and promoter of all unproductive ("rent-seeking") activities'.

According to Sathyamurthy, this presupposition ignores the numerous devices at the disposal of dominant elements in the ruling classes (including the bureaucratic apparatus of the state itself) to manipulate the state apparatus. A final point in relation to economic growth which emerges for the books under review is the skewed distribution of demand. The fact of unequal distribution of land and assets in agriculture has meant that demand originating from within agriculture for domestically produced industrial goods only grows slowly. The limited demand base for these goods is evident from the fact that the poorest 50 per cent in rural and urban areas account for only about 20 per cent of industrial consumption.

Let me now turn to the suggested causes of poverty. The state is again seen to be central, with neo-liberal policy contributing in several ways. In order to limit the quantum of food subsidy at existing levels so as to contain the fiscal deficit, issue prices of food grains have been revised upwards consequent upon the upward revision of minimum support prices fixed by the government. Of course, the higher price of food adversely affects the poor who are net buyers of food. There has also been a further compression of demand following reduction in government spending and restrictions on the import of raw materials and capital goods. This slows down the general rate of growth which means slow employment growth.

The poor are especially dependent on public expenditure for employment and so cuts in public expenditure have hurt them. In general too, high inflation, caused partly by devaluation and the rising revenue deficit which are parts of the neo-liberal reform package, has eroded the real incomes of the poor. Indeed, the vocabulary of poverty alleviation is absent from the rhetoric of liberalisation. But even historically according to Chandhuri, it seems 'unlikely that government policy has from the beginning been consciously designed to benefit large sections of the rural population'. 'No influential person in government has suggested that the anti-poverty programmes should be given priority in the same way as power generation.'

Programmes that directly benefit the poorest communities in India tend to have been sacrificed at the altar of growth. Dreze and Sen and Gupta point out that growth is necessary for poverty and that growth does trickle down. But Gupta notes that percolation to the poor from growth only becomes effective when growth accelerates to at least 7–8 per cent per annum. To the extent that growth is slow for the reasons just discussed, it contributes to poverty. Until growth reaches the level identified, positive poverty alleviation policies are needed. Yet these policies also have had only limited success, in part because they have largely been administered 'from above' without any proper assessment of needs and resources at the local level and partly because of leakages (major benefits from these programmes have gone to the non-poor).

Several writers in the Sathyamurthy volume suggest that the state has promoted capitalism (for example Baru, Patnaik and Hasan). But, as Kurien rightly suggests, the vast majority of the people have very little resource power to take advantage of the 'prosperity' that capitalism has brought about; they can, at best, be passive participants in it and they frequently and that the only commodity they have for sale—their labour power—is not saleable. As is usually the case, the benefits of growth have accrued to those who control land and capital at the expense of the poor.

Finally, the lack of pressure from the masses is considered to be a cause of poverty. Dre'ze and Sen comment that 'successive governments in India have had reason enough to rely on the unending patience of the neglected and deprived millions in India, who have not risen in fury' about their socioeconomic problems. In a similar vein, Varshney says that the rural poor are not organized enough to pressure the government to allocate more resources to rural development. This last argument does seem rather to smack of a 'blame-the-poor 'approach since little consideration is given to the way absolute poverty itself can impede organisation.

Political Economy of India's Special Economic Zones

Every country stands for its own development. For this purpose the state introduces and implements new policies and programmes such as Special Economic Zones Act. After 60 years of its independence India with its 110 core population has evolved a new paradigm of its political economy which is confusing. The policies and programmes initiated by Indian government to create a 'global village' based on free market economy and free trade among nations cutting across all barriers, abolition of national boundaries and dismantling the nation –state system giving priority to 'market' over the 'state'. After the enactment of Special Economic Zone Act 2005, it created tremendous effects on political economy of the country.

The term 'political economy' came from the two Greek words 'Politiko' and 'Oikonomia, where 'Politiko' stands for the state and society and 'Oikonomia'means managing the household economy. Political economy thus means a study of the state, society and household economy. The concept of political economy arose historically as the economic doctrine of a new class – the capitalist class. It has been evolved since the days of Aristotle who gave a model of public good through guaranteeing each person private possession of what he was rationally and morally entitled. Private property was elaborated later by Locke, Adam Smith, Ricardo and the physiocrates, who came to be known as the *Laissez fairists* in Economics, or, the liberal democrats in politics. Adam Smith referred to political economy as a branch of the system of civil government. It was concerned with public policy.

In Marxian view, political economy can be regarded as a subject which studies the social relations evolves between different classes of people in course of production, distri-bution, exchange and consumption. Political economy belongs to the broad land of economics, which opens on to political science. After a prolonged period of hibernation, the subject has again been resurrected. Marxist political economy makes a study of how the productive forces are used under the given relations of production taking account of the lines and trends in technical progress; political economy studies the influence of production relations on such progress and its socio economic consequences. Marxist political economy starts from the assumption that human vital activity is objectively based on social material production which includes man's interactions with the nature and whole range of relations which arise in the process.

It has been realized that every political action has its obvious economic repercussion, and every economic action has had its political implications. The liberal school of political economy offers economic implications of political facts and factors. The liberal school has economized politics. The liberal system focuses on the atomistic individual as the relevant unit, on the description of economic behaviour in terms of subject choices among alternatives, on the notion of social welfare as the maximizations of individual utility sums. The socialist system views the entire economic system as the basic unit, views economic progress in terms of the growth of the forces of production and focuses on 'relations of production' 'surplus value' and the rapid increase of social product.

By contrast the Gandhian system eschews both the notions of the atomistic autonomous individual maximizing his utility in a self regulating economy and the notion of processes of production autonomously effecting changes in the organization of production ,class relationship and the magnitude and distribution of social product instead of the Gandhian model suggest that the fundamental attribute of human economic behaviour lies in the relationship of individual to socioeconomic micro groups and the relationship of micro groups to society .The basic economic act is neither the choice between economic alternatives nor the social division of natural products, but the adjustment between individual and the micro groups to which they belong, and of those micro groups to society .It is this collaboration which is the basic theme of the Gandhian system of political economy.

The Gandhian system is viewed in micro groups that are fundamental constituents of the economic system and given full scope to develop their potential in the context of no coercive forms of political control. Social welfare is defined in terms of the functioning of the collaborative micro groups *vis –a-vis* its members. Gandhi believed that the introduction of technology and patterns of development must be consistent with the full employment objective. Today economist speaks of sustainable development and ecological values. Gandhi was not against industry but as he predicted it could not give people more employment. His constructive programmes were to give employment to all people whether it be *khadi, gobar* gas or tree plantations, where all can be engaged in constructive work.

Gandhian economics is an alternative to overcome the exploitation of both capitalism and communism for the exponents of human social order. He was against the large scale use of machinery which kept millions without work. Swadeshi is one of the core elements in the socio-economic organisation of Gandhian system.

Gandhi Observes

"Life here will not be a pyramid with the apex sustained by the bottom, but it will be an oceanic circle whose centre will be the individual, always ready to perish for the village, the latter ready to perish for the circle of the villages, till at last the whole becomes one life composed of individual, never aggressive in their arrogance, but ever humble sharing the majesty of the oceanic circle of which they are integral units'. The idea of the circle stands for integrating, fullness and self-sufficiency. He wrote that independence must begin at the bottom. Thus every village will be a republic or *Panchayat* having full powers. It follows therefore, that every village has to be self sustained and capable of managing its affairs even to the extent of defending itself against the whole world."

Politics and economy are considered as two basic factors in determining the nature of the state and society. They are interrelated to such an extent that the changes in one affect the other, and hence both are 'dynamic' and 'flexible' ingredients of the national and the international systems. Politics and economy taken together as political economy refers to 'managing the economy of the state' and conceptually political economy connotes the relationship between the state, society and the economy, the cause–effect relationship between technological change and the process of development, the economic relations among the different nations of the world.

Definition of Special Economic Zone

A special economic zone is a geographical region that has economic; laws more liberal than a countries typical economic laws. According to the SEZ Act 2005, A SEZ is a 'specially delineated duty free enclave and shall be deemed to be foreign territory for the purpose of trade operations and duties and tariffs. A SEZ also been viewed as "a geographical region with different economic laws than a countries typical economic laws with the main goal of attracting foreign investment'. "A SEZ or a Free Trade Zone (FTZ) is typically an enclave of units operating in a well – defined area within the geographical boundary of a country where certain economic activities are promoted by a set of policy measures that are generally not applicable to the rest of the country".

The concept of special economic zones is not new. In an International Labour Organization (ILO) report traces the roots of the concept to 13th centaury Spain and in more recent times to Ireland and Puerto Rico, which established Export Processing Zones (EPZ). Export Processing Zones is the former name of the Special Economic Zones. The countries like China, United Arab Emirates, Malaysia, India, Jordan, Philippines and Russia have utilized the concept of SEZ. In 1986, there were 176 zones across 47 countries. Now the number has increased to over 5000 across 147 countries. The zones are known by different names in different parts of the world. Most often these are Free Trade Zones (FTZ), Industrial Free Zones (IFS) Export Processing Zones (EPZ) Bonded Free Zones and Special Economic Zones (SEZ).

Export Processing Zone is the ancestor of SEZ. An Export Processing Zone is relatively small geographically spread area within a country. The purpose of which is to attract export oriented industries, by offering them especially favorable investment and trade conditions as compared with the reminder of the host country. The EPZ is just an industrial enclave but SEZ is an integrated township with fully developed infrastructure. The UN Industrial Development Organization (UNID) identifies five basic attributes of EPZ s are:

- EPZs are dominated by market mechanisms.
- EPZ are restricted to a limited region.

- EPZs specialize in the production of exports goods and offer special incentives for such production.
- Their major aims are to attract foreign investments, earn foreign exchange and to generate employment.
- Secondary aims are technology transfer, development linkages and regional development.

Policies taken by the governments for the development of the nation obviously affect the people. SEZ policies are for the development of the country. These Developmental projects have economic, political and social impact. In Gandhian political economy, village level development is needed. Land needed for the establishment of the SEZs projects also affected the political economy of the country. Tax incentives, Foreign Direct Investment, New type of employment generation also affect the political economy of the country. The macro economic changes driven by SEZs will push the countries down the path of increasing socio-political crisis. Every country stands for its own development. For this purpose the state introduces and implements new policies and programmes such as Special Economic Zones Act.

India became independent in 1947 and chose self-sufficiency along with economic autonomy. The Industrial Policy Resolution of 1948 marked the beginning of the evolution of the Indian Industrial policy. The Resolution not only defined the broad contours of the policy. But it delineated the role authority of the state in industrial development both as an entrepreneur and as an authority. The industrial policy Resolution of 1956 gave the public sector a strategic role in the economy. It categorized industries, which would be the exclusive responsibility of the state or would progressively come under state control and others. Earmarking the pre-eminent position of the public sector, it envisaged private sector coexisting with the state and thus attempted to give the policy framework flexibility.

India opted for a planned economy with emphasis on state sponsored industrialization. The argument was that capital being scare in India, it was essential to regulate the flow of the available capital in to socially desirable channels. This was achieved by an elaborate system of industrial licensing and state monopoly and control over key industries. More than 80% of the Indian population is still living in agricultural field. Agri-centered model of development was prevalent during the 1950sand the 60s. Agriculture contributes approximately one-fifth of total gross domestic product (GDP). It provides the means of livelihood to about two-thirds of the country's population. The Sector provides employment to 59 percent of the countries workforce and is the single largest private sector occupation. Agriculture accounts for about 10 percent of the total export earnings and provides raw material to a large number of industries.

During the Jawaharlal Nehru's period, foreign collaborations were promoted in certain sectors and foreign investment was encouraged. First Export Processing Zone (EPZ) was set up in 1965 at Kandla, in Gujarat. This was a predecessor of the Special Economic Zone in India. The Santa Cruz EPZ in Mumbai became operational in 1973. After the death of Jawaharlal Nehru, Indira Gandhi became the prime Minister of India in 1966. She also did a lot for the economic development of the country. The Foreign Investment Board was set up in 1968. In 1973, Foreign Exchange Regulation Act (FERA) was enacted.. India set up the Santa Cruz Electronics Export Processing Zone (SEEPZ) between1973-74. It was the first EPZ which was dedicated to the electronic industry.

Doors of the Indian economy were opened during the 1980s, by Indira Gandhi and later by Rajiv Gandhi. From 1984 to 1989, the policy was to enable the middle class to consume more so as to raise the internal demand. This resulted in the raise of imports and the growth of Foreign Direct Investment. The government tried to raise the level of exports in order to balance this phenomenon. In 1984, the Free Zone policy received a fresh start. By 1991, the Indian economy was opened up for linking up the Indian market with the world leading to free flow of trade and commerce. The multilateral Financial Institutions like the World Bank and the International Monetary Fund while assisting the developing countries like India also insisted upon restructuring the polity and the administrative machinery.

Following a change in the policy regime in this period and the formation of the World Trade Organization (WTO) with India becoming its founder member, it opted for a liberalized capitalist strategy. There had been introducing policies since July 1991 particularly in the industrial sector. De-reservation of industries for the public sector was one of the major step taken by the government as part of the policy changes in the industrial sector. It was against the earlier 17 industries were reserved, there are now industries like defense production, atomic energy, coal and lignite, railways and mineral oils reserved for the public sector. Core industries like iron and steel, electricity, air transport, shipbuilding, and heavy machinery industries such as heavy electrical plants telecommunication cables and instruments are now open to private sector participation. Besides, equities held by the government in selected public sector enterprises like ONGC etc are now available to mutual funds, financial institutions, the general public and workers through a policy of divestment. In1998, the first private SEZ started its operations in Surat.

This was under the jurisdiction of the Mumbai (SEEPZ) Development Commissioner, who was a nominee of the central Government. From the beginning of the 21st century, most of the developing countries in the world have recognized the importance of facilitating international trade for the sustained growth of the economy and increased contribution to the GDP of the nation. As part of its continuing commitment to liberalisation, the Government of India has also adopted a multi-pronged approach to promote foreign investment in India. The Government of India has pushed ahead with second-generation reforms and has made several policy changes to achieve this objective. The annual growth rate ranged between six and nine percent. Bharatiya Janatha Party (BJP) government decided to re-launch the Free Trade Zone Policy in 2000. It changed the name of Export Processing Zone (EPZ) to Special Economic Zone (SEZ). The policy intended to make SEZs an engine for economic growth supported by quality infrastructure complemented by an attractive fiscal package both at the Centre and the State level with the minimum possible regulations.

The salient features of the SEZ scheme are:

- No licenses required for import.
- Manufacturing or service activities allowed.
- SEZ units to be positive net foreign exchange earner within three years.
- Domestic sales subject to full customs duty and import policy in force.
- Full freedom for sub contracting.
- No routine examination by customs authorities of export/ import cargo.

The United Progressive Alliance (UPA) government currently in power enacted Special Economic Zone Act, 2005 which was passed in June 2005 and came into force on 10th February 2006 with the notification of the SEZ Rule in 2006. The Act provides for drastic simplification of rules and single window clearance on matters relating to the union and state governments .The state governments have also been enacted their own SEZ laws to cover State subjects. The Act provides for single window clearance mechanisms for developers and operators for ensuring orderly development of SEZs, the responsibility is assigned to the Board of Approval, constituted by the union Government. The Union Government may set up a SEZ on its own or on the basis of proposals of the state government or private developers after the Board of Approval has duly screened them.

At the regional level, the Development Commissioner and his /her office will exercise administrative control of SEZs.

The Labour Commissioner's power is also delegated to the Development Commissioner. There is an approval committee to approve /reject /modify proposals for setting up units in SEZs. All suits of civil nature and notified offences in SEZs will be tried and settled by specially notified courts and affected parties may appeal to high courts against the orders of the designated courts. The corporate units operating under SEZs will enjoy special privileges and protection granted by law. The Act offers a special fiscal package to the units set up in the SEZs.

This package includes, exemption from customs duties, central excise duties, service tax, central sales taxes, and securities transaction tax to both the developer and the units set-up, tax holiday for 15 years like 100 percent tax exemption for five years, 50 percent for next five years, and 50 percent for the ploughed back export profits for the next five years.100percent income tax exemption for 10 years in a block of 15 years for SEZ developers. There is a three-tier administrative structure. On the top, a Board of Approval at the level of the Union Government has been set up for the functioning of the SEZs. Next an authority has been created by the state governments for creation and promotion of the infrastructure within each state.

Finally, in SEZ mechanism /authority is provided for single window approval. According to the 2005 Act, these zones can be set up by the developers, who could be private real persons, companies, both Indian and foreign, as also the State governments or the central government by themselves or jointly with private parties. It is also being envisaged that some of the existing Export Processing Zones would be converted into Special Economic Zones. The SEZ Act, 2005 supported by SEZ Rules, has come in to effect on 10th February 2006.

Three Categories of SEZ

In India SEZs are divided into three categories, Multi-product SEZs Sector specific SEZs, Free Trade and Ware housing Zone (FTWZ). The first category signifies a SEZ where units may be set up for manufacture/rendering of services of two or more goods in a sector or good/services falling in two or more sectors. For multi-product service SEZ, a contiguous area of 100 hectares or more is required. The second category defined as a zone meant exclusively for one or more product/services. The minimum area requirement is 100 hectors of contiguous and vacant land. Within sector specific SEZs, Bio-technology, Gems and Jewellery, Non conventional energy, electronics, hardware and software SEZ-including IT can be set up with minimum area has been relaxed to 50 hectares for Assam, Meghalaya, Nagaland and, Arunachalpradesh, Uttarakhand, Sikkim, J&K, Goa and the Union Territories.

Free trade and warehousing zone (FTWZ) is the third category which minimum area requirement is 40 hectares of contiguous and vacant land. Built up area should not be less than 10 hectares. There are 19 functional SEZs in the country which were set up prior to SEZ Act, and 154 SEZs that were notified under SEZ Act 2005. The maximum numbers of SEZs are coming up in the IT sector. The total land requirement for the formal approvals granted till date is approximately 44,268 hectares. Out of this, about 87 approvals are for State Industrial Development Corporations (SIDCs) State Government ventures which account for over 21,169 hectares.

Issues Relating SEZs in India

One of the main issue is related with SEZ is locating land for SEZs. Many state governments are in the process of establishing SEZs. The issue of displacement, that of compensation or land price, rehabilitation, residential property development and land speculation, the threat of possible relocation of units from other parts of the state to SEZs and the consequent loss of revenue have been flagged . Farmers are protesting against the forced acquisition of their lands. The development of SEZs would lead to the destruction of employment of peasants whose land will be acquired and will create very little employment for high tech or high skilled persons and total net employment generated may well be negative.

Handing over thousands of hectares of land cheaply to promoters of industry and relaxing the laws of the land, including those that relate to the welfare of the industrial workers, protection of the environment, taxation, etc, would automatically promote industrialization and solve the nagging unemployment problem of the country overnight. The farmers/peasants in various states such as West Bengal, Orissa, Maharastra, and Punjab have opposed acquisition of their land for SEZs. The highest level of opposition has been observed in West Bengal when land was acquired by the state government for the Tata group at Singur and Salim group of Indonesia at Nandigram. Besides the loss of agriculture land, concerns have also been raised about the project affected People.

Using water for SEZs is one of the major problems rising from different parts of the country. Mundra SEZ as per official website of the SEZ, it expects to get at least 6 million liters per day from the Sardar Sarovar project, as promised by Gujarat water infrastructure Ltd. Another main issue is rising from different parts of the country, the labour laws applicable to the rest of the country have been relaxed for the SEZs. The existing laws are well intentioned and they promote worker welfare. Relaxing such laws exclusively for the SEZs shows the government's lack of conviction in its own commitment to social justice.

In some SEZs, the state governments are joint venture partners. In the case of some, special incentives by way of concessional electricity and water tariffs have been offered. In almost all the cases, valuable lands have been given away at concessional prices. Considering the SEZ Act, it violates the letter and spirit of the Indian Constitution; it infringes the Fundamental Rights of the citizen guaranteed in part

3rd of the Constitution. Relaxation /inapplicability of many labour Laws (including under the Industrial Dispute Act, Contract Labour Act, Factories Act, Minimum wages Act, Trade Union Act), Environment (Protection) Act is inapplicable to SEZs and no environmental clearance needed to violates Panchayat Raj Act (1996) for local self government, violating laws granting rights and control to adivasi communities over their land, violating many international conventions on human rights. To sum up, SEZs and other emerging developmental issues can be seen in a broad perspective and theoretical underpinnings of neo-liberalism.

As far as Indian polity is considered the implications emerging from SEZs may cause increasing socio-political crisis because the society is far more complex than we assumed and that will result in organized or unorganized resistance and that may even cause anti-neo liberal political forces. So, in order to avoid the polarization of the society, civil society should engage to create a consensus on developmental issues. More over, in order to understand the continuities and changes that are taking place in the developmental scenario it needs further study.

Political Economy and Social Movements

In the context of the recent declaration of emergency, a suspension of the constitution and the assumption of all executive powers by the monarch, attention have once again focused on the Maoist insurgency in Nepal. Most analysts, particularly foreign, have tended to treat the Maoists as terrorists, insufficiently appreciating the social conditions which have given rise to a range of social movements from below. The situation has become more complex since multiparty democracy, theoretically expected to provide space for legitimate ventilation of grievances and increase participation in governance, is seen by the more marginalized strata as a failure. Now with even this avenue blocked, we are likely to experience an escalation in extra-parliamentary protest. This brief note explores links between the political economy of the Nepali state and the growth of radical social movements for transformation.

The basic economic foundation of Nepalese society is agriculture; more than 81% of the labour force is engaged in agriculture and close to 90% of Nepalese people live in rural areas. The dominance of agriculture also appears in the accumulation process, though the productive forces in Nepalese agriculture are backward and primitive. It is still the case that nearly 99% of the total investment in Nepalese agriculture is made in land, human and animal labour and primitive equipment and only 1% in modern means of production. Nepalese agrarian production relations are complex. Alongside pre-feudal societies such as Chepang, Raute and Kusunda there are sophisticated capitalist farmers who farm for the market and employ agricultural wage labour, albeit in small numbers.

Despite major political changes since the overthrow of the Ranas, the basic structure of the rural political economy, of western Nepal (at least), remains surprisingly unchanged in terms of the continuing survival of what might be termed a 'middle peasantry' - exposing a significant proportion of rural people to acute livelihood and rights vulnerabilities. Equally, Nepalese political economy remains under- developed and slow moving (stagnant), constrained both from within by archaic and repressive sociopolitical structures and from outside by its particular relationship with India through which global forces are mediated. It is unlikely that economic growth in itself will be sufficient to significantly reduce vulnerabilities, though the abolition of *Birta* system in 1959 and subsequent introduction of the Land Reform Act 1964 reduced big landholding, some large absentee landowners still covertly hold large areas of land.

These landowners are likely to be senior government officials, members of the Rana nobility and other representatives of upper castes whose land claims date back to the past. This is more prominent in the terai and less in the hill and mountain regions. Around 8% of Nepalese are totally landless and of those who have land, 65% are poor peasants owning only 10% of land. In the terai, big landlords, owning more than 10 hectares each, control more than half the land. This data suggests that the main impulse behind social movements in rural Nepal is lack of ownership of land and secure land titles by a significant, but not overwhelming, group of rural people. It is these groups who are the focus of the various social movements. But they are not a majority, which makes mobilisation a special challenge, despite the fact that overall control over land is concentrated in the hands of a small minority. Nepalese agrarian production relations can be broadly classified as peasant, semi-feudal and capitalist forms of production.

Since the vast majorities are peasants who own means of production such as land, farm animals and farm implements, peasant forms of production relation are central to understanding class relations and the political economy of Nepal. They are primarily 'owner-cultivators', tenant and tenant-cum-owner cultivators who own small pieces of land, produce for their own consumption and depend largely on family or exchange labour, *parma* , within their own communities. However, in some cases they employ occasional and permanent labourers such as *haliya, kamaiyas* and *haruwas*. They maintain patron-client relationships with various occupational castes such as blacksmiths, tailors and sometimes shoemakers. The totally landless poor, whose number is small in rural Nepal, largely depend on wage labour, though tenancy and share cropping may also figure in their livelihoods.

Semi-feudal relations still play a significant role in the underdevelopment of Nepalese agriculture and economy of the country and nearly two-thirds of those who are wholly tenants till the land on a sharecropping basis, with the rest operating on fixed rent, either cash or kind and other tenurial arrangements. Most tenants are forced to till larger landowners' land and the surplus is not accumulated and reinvested as capitalist profit. They work for bare subsistence family needs. Further, the vulnerable people who gain access to some land can still be tied to landowners through usury and bonded labour conditions. Capitalist production relations in Nepal are based on the appropriation of surplus labour employed as causal and wage labour. However, the number of people involved in capitalist production relations producing primarily for the markets is very small. The Golchha, Dugar, Chaudhary and Jyoti groups and some members of the royal family are a few examples of employers engaged in such relations. They manage big commercial farms and tea estates, grow off-season vegetables and run cut-flower businesses exclusively for the market, employing once, now displaced, occupational castes that are unable to earn their livelihood in their traditional occupations.

In the terai, they also employ a large number of migrant Indian labourers who enter Nepal in the hope of illegally settling down. In Nepal, the upper level leadership of all the political parties, including the Communists, is dominated for the most part by the landed class. This landed gentry not only controls politics and bureaucracy but also industries such as hotels, tourism, carpets, garments and trade. Though some surplus from agriculture is invested in trade and industry by the ruling elites, they have not been able to establish themselves as an independent national bourgeoisie. They are far more involved in the expansion of international capitalism through the promotion of foreign industrial capital. In other words, they serve not the interest of Nepalese people and nation, but the transnational corporate regime as traders, businessmen, industrialists and commission agents. In brief, Nepalese merchant capital has been transformed into comprador capital instead of developing into national industrial capital and thus does not play a progressive social role.

In the popular political debates on state development strategies, the CPN (UML) argues that the semi-feudal and semi-colonial nature of exploitation and oppression in Nepalese society has been hindering the progress and prosperity of the people and the country. Despite several changes in the politics of the country, the fundamental aspects of the national economic, social and cultural situation has not significantly changed. Similarly, the CPN (Maoist) too sees Nepal as a semi-feudal and semi-colonial state and a country that is fettered by various semi-colonial unequal treaties with foreign powers (particularly India). Irrespective of the living standard of the family or the level of adoption of modern amenities, the mentality of the upper social classes continues to be feudal. As a result, the present form of the state has increasingly failed to manage these multifarious classes, national and other contradictions within the ambit of its old structure.

Therefore, it can be said that there is a structural contradiction between the well-being of the general masses of people and feudalism and comprador capitalism dominating social dynamics in Nepal. The present crisis-ridden conditions can be understood as the development of contradictions between the exploitation and oppression of the people by the state machinery under the control of feudal, comprador and bureaucratic capitalist classes and the continued struggle of the people. Throughout its modern history, the Nepalese people have struggled against the state. For example, they fought against the 104 years of Rana autocracy (1846-1950), the so called multiparty system (1950-1959), party less *panchayat* (1960-1990) and the current multiparty system under a constitutional monarchy.

Despite political changes in 1951, 1960 and 1990, the basic structure of the state has remained unchanged. The role of the state has been to maintain internal security and appropriate the surplus produced by peasants and other social classes in the form of taxes to maintain the state apparatus and continued control of the ruling classes. Even after the major political changes of 1990, an aristocracy continued to control national politics and state affairs, with major landowners and comprador bourgeoisie dominating the higher ranks of police, military and bureaucracy. This is because as the class controlling large amounts of land, it could afford better education and nepotistically access the political power of the state. It can be said that ordinary people in Nepal never had an opportunity to become *thalu* or *thulo manchhe* even after the restoration of multiparty democracy.

The political structure established as an outcome of the 1990s democratic movement also failed to ensure a sharing of power and resources among ordinary people. The *Janastha,* a vernacular weekly (4 February 2000) stated that 60% of the former *pancha* , who ruled Nepal for 30 years under the autocratic *panchayat* prior to 1990, had joined Nepali Congress, the ruling party of Nepal, 20% joined the CPN (UML), ML and Sadbhawana parties with the rest in the Rastria Prajatantrik Party. According to the new constitution, the three key organs of the Nepali state are the executive, the legislature and the judiciary. In theory, the executive power of the kingdom of Nepal is vested in the Council of Ministers and all functions of the king and royal palace, except those to be discharged by him, should be carried out with the advice and consent of the council of ministers through the prime minister.

However, in practice the king still holds the key to power in the country as the chief of the military. He appoints the leader of the majority parliamentary party in the House of Representatives as prime minister and forms a council of ministers under his chairmanship. The legislature of Nepal consists of the king, the House of Representatives and the National Assembly called the Parliament. There are 205 members in the HoR elected from each district constituency on the basis of direct voting. The National Assembly, sometimes known as the 'Upper House' consists of 60 members, including 10 members nominated by the king. The experience of the last 10 years has been that most candidates for the parliamentary election are selected by party bosses and party bureaucrats as per the interests of the party 'sponsors' and thus show little practical accountability to the people who elect them.

The judiciary consists of the Supreme Court, appellate court and the district courts. The king appoints the Chief Justice on the recommendation of the Constitutional Council and the judges of the Supreme Court on the recommendation of the Judicial Council. However, most judges are sons and daughters of big landowners and merchants and other ruling elites. They are not only representatives of the upper class of Nepalese society but also upper caste, mainly Brahmins, Chhetries and Newars. Occasionally, they are publicly criticised for their proximity to mainstream political parties and corruption. The state machinery, which movements from below encounter at the district and village levels, consists of the chief district officer, district development committee (DDC), village development committee (VDC), and the police and military.

The chief district officer is also responsible for overall coordination of peace and security of the district since he or she is also chief of police and military at the district level. However, in most cases, they receive direct instruction from the Ministry of Home and Police Headquarters in case of police and Ministry of Defence and Royal Palace and Military Headquarters in the case of the Royal Nepal Army. In other words, they represent the ruling class at the district and village level. Though most junior police and military officials are sons and daughters of poor and oppressed middle peasantry, senior officials of the military and police are usually related to the members of the royal family and belong to the upper castes such as Rana, Shah and Thakuri.

Those who are loyal to the ruling elites are sent to the accessible urban centres and lucrative places for corruption and bribery. But those without 'connections' are packed off to more problematic sites such as Maoist insurgency areas, where killing and violence are an everyday phenomenon. Therefore, it can be said that the police officials killed in the Maoist insurgency come from poor and oppressed social classes who are themselves already exploited by their own bureaucracy. This could be one reason why the Maoists were so easily able to defeat the police in remoter villages. Another section of the state apparatus that rural social movement confronts is the district forest office. In the name of protecting forests, aided by police and military, they are often involved in the eviction and exploitation of landless settlers, bonded labour and other poor peasants whose livelihood depends upon forest products and resources. They engage in logging forest products in partnership with other rural elites and their accomplices.

The DDCs and VDCs are elected government bodies, responsible for the social welfare and local development in their respective constituencies. Baring a few DDCs and VDCs, where more progressive and left village level activists are elected, most officials are rural elites, relatively large landowners and village money lenders, who exploit landless and bonded labour and other rural proletariat. As a result, in the struggle for land rights and movements against other forms of exploitation, these officials usually side with the police, military and landowners. There is widespread agreement that the entire system is corrupt, and ordinary people have little hope from the state machinery for ensuring equity, justice and sustainable rural livelihoods. Overall the state appears incompetent to do anything about combating corruption, since the state machinery itself is engulfed by corruption and its important actors sustain themselves through alliances with criminal elements of different kinds.

In addition to state machinery, NGOs and INGOs are also active in the Nepalese socioeconomic and political lives. Successful NGOs in Nepal have organised communities into groups for self-help and self-development that help build solidarity among and empower community members. Until

1990, the *panchayat* system government discouraged independent and autonomous NGOs. However, after the restoration of multiparty democracy in 1990, the number of NGOs significantly increased, from 10 in 1960, to 37 in 1977, 193 in 1989, and to 10,555 in April 2000. It needs to be admitted that few NGOs are active in socioeconomic develop-ment, a vast majority just holding legal status. Many 'inactive' NGOs are initiated by senior politicians and government bureaucrats in order to secure foreign funds for their own vested interest rather than deal with socioeconomic and political challenges.

Those active in the remote villages for building or supporting people's organizations rarely enjoy good relations with the state machinery and are seen as competitors rather than playing a complementary role in socioeconomic development. Despite their limited numbers, these NGOs have worked in favour of struggles from below and against the state-led repression of the rural social movement. Sometimes INGOs, UN agencies and donors such as USAID and DFID have taken an interest in improving some aspects of human rights and social justice in Nepal. Nevertheless, their overall role has been marked by (i) a lack of influence on poverty alleviation schemes, (ii) target failure, (iii) unsustainability of projects and (iv) corruption. Their efforts are seen as donor-driven and supply-led, implemented without a proper understanding of the forces that create and perpetuate poverty and injustice in Nepal.

Nevertheless USAID pressure on the Nepal government to implement land reforms in the 1960s and 1970s did help to minimise the land holding gap between rich and poor peasants. In contrast, USAID also assisted the development of the public school system, formally modelled on the American colleges of education and agricultural extension, which had little relevance to the experience and needs of the people. The programme devalued local knowledge and culture and taught young people, most of them farmers, to despise farming and rural life. Donor assisted NGOs are often considered as agents that promote globalization and the opening up of the Nepalese economy and market in the interest of global financial regimes.

Most work more closely with the state machinery rather than the people and members of the emerging civil societies. Although most foreign aid to Nepal poured in to promote human rights and democracy, it failed to ensure either, even as Nepal became dependent on foreign aid even to meet its basic annual expenditure. Accounting for more than 60% of the development budget, foreign aid, constitutes a major instrument to escape the low income, poor savings and low investment trap. Further, international financial institutions such as the World Bank, IMF and Asian Development Bank are involved in financing several developmental initiatives which, though meant to reduce poverty, have not only failed to achieve their declared objectives but contributed to a growth in state-led corruption and indebtedness, as also growing inequalities. But more than these donors and INGOs, it is the role of India that is significant in shaping political and economic conditions. In every major political change - 1846, 1950 or 1990 - India's role was central.

For example, it is widely believed that the autocratic Rana regime received support from British-India, the Nepali Congress-led movement against the Rana regime in 1950 was supported by independent India, and the political change of 1990s was also influenced by major political forces in India. Somewhat ironically, different social movements, including the ongoing Maoist 'people's war', have taken shelter in India, training their activists to fight for democracy and human rights in Nepal. Commenting on the role of the Indian state in the ongoing Maoist people's war, the president of Nepali Congress publicly charged that the Indian state was providing shelter to Maoist rebels. In response, the Indian government decided to deploy more than 10,000 Indian soldiers along the Nepal-India border to discourage the Maoists and their activities on Indian soil.

This act definitely influenced the current strategy of CPN (Maoist) to deepen the pace of their struggle. India is not only politically influential but also dominant in the country's finance and trade. More than one-third (35%) of foreign direct investment originates from India, followed by the USA (18%). Not surprisingly, Bhattarai, a senior CPN (Maoist) leader, writes that the Nepalese comprador class, in total alignment with Indian expansionism, finds it more fruitful to invest in foreign trade or to work as agents for foreign capital rather than develop national industrial capitalism. Similarly, the CPN-UML too maintains that Nepal is a market for Indian capitalists to invest, exploit and make profit and that India exercises more control in Nepal than any other South Asian country. Therefore, India's role is crucial not only in shaping the socioeconomic and political agenda but equally in ensuring the success or failure of various movements from below.

This brief note attempts to analyse the social and political environment in which the various social movements, including the Maoist struggle, have emerged. It is Nepal's misfortune that despite a popular struggle that helped usher in multiparty democracy in 1990, the various governments failed to meet the aspirations of the people and handle the deep-seated social contradictions. This is true not only of the Nepali Congress but also the 'left-wing' UML which ruled for a brief period in 1995. No wonder the broad masses of the people seem to have lost faith in mainstream political parties. It is this combined failure of both the state and political parties which explains the growing hold of radical social movements from below.

Bibliography

Andrews, B., Brewin, C. R., Rose, S., et al. 2000. "Predicting PTSD Symptoms in Victims of Violent Crime: The Role of Shame, Anger, and Childhood Abuse." *Journal of abnormal psychology* 109: 69-73.

Baldinger, B. G., and Nelson, D. T. 1995. "Crime Victims and Psychological Injuries." *Trial* 31: 56.

Bisson, J. I., and Shepherd, J. P. 1995. "Psychological reactions of victims of violent crime." *The British journal of psychiatry* 167: 718.

Bjerregaard, B. 2000. "An Empirical Study of Stalking Victimization." Violence and Victims 15: 389-406.

Black, J. 1995. "Rethinking the naming of sex crime victims." *Newspaper Research Journal* 16: 96.

Blackburn, S. 1999. "Gender Violence and the Indonesian Political Transition." *Asian Studies Review* 23: 433-448.

Breault, K. D., and Kposowa, A. J. 1997. "The Effects of Marital Status on Adult Female Homicides in the United States." *Journal of Quantitative Criminology* 13: 217-230.

Bubar, Roe, and Pamela Jumper Thurman. 2004. "Violence Against Native Women." *Social justice: a journal of crime, conflict & world order*. 31(4): 70 (17 pages).

Chilton, R., and Jarvis, J. 1999. "Victims and Offenders in Two Crime Statistics Programs: A Comparison of the National Incident-Based Reporting System (NIBRS) and the National Crime Victimization Survey (NCVS)." *Journal of Quantitative Criminology* 15: 193-205.

Cling, B. J., *Sexualized Violence against Women and Children: A Psychology and Law Perspective*. The Guilford Press: 2004.

Davis, K. E., and Frieze, I. H. 2000. "Research on Stalking: What Do We Know and Where Do We Go?" *Violence and Victims* 15: 473-487.

Denkers, A. J .M., and Winkel., F. W. 1998. "Crime victims well being and fear in a prospective and longitudinal study." *Sage Urban Studies Abstracts* 26.

Dunn, J. L. 2001. "Innocence Lost: Accomplishing Victimization in Intimate Stalking Cases." *Symbolic Interaction* 24: 285-313.

Dwyer, D. C. 1995. "Response to the Victims of Domestic Violence: Analysis and Implications of the British Experience." *Crime and Delinquency* 41: 527-541.

Epstein, J. N., Saunders, B. E., and Kilpatrick, D. G. 1997. "Predicting PTSD in Women with a History of Childhood Rape." *Journal of Traumatic Stress* 10: 573-588.

Erez, E., Laster, K. 1999. "Neutralizing Victim Reform: Legal Professionals' Perspectives on Victims and Impact Statements." *Crime & Delinquency* 45: 530-553.

Fenwick, H. 1996. "The rights of victims of crime: Protection from harassment and intimidation?" *The Journal of criminal law* 60: 84-93.

Gartner, R., Dawson, M., and Crawford, M. 1998/1999. "Woman Killing: Intimate Femicide in Ontario, 19741994." *Resources for Feminist Research* 26: 151-173.

Gaumer, C. P. 1995. "Protecting the Innocent: Victim-Witness Rights in Illinois." *Illinois bar journal* 83: 568.

Hart, B. In: Eds. 1996. *Battered Women and the Criminal Justice System.* Thousand Oaks, CA: Sage Publications, pp 98-114.

Herman, S., and Wasserman, C. 2001. "A Role for Victims in Offender Reentry." *Crime & Delinquency* 47:428-445.

Johnson, K. W. 1997. "Professional Help and Crime Victims." *The Social service review* 71: 89-109.

Kalaher, K. 1997. "The Proposed Victim's Rights Amendment: Taking a Bite Out of Crime or a Dog With No Teeth?" *Seton Hall legislative journal* 22: 317.

Kamphuis, J. H., and Emmelkamp, P. M. G. 1998. "Crime-Related Trauma: Psychological Distress in Victims of Bankrobbery." *Journal of anxiety disorders* 12: 199-208.

Katz, J. 1997. "Staying Alive: Women Who Saved Their Own Lives." *Cosmopolitan* 222: 188.

Kenney, J. S. 2002. "Victims of Crime and Labeling Theory: A Parallel Process?" *Deviant behavior* 23: 235-266.

Kumar, G. S. J. 1997. "Victimization of Women: Coping with Violence." *International Journal of Sociology of the Family* 27: 139-155.

Kury , H. Ferdinand., T. 1998. "The Victim's Experience and Fear of Crime." *Sage Urban Studies Abstracts* 26.

Lowenstein, L. F. 2000. "Victims of Violent Crime Leading to Post-Traumatic Stress Disorders." *The Police journal* 73: 256-262.

Lurigio, A. J. 2000. "Are all victims alike? The adverse, generalized and differential impact of crime." *Violence and Abuse Abstracts* 6.

Madriz, E. I. 1997. "Images of Criminals and Victims: A Study on Women's Fear and Social Control." *Gender & Society* 11: 342-356.

Marietta, J. D., and Rowe, G. S. 1999. "Violent Crime, Victims, and Society in Pennsylvania, 1682-1800." *Pennsylvania history* 66.

Martens, P. L. 2002. "Immigrants as victims of crime." *Violence & Abuse Abstracts* 8: 3-84.

McPhail, Beverly A. 2002. "Gender-Bias Hate Crimes: A Review." *Trauma, Violence, & Abuse: A Review Journal* 3: 125-143.

Mesch, G. S. 2000. "Women's Fear of Crime: The Role of Fear for the Well-Being of Significant Others." *Violence and Victims* 15: 323-336.

Nettleton, H., Walklate, S., and Williams, B. 1997. "Three Models of Probation Involvement with Victims of Crime." *The Liverpool law review* 19: 203.

Peltzer, K. 2000. "Risk for traumatization among violent crime victims in an urban community sample in South Africa." *Curationis* 23: 22-27.

Petersilia, J. R. 2001. "Crime Victims With Developmental Disabilities: A Review Essay." *Criminal Justice and Behavior* 28: 655-694.

Pino, N. W., and Meier, R. F. 1999. "Gender Differences in Rape Reporting." *Sex Roles* 40: 979-990.

Ruback, R. B., Menard, K. S., Outlaw, M. C., et al. 1999. "Normative Advice to Campus Crime Victims: Effects of Gender, Age, and Alcohol." *Violence and victims* 14: 381-396.

Sebba, L. 2001. "On the relationship between criminological research and policy: The case of crime victims." *Criminal Justice* 1: 27-58.

Wadham, J., and Arkinstall, J. 2000. "Rights of victims of crime explain how victims' rights will be affected by the Human Rights Act." *The New law journal* 6943: 1023-1024.

Weinrath, M., and Gartrell, J. 1996. "Victimization and Fear of Crime." *Violence and Victims* 11: 187-197.

Weisman, C. S. 1995. "Armed by Fear: Self-Defense Handguns and Women's Health." *Women's Health Issues* 5: 3-7.

Yee, J. L., and Greenberg, M. S. 1998. "Reactions to Crime Victims: Effects of Victims' Emotional State and Type of Relationship." *Journal of Social and Clinical Psychology* 17: 209-226.

Index

I

K

M

N

P